Implementing Sport Policy

This book critically examines the roles and contributions of different organisations in the implementation of sport policy in the UK and, therefore, provides an important guide to the complexities of implementing sport policy and of achieving policy goals through, and for, sport.

Presenting analytical chapters by leading sport researchers alongside shorter commentaries by practitioners working in the field, this book outlines the uneven path between policy planning and real-world outcomes. Adopting a multi-level analysis, this book examines the interlocking structures and challenges of organisations, from grassroots voluntary sport to national governing bodies and professional clubs, and considers the most important issues affecting UK sport policy today.

This is fascinating reading for any student, researcher or practitioner working in sport policy, sport for development, sport management, sport coaching, physical education and related areas of policy such as public health, community development, social policy, public policy and education.

Marc Keech is Principal Lecturer at the University of Brighton, UK, teaching and researching Sport Policy and Sport Management. Marc has acted as a consultant and researcher for a range of organisations for 30 years. A Senior Fellow of the Higher Education Academy, Marc was the Higher Education (HE) representative on the national CIMSPA (the Chartered Institute for the Management of Sport and Physical Activity) Professional Development Board from 2018 to 2020. He has been the HE representative on the Professional Development Committee for Community Sport since 2021.

Iain Lindsey is Associate Professor in the Department of Sport and Exercise Sciences at Durham University, UK. Iain's research has primarily examined sport policy and development, especially youth sport policy in the UK and the use of sport for development in Africa. This research has been undertaken at both global and national levels as well as in a variety of local and community contexts. Iain's research is underpinned by theories and methodologies from the fields of political science and international development.

John Hayton is Assistant Professor in Sport Development in the Department of Sport, Exercise and Rehabilitation at Northumbria University, UK. John's research has coalesced around the policy, delivery and management of sport in and by the non-profit and voluntary sector. John has published widely in areas such as sport volunteering, sport-based interventions, austerity and sport, and the role and management of non-profit organisations in the delivery of sport, physical activity and physical recreation.

Routledge Research in Sport Business and Management

Embedded Multi-Level Leadership in Elite Sport
Edited by Svein S. Andersen, Per Øystein Hansen and Barrie Houlihan

Good Governance in Sport
Critical Reflections
Edited by Arnout Geeraert and Frank van Eekeren

Stakeholder Analysis and Sport Organisations
Edited by Anna-Maria Strittmatter, Josef Fahlén and Barrie Houlihan

Sport and Brexit
Regulatory Challenges and Legacies
Edited by Jacob Kornbeck

Sport Management Education
Global Perspectives and Implications for Practice
Edited by Mike Rayner and Tom Webb

Digital Business Models in Sport
Edited by Mateusz Tomanek, Wojciech Cieśliński and Michał Polasik

Sport Management, Innovation and the COVID-19 Crisis
Edited by Gözde Ersöz and Meltem Ince Yenilmez

Sport in the Iberian Peninsula
Management, Economics and Policy
Edited by Jerónimo García-Fernández, Moisés Grimaldi-Puyana and Gonzalo A. Bravo

EU Antitrust Law and Sport Governance
The Next Frontier?
Edited by Jacob Kornbeck

Implementing Sport Policy
Organisational Perspectives on the UK Sport System
Edited by Marc Keech, Iain Lindsey and John Hayton

For more information about this series, please visit https://www.routledge.com/
Routledge-Research-in-Sport-Business-and-Management/book-series/RRSBM

Implementing Sport Policy

Organisational Perspectives on the UK Sport System

Edited by Marc Keech, Iain Lindsey and John Hayton

LONDON AND NEW YORK

First published 2024
by Routledge
4 Park Square, Milton Park, Abingdon, Oxon OX14 4RN

and by Routledge
605 Third Avenue, New York, NY 10158

Routledge is an imprint of the Taylor & Francis Group, an informa business

© 2024 selection and editorial matter, Marc Keech, Iain Lindsey and John Hayton; individual chapters, the contributors

The right of Marc Keech, Iain Lindsey and John Hayton to be identified as the authors of the editorial material, and of the authors for their individual chapters, has been asserted in accordance with sections 77 and 78 of the Copyright, Designs and Patents Act 1988.

All rights reserved. No part of this book may be reprinted or reproduced or utilised in any form or by any electronic, mechanical, or other means, now known or hereafter invented, including photocopying and recording, or in any information storage or retrieval system, without permission in writing from the publishers.

Trademark notice: Product or corporate names may be trademarks or registered trademarks, and are used only for identification and explanation without intent to infringe.

British Library Cataloguing-in-Publication Data
A catalogue record for this book is available from the British Library

Library of Congress Cataloging-in-Publication Data
Names: Keech, Marc, editor. | Lindsey, Iain, editor. | Hayton, John, editor.
Title: Implementing sport policy : organisational perspectives on the UK sport system / Edited by Marc Keech, Iain Lindsey, and John Hayton.
Description: Abingdon, Oxon ; New York, NY : Routledge, 2023. | Series: Routledge research in sport business and management | Includes bibliographical references and index. |
Identifiers: LCCN 2023003319 | ISBN 9780367755027 (hardback) | ISBN 9780367755041 (paperback) | ISBN 9781003162728 (ebook)
Subjects: LCSH: Sports and state—Great Britain. | Sports administration—Great Britain.
Classification: LCC GV706.35 .I47 2023 | DDC 796.0942—dc23/eng/20230206
LC record available at https://lccn.loc.gov/2023003319

ISBN: 978-0-367-75502-7 (hbk)
ISBN: 978-0-367-75504-1 (pbk)
ISBN: 978-1-003-16272-8 (ebk)

DOI: 10.4324/9781003162728

Typeset in Times New Roman
by Deanta Global Publishing Services, Chennai, India

Contents

List of Tables	*vii*
List of Boxes	*viii*
List of Acronyms and Abbreviations	*ix*
Preface	*xii*
Acknowledgements	*xiv*
List of Contributors	*xv*

1 Introduction   1
IAIN LINDSEY, MARC KEECH AND JOHN HAYTON

2 National Sports Agencies   20
PIPPA CHAPMAN
Practitioner Reflection and Insights: Andy J Reed OBE   31

3 National Governing Bodies of Sport   37
MATHEW DOWLING AND SPENCER HARRIS
Practitioner Reflection and Insights: Ian Freeman   51

4 The Active Partnerships   57
MARC KEECH AND JACK WILKINSON
Practitioner Reflection and Insights: Maxine Rhodes   70

5 Local Authorities and the Implementation of Sport Policy   76
JANINE PARTINGTON, STEPHEN ROBSON AND LOUISE MORBY
Practitioner Reflection and Insights: Katy Bowden   86

vi Contents

6 Public Health Agencies and Policy Implementation in Sport
and Physical Activity: Re-thinking Partnerships and Priorities 94
PHIL BROWN AND AARON BEACOM
Practitioner Reflection and Insights: Dwain Morgan 107

7 Implementation of Equality Policies: From Legislation to
Lived Practices 116
LAUREN KAMPERMAN AND A. J. RANKIN-WRIGHT
Practitioner Reflection and Insights: Kirsty Clarke 125

8 Sporting Charities and Non-sporting Community Agencies 134
KATE MORI
Practitioner Reflection and Insights: Kevin McPherson 144

9 Schools 152
HELEN IVES
Practitioner Reflection and Insights: Alan Watkinson 162

10 Voluntary Sports Clubs 171
ANDREW ADAMS
Practitioner Reflection and Insights: Daniel Edson 182

11 Professional Football Clubs and Policy Implementation and
Enactment 190
JIMMY O'GORMAN
Practitioner Reflection and Insights (1): Steve Williams and
Louise Edwards 199
Practitioner Reflection and Insights (2): Paul Morrison 201

12 Conclusions: Learning Lessons from Implementing Sport Policy 208
JOHN HAYTON, IAIN LINDSEY AND MARC KEECH

Index 227

Tables

1.1	Policy actors and policy work	15
3.1	National Governing Body of sport funding 2008–2016	46

Boxes

1.1	Sabatier and Mazmanian Identified Five Conditions for Effective Implementation	7
1.2	Why Policy Changes or Fails	8

Acronyms and Abbreviations

ABCD	Asset-Based Community Development
ACF	Advocacy Coalition Framework
ACT	Argyle Community Trust
ADSP	Athlete Development Support Pathway
APPGFHC	All-Party Parliamentary Group for a Fit and Healthy Childhood
ATF	Active Through Football
BLM	Black Lives Matter
CCG	Clinical Commissioning Group
CCPR	Central Council of Physical Recreation
CCT	Compulsory Competitive Tendering
CDS	County Durham Sport
CMO	Chief Medical Officer
CoE	Council of Europe
CRE	Commission for Race Equality
CSD	Community Sport Development
CSP	County Sport Partnership
CSR	Corporate Social Responsibility
DCMS	Department of Digital, Culture, Media and Sport
DDA	Disability Discrimination Act
DfE	Department for Education
DfES	Department for Education and Skills
DNH	Department of National Heritage
DRC	Disability Rights Commission
DSG	Direct Schools Grant
EDI	Equality, Diversity, and Inclusion
EFL	English Football League
EFLT	English Football League Trust
EHRC	Equality and Human Rights Commission
EOC	Equal Opportunities Commission
EPL	English Premier League
EPPP	Elite Player Performance Plan

x Acronyms and Abbreviations

FA	Football Association
FFIT	Football Fans in Training
FiTC	Football in the Community
HotN	Health of the Nation
IMD	Index of Multiple Deprivation
KPI	Key Performance Indicator
LAA	Local Area Agreement
LDP	Local Delivery Pilot (Sport England from 2018 to present date)
LDP	Local Delivery Plan (for public health)
LEAP	Local Exercise Action Pilot
LGA	Local Government Association
LGM	Let's Get Moving
LGMA	Local Government Modernisation Agenda
LSP	Local Strategic Partnership
LTAD	Long-Term Athlete Development
MSF	Multiple Streams Framework
NGBs	National Governing Bodies (of sport)
NHS	National Health Service
NPM	New Public Management
NSO	National Sport Organisation
OFSTED	Office for Standards in Education
OTS	Office of the Third Sector
PA	Physical Activity
PAFC	Plymouth Argyle Football Club
PATs	Policy Action Teams
PCT	Primary Care Trust
PDM	Partnership Development Manager
PE	Physical Education
PESS	Physical Education and School Sport
PESSCL	Physical Education, School Sport and Club Links
PESSYP	Physical Education and Sport Strategy for Young People
PFA	Professional Footballers' Association
PLCF	Premier League Charitable Fund
PLT	Primary Link Teacher
POS	Political Opportunity Structure
PPA	Planning, Preparation and Assessment
PSA	Public Service Agreement
RRI	Race Representation Index
SDC	Sports Development Council
SDO	Sport Development Officer
SE	Sport England
SEM	Socio-Ecological Model
SGO	School Games Organiser
SHA	Strategic Health Authority

SLBt	Street Level Bureaucrats
SLBy	Street Level Bureaucracy
SROI	Social Returns on Investment
SSC	Specialist Sports College
SSCo	School Sport Coordinator
SSP	School Sport Partnership
TAES	Towards an Excellent Service
TSOs	Third Sector Organisations
UK	United Kingdom
VSC	Voluntary Sports Club
WCP	World Class Programme
WCPP	World Class Performance Programme
WHO	World Health Organisation
YST	Youth Sport Trust

Preface

The origins of this book emanated from long-standing discussions, dating back as far as 2005, between the editors about the changing nature and purpose of the relationship between the academic study of and the professional practice inherent in the implementation of sport policies. Those origins can be summarised as four overlapping points of departure.

First, since the mid-1990s, successive governments in the UK have accorded sport a relatively high level of priority, without sport obtaining the status of a primary policy concern like health or education. Governments of different political parties have thus developed various policies and strategies to promote the benefits, value and practice of sport as a secondary goal which has the potential to contribute to primary policy goals. Consequently, there have been numerous examples of continuities and changes in approaches to the implementation of sport policies, as well as to the roles of various organisations which have been involved and charged with contributing to the delivery of sport policy objectives. As such, the nature of sports organisations is defined by their abilities to constantly adapt to changes.

Second, as a result of the point above, it has become the norm to view policy implementation in sport through the lens of the organisations themselves accorded with the responsibility of translating policy objectives into practice. As sport policy has evolved into a more complex network of practices, responding to a growing number of issues, each with their own levels of complexity, the importance of the professional practice through which policy is implemented has become increasingly important. Fundamentally, understanding the environment and conditions in which key organisations operate within is essential to understanding the relative efficacy of individual policies.

Third, the interface between the academic study and professional practices of sport has been a long-standing concern for the editors. The notion of practitioner commentary was particularly highlighted by Hayhurst, Kay and Chawansky (2016) in their edited collection *Beyond Sport for Development and Peace: Transnational Perspectives on Theory, Policy and Practice*. By bringing together the views of academics and professionals (which as Hayhurst et al. note are 'categories which are not always uniquely separate or distinct,' 2016, p. 3), each academic contribution receives a response from a professional who has been involved in policy implementation. As academic interest in sport policy has increased, each of the academic authors in this collection has a record of either having worked in sport policy/development, before making the transition to academic employment or working in partnership with sport policy and development professionals through a range of programmes and projects. Yet the knowledge and understanding facilitated by these connections often are not always translated into written evidence to facilitate learning. On the other hand, all the practitioners who have contributed to this book have at some point given talks in schools, colleges and universities but often, except for the students who attend, there is little legacy from the visiting speakers. These contributions will provide readers with a rare opportunity to listen to an integrated dialogue amongst divergent and occasionally separated viewpoints in a written format.

Fourth, and finally, the editors wanted to pay tribute to some of the foremost scholars who have paved the way for many of the contributors to take up the mantle. In the same way that many of the first generation of sport (or leisure or recreation) managers have left legacies to help understand the present from the past (see https://sportsleisurelegacy.co.uk), people such as Barrie Houlihan, Mike Collins, Ian Henry, Tess Kay, Kevin Hylton, Jonathan Long, Mick Green and others pioneered the study of sport policy in the UK. These people enabled the contributors to take up the mantle of furthering the study of sport policy in the UK and have offered a landscape through which academics have analysed issues inherently related to the notion that policy commitments do not exist in a political vacuum, but emerge out of a deeper structure of norms, values and belief systems. In this regard, there has been substantive analysis of processes by which sport policies have emerged and also of the implications of such policies. But there have been relatively few studies, in the UK or in other contexts, that have analysed sport policy implementation. The editors and all the contributors hope that this book contributes further understanding to the area of study.

Reference

Hayhurst, L., Kay, T., & Chawansky, M. (2016). In Hayhurst L., Kay T., and Chawansky M. (Eds.), *Beyond sport for development and peace: Transnational perspectives on theory, policy and practice*. Routledge. https://doi.org/10.4324/9781315751559

Acknowledgements

The editors would like to say thank you to all the authors for their time, patience, thought and willingness to contribute to the challenges this book set. In particular, the editors would especially like to acknowledge the practitioners who responded for volunteering to take on their responses to the academic contributions. The book has had a long gestation since prospective authors were initially approached. The period has covered the Covid pandemic and also increasing and multiple pressures in society, academia and the sport industry. These pressures have had notable and challenging impacts on authors and practitioners in the book, and also some who may otherwise have been involved.

The editors would also like to say thank you to Dr Ben Hildred for his diligence and editorial assistance in the latter stages of the project.

Thank you, as always, to Taylor & Francis Senior Publisher Simon Whitmore for commissioning the project and believing in the initial idea and to Taylor & Francis Editorial Assistant Rebecca Connor for her endless patience and unstinting support through the duration.

Contributors

Andrew Adams is Senior Lecturer in Sports Management in the Department of Sport and Event Management at Bournemouth University, UK.

Aaron Beacom is Reader in Sport and International Relations at Plymouth Marjon University, UK.

Katy Bowden is Development Manager at Active Leeds, UK.

Phil Brown is Senior Lecturer in Sport Development at Plymouth Marjon University, UK.

Pippa Chapman is Lecturer in Sport Management & Sport Development at the University of Edinburgh, UK.

Kirsty Clarke is Director for Innovation and Business Development at the Activity Alliance, UK.

Mathew Dowling is Senior Lecturer in the Cambridge Centre for Sport and Exercise Sciences at Anglia Ruskin University, UK.

Daniel Edson is Sport Development Officer and Rugby Development Officer and a Rugby Voluntary Sport Club Head Coach, UK.

Louise Edwards is Community Officer for Tranmere Rovers in the Community, UK.

Ian Freeman is Higher Education Lead in Sport and Exercise Science (Coaching) at Grantham College, UK, and was previously Coaching Systems Officer and Athlete Development (Technical Lead) (2005–2019) for Swim England, UK.

Spencer Harris is Associate Professor of Sport Management at the University of Colorado, Colorado Springs, USA.

Helen Ives is Senior Lecturer in Sport, Health and Exercise Sciences (Pedagogy and Youth Sport) at Brunel University, UK. Helen has first-hand experience of implementing physical education (PE) and sport policy in schools, having previously worked as a Partnership Development Manager in West London.

xvi Contributors

Lauren M. Kamperman is a PhD candidate in the Department of Sport and Exercise Sciences at Durham University, UK, co-funded by the Talented Athlete Scholarship Scheme (TASS).

Kevin McPherson is Director of Square Impact, a Third Sector and Sports Development Consultancy in the UK.

Louise Morby is Senior Lecturer in Sport Development at Leeds Beckett University, UK.

Dwain Morgan is Head of Business and Impact for Argyle Community Trust, Plymouth, UK.

Kate Mori is Academic Engagement Manager, Membership, Quality Enhancements & Standards Quality Assurance Agency for Higher Education, UK.

Paul Morrison is Head of Football/Futsal Operations and Safeguarding for Tranmere Rovers in the Community, UK.

Jimmy O'Gorman is Senior Lecturer in Sports Development, Management and Coaching in the Department of Sport and Physical Activity at Edge Hill University, UK.

Janine Partington is Senior Lecturer in Sport Development at Leeds Beckett University, UK.

A. J. Rankin-Wright was formerly Assistant Professor of Equality, Diversity and Inclusion in Sport in the Department of Sport and Exercise Sciences, Durham University, UK.

Andy J. Reed OBE is Founder of the Sports Think Tank and Chair of the Sport for Development Coalition. Previously, he has been the Member of Parliament (MP) for Loughborough, UK, and Chair of the Sport and Recreation Alliance and Chartered Institute for the Management of Sport and Physical Activity. He served in the Department for Culture, Media and Sport and Treasury Ministerial Teams in the 1997–2010 Labour government.

Maxine Rhodes is Managing Director of County Durham Sport, UK.

Stephen Robson is Course Director in Sport Development at Leeds Beckett University, UK.

Alan Watkinson is Founder of Sport Impact, Co-founder of the Schools Active Movement and Mo Farah's PE teacher. Alan works in partnership with schools to improve the quality and quantity of physical education and school sport.

Jack Wilkinson is a former Lead Regional Manager for Sport England and former Chair of the Board of Trustees for Active Sussex, UK.

Steve Williams is Community Development Officer for Tranmere Rovers in the Community, UK.

Chapter 1

Introduction

Iain Lindsey, Marc Keech and John Hayton

Approaches to implementing sport policies are vital to the ultimate outcomes and effectiveness of these policies. Understanding drawn from sport policy research has certainly developed significantly in the UK and in other countries over the past decades, most significantly giving attention to the processes by which sport policies come to be made and the wider factors and priorities influencing their objectives. However, understanding of implementation processes remains far less comprehensive. Studies of sport policy implementation in both the UK and elsewhere have instead tended to focus on specific policies, initiatives or issues, or else on particular types of organisations affected by sport policies. These limitations have provided the motivation for this book which seeks to contribute to developing a more overarching understanding of sport policy implementation. Through considering the roles and contributions of the range of key organisations in the implementation of sport policy in the UK, the book and all of its chapters will specifically and critically examine:

- changes and continuities in the positioning of different organisations in national sport policies and respective implementation approaches over time;
- the consequences of national sport policies and implementation approaches for different organisations engaged with sport;
- how recognised sport policy outcomes reflect approaches towards implementation through different organisations.

In doing so, we hope the book will add to both academic and practical understanding both in the UK and for those considering sport policy implementation in other countries. To contextualise this understanding, we begin by providing an overview of sport policies and the overarching implementation approaches pursued in the UK over time.

Trends in UK Sport Policy and Implementation

The orientation and extent of governmental interest and intervention are the starting point for any consideration of implementation in a particular policy sector.

DOI: 10.4324/9781003162728-1

Broadly summarised, the overarching trend in sport policy in the UK from as far back as the 1960s has been 'a steady, though uneven, expansion in the role of the state in sport' (Houlihan & Lindsey, 2013, p. 188). It was the publication of *Sport: Raising the Game* in 1995 by John Major's Conservative government (DNH, 1995) that remains most commonly regarded as a particular landmark in the increasing salience of sport for central government in the UK (Green & Houlihan, 2006). Subsequently, there has been broad continuity in policy priority given to sport by successive Labour and Conservative-led governments that have commonly linked sport to a variety of wider policy and political goals.

Increases in national, public funding for sport followed the increased priority given to it by central governments. It was, again, John Major's instigation of the National Lottery in 1994 that was perhaps the most crucial policy development in providing a consistent source of funding to support governmental objectives for sport. However, this is not to say that resources have been spread evenly across different agencies responsible for different aspects of sport provision. The implementation of austerity by Conservative-led governments from 2010 imposed particularly steep cuts on overall local government budgets, with specific spending on sport and recreation estimated to have reduced by 70% on average between 2009–2010 and 2019–2020 (Harris et al., 2019). By contrast, funding for UK Sport and Sport England, the two non-departmental public bodies responsible for elite and community sport, respectively, increased to historically high levels. National public funds distributed by UK Sport in pursuit of success in summer Olympic and Paralympic Games jumped from £69m in the four years leading up to Sydney 2000 to £265m for the Beijing 2008 cycle and have been in excess of £300m for subsequent summer games cycles (UK Sport, n.d.). Comparative funding for Sport England to pursue policy goals for community sport and physical activity increased in cash terms from a total of £261.3m in the financial year of 2009/2010 to £332m in 2019/2020, of which 67% came from the National Lottery and 33% directly from the government (Sport England Annual Report, 2010, 2020).

If the period of John Major's premiership can be identified as the key departure point for increased salience and funding for sport, then it was the subsequent Labour governments from 1997 that significantly reshaped the implementation approaches utilised in pursuit of sport policy aspirations. Tony Blair, as Prime Minister, and his Labour governments strongly pursued an agenda of 'modernisation' of public services which extended into national policy approaches towards sport. The core features and implications of Labour's approach to modernisation have been subject to much debate. On the one hand, aspects of modernisation represented the continuation of the previous Conservative governments' implementation of 'New Public Management' (NPM) approaches that sought to instil private sector, business management practices into the operation of public services. On a somewhat different tack, aspects of Labour's impetus towards modernisation can be viewed as a response to the 'hollowing out' of state capacities that had occurred under the Conservatives, and the fragmentation that had occurred as previously public services had increasingly become delivered by a widening array of different organisations across the public, private and voluntary sectors. As shall be considered further, different aspects of Labour's modernisation agenda were not necessarily coherent but rather operated in paradoxical ways.

Impetus for 'modernisation' across the sport sector came not only from the increased political salience and public funding of sport but also from the Labour government's problematisation of longstanding practices and modes of operation of sport organisations. The first sport policy documents published by the Labour governments, *A Sporting Future for All* (DCMS, 2000, 2001) and *Game Plan* (DCMS/Strategy Unit, 2002), represented a clear departure from previous sport policy in articulating the political view that the 'organisational infrastructure of sport was considered to be an impediment to achieving primary policy goals' for sport (Houlihan & Lindsey, 2013, p. 66). The government's call for what it termed a 'modernising partnership' with sport organisations was, therefore, founded on the premise that 'a radical rethink of the way we fund and organise sport' was required (DCMS, 2000, p. 19). As the following paragraphs explain, it was through enactment of different governmental tools and techniques, that were utilised in other areas of public policy as well as sport, that the shift towards a 'modernised' approach to implementation in sport became realised.

Labour's prioritisation of 'partnerships' as a core mechanism for policy coordination and implementation responded to the challenges resulting from previous fragmentation and the aspiration to develop more 'joined up' approaches to the delivery of public services. At different levels of policymaking and implementation, the government mandated and funded the creation of an expansive array of partnerships, with these commonly being developed as new, formalised structures comprised of representatives from different policy areas and from public, private and voluntary sectors (Coaffee & Johnson, 2005; Diamond, 2006). This institutionalisation of partnerships as an organisational form was replicated in and across sport. Active Sport Partnerships (subsequently retitled as County Sport Partnerships and then Active Partnerships) and School Sport Partnerships were but two of the most prominent new structures that were universally instigated across England. Other, more short-lived, partnerships became central in the operation of other nationally-funded initiatives, such as Sports Action Zones and the New Opportunities for physical education (PE) and Sport programme (for examples, see Lindsey, 2011).

If this emphasis on implementation through partnerships differed from previous Conservative governments, there was a greater degree of continuity in Labour's utilisation and extension of performance management techniques. Broadly and rhetorically, Labour governments consistently advocated the pursuit of 'evidence-based policy' (Coalter, 2017). In practice, what was more widely realised was what Kurunmäki and Miller (2006, p. 97) described as an 'avalanche of performance indicators, performance reviews, audits and inspections in the UK public sector.' Across sport, setting and reporting of targets and performance indicators became commonplace. Systems of measurement against these targets were also established, with a key example being the instigation of the national Active People Survey in

2005 to provide national and local indicators of participation in sport. The power of government and its national agencies to determine and measure targets for organisations in sport meant that these mechanisms served to strengthen and centralise accountability towards the national level.

Furthermore, the linking of funding decisions with performance measures further inculcated top-down, governmental control over sport. The Labour government's pursuit of a 'modernising partnership' was predicated on funding arrangements in which sport organisations could 'gain more responsibility' but on the condition that 'if they fail to perform against agreed targets, then funding arrangements will be reviewed' (DCMS, 2000, p. 20). A key, and continuing, paradox that ran through sport policy was thus established. On the one hand, the Labour government sought to portray modernisation as enabling organisations to become more responsive to the needs of service users. On the other hand, top-down control over the provision or withdrawal of funding upon which many sports organisations had become dependent meant that the government exerted increasingly widespread influence over the sport sector (Houlihan & Green, 2009). As expressed by Phillpots et al. (2011, p. 266), this paradox was embedded in:

> *a model of governance in which managerial power is ostensibly dispersed amongst a range of agencies at local levels, yet government exercises top-down control over policy development and implementation through tight fiscal control based on principles of reward and punishment.*

The replacement of Labour with Conservative-led governments from 2010 brought a number of significant political and sporting developments, including the enforcement of austerity and London playing host to the 2012 Olympics and Paralympic Games as a consequence of a bid process won seven years earlier under the Labour government. Taking a broad lens, however, changes in sport policy implementation since 2010 may be considered as shifts in emphasis rather than overarching divergence from Labour's preceding approach. Political and policy discourse from the Coalition government that came to power in 2010 promised a change from the centralisation evident under Labour towards more localised approaches to implementation. This rhetorical commitment was initially symbolised by David Cameron's short-lived 'Big Society' initiative and was also represented in the most substantive sport policy document of the period, *Sporting Future: A New Strategy for an Active Nation* (HM Government, 2015). Nevertheless, there remained counteracting top-down influence particularly through the early Conservative government continuation of systems by which funding for sport was distributed to different organisations according to nationally-set measures of effectiveness and accountability.

Different elements that had been central to Labour's 'modernisation' agenda were extended or weakened by Conservative-led governments to differing extents. The New Public Management impetus for embedding private sector management practices within the sport sector was further strengthened under the Conservatives. In particular, approaches centred on considering and treating persons (potentially) involved in sport as 'customers' were strongly emphasised in *Sporting Future* (HM Government, 2015) and other policy initiatives. Sporting organisations were also urged to cultivate new sources of private sector income in order to address what was considered as an embedded 'over-reliance' on public funding. Governmental impetus towards partnerships as a key mechanism for policy implementation was, on the other hand, more equivocal. The language of 'working in partnership' and 'collaboration' did remain prevalent within policy documents such as *Sporting Future*. However, support for formalised partnership structures created by the preceding Labour government was mixed, at best, with the removal of direct government funding from School Sport Partnerships, symbolising divergence from a key element of Labour's sport policy infrastructure.

The example of School Sport Partnerships also draws attention to the ways in which overarching approaches to policy and implementation considered in this section thus far have differentially affected and been enacted in different sport policy areas. It is perhaps the area of PE and school sport policy that saw the most significant shift in policy and implementation approach across the period covered by this book. As discussed further in Chapter 9, the standardised and nationally-controlled system of School Sport Partnerships was changed in the early years of Conservative-led government towards a highly decentralised approach by which spending on the government's PE and Sport Premium became delegated to primary schools. There has, on the other hand, been a greater degree of continuity in national policy goals associating PE and school sport with the achievement of a range of other social policy goals, with health in particular becoming increasingly prominent over time (Lindsey, 2020). The influence of ongoing faith from policymakers in the wider benefits that may derive from young people's involvement in sport can also be seen in the advance of the 'sport for development' sector, as highlighted in Chapter 8.

It has been community sport and physical activity that has, perhaps, been most marked by inconsistency in policy and implementation approaches over time. The extent to which policies for sport have also addressed physical activity has varied considerably, for example from the prioritisation of 'sport for sport's sake' in the years immediately prior to London 2012 Olympics (Collins, 2010) towards subsequent policy statements and actions which have increasingly focused on physical activity and broader orientations towards health. Impetus towards New Public Management and other aspects of national implementation approaches have, however, been influential in the community sport sector over time. As a result, it is arguable that this sport policy area has also been subject to top-down influence to a notable degree. More recent policy statements from *Sporting Future* (HM Government, 2015) and especially the Sport England (2021) strategy, *Uniting the Movement*, appear to signal a potential rebalancing of implementation relations towards a greater degree of localism, which will be given consideration in Chapters 2, 4 and 5.

Finally, in the area of elite sport, the UK's levels of Olympic and Paralympic success since 2008 onwards have broadly led to the continuation of a policy and implementation approach that had been significantly transformed through the early part of the Labour government. Policy towards large professional and other, smaller non-Olympics sports may have been more inconsistent, but top-down influence and control have otherwise been strongly evident in the elite sport sector. Funding increases identified earlier in the section have been consistently conditional on recipient national governing bodies (NGBs) and athletes both delivering on medal targets and also nationally-mandated organisational reforms. The extent of success accompanying this 'no compromise' approach has not come without criticism. For example, concerns regarding sporting integrity as well as pressure and limited diversity amongst athletes and others working in the UK's elite sport system have led to shifts in funding allocation towards the Paris 2024 Olympics. The extent to which these shifts may become embedded as a distinctively different policy implementation approach will be considered as part of Chapter 2.

Implementing Sport Policy

A feature of the evolution of sport policy outlined above has been the emergence of a variety of agencies, predominantly non-state actors, working in partnership to implement policy (Lindsey, 2009; McDonald, 2005). Partnership approaches were widely adopted as a means of addressing the complex and multifaceted issues inculcated under the banner of sport policy, yet such approaches led to significant challenges in terms of the interplay between implementation, activities and outcomes (Baker et al., 2016). Consequently, a concern identified both theoretically and in practice was to identify how organisations interact with each other and their environment in the implementation and delivery of policy. In its simplest form, implementation is the process of turning policy decisions into practice. Whilst a policy decision 'identifies the problem(s) to be addressed, stipulates the objective(s) to be pursued and structures the implementation process' (Sabatier & Mazmanian, 1980, p. 540), it is common to observe an 'implementation gap' between what was planned and what actually occurred as a result of a policy (O'Gorman, 2011). The complexity of these processes is captured by Mazmanian and Sabatier's widely recognised definition which notes that implementation is the carrying out of a basic policy decision, usually incorporated in a statute but which can also take the form of important executive orders or court decisions (1983), p. 20). Given the complexity and multi-actor nature of its implementation, the sport policy landscape which has emerged is characterised by different levels of implementation, which in itself takes different forms in different cultural, institutional and organisational settings.

It is a challenging task explaining the complex structures of sport in the UK. The sheer number of agencies and professional organisations involved can only superficially illustrate the nature of partnership working required in order to deliver services and sporting opportunities. The rapid and fluid changes witnessed in UK sport policy in recent years mean that the structure of sport is subject to constant refinement in response to changing policy priorities and the shifting responsibilities of organisations (Keech & Nauright, 2018, pp. 453–454). Policies formulated at national level may face the challenge of ensuring some degree of consistency in delivery at subnational level especially. A particular example of this is where local authorities have jurisdiction over local spatial resources or local strategies to increase participation in physical activity, but a national governing body may have overall responsibility for increasing participation in a single sport. Policy implementation, therefore, is a process that is especially fraught where the subnational level has some separate degree of political authority. This context in sport strongly reflects broader changes in which processes of 'government' have transformed into 'governance,' whereby a wide range of actors may be participating in policy processes. As a result, simplistic hierarchical models of implementation have far less relevance than previously (Hill & Hupe, 2015), and there is a strong need to understand the contributions of, and constraints on, all organisations involved with governance and policy implementation.

Implementation is a complex and multidimensional process. Theoretically, top-down, bottom-up and principal–agent models represent three major strands of theorising on policy implementation which continue to shape prominent debates. The top-down approach, exemplified in work such as that below by Sabatier and Mazmanian (1979), sees policy formation/formulation and policy execution as distinct activities.

Box 1.1: Sabatier and Mazmanian Identified Five Conditions for Effective Implementation

- The programme is based on a sound theory relating to changes in target group behaviour.
- Policy decisions have to contain unambiguous policy directives and structure the implementation process in a way that increases the chances of good performance of target groups.
- The leaders and implementing agencies require significant managerial and political skills and commitment to the goals.
- The programme also needs to be supported by organised constituency groups and few key legislators throughout the process.
- The priority of objectives is not undermined over time by conflicting public policies or changes in socioeconomic conditions.

(Sabatier & Mazmanian, 1979, pp. 484–485)

In top-down approaches, policies are set at higher levels in a political process and are then communicated to subordinate levels which are then charged with the

8   Iain Lindsey et al.

organisational technical, managerial and administrative tasks of putting policy into practice. Contributions from Sabatier and Mazmanian in Box 1.1 and Cairney's summary of top-down perspectives in Box 1.2 illustrate the interest of theorists in seeking to identify the conditions required for policies developed and implemented from the top-down to be effective in reaching desired outcomes. Problems associated with the top-down approach, however, include the unlikelihood that all pre-conditions would be present at the same time and that the approach only adopts perspectives of those in higher levels of government and neglects the role of other actors and therefore risks overestimating the impact of government action (neglecting other factors). Top-down change is also difficult to apply where no single, dominant policy or agency is involved, and inherently, policies change as they are being implemented.

Box 1.2: Why Policy Changes or Fails

Top-down approaches seek standardised explanations that 'highlight the conditions that have to be met to ensure "perfect" implementation success' (Hood, 1976, p. 6; Hogwood & Gunn, 1984, p. 198; Sabatier, 1986, pp. 23–24; Cairney, 2009, p. 357). The understanding is that, in fact, they explain why policies fail or achieve partial success:

1. The policy's objectives are clear, consistent and well communicated and understood. A clear policy provides legal weight and acts as a 'standard of evaluation' (Sabatier, 1986, pp. 23–24). A vague policy is subject to multiple interpretations and the potential for bad execution even by implementers with the best of intentions. For Hogwood and Gunn (1984, pp. 204–206), perfect implementation requires that policymakers: agree on a common understanding of objectives; fully specify those objectives in the correct sequence; and, coordinate the implementation process with no breakdown in communication.
2. The policy will work as intended when implemented. The policy must be a good solution to the problem, based on a 'valid theory of cause and effect' (if we do X, the result will be Y).
3. The required resources are committed to the programme. Commitment can refer to money, staffing and physical materials, or giving the task to an organization that 'would be supportive and give it a high priority,' providing the right legal and economic sanctions and incentives to 'overcome resistance' (Sabatier, 1986, p. 23), and investing attention and political will to an issue over the longer term.
4. Policy is implemented by skilful and compliant officials. The term 'perfect obedience' (Hogwood & Gunn, 1984, p. 206) reminds us that we are

> discussing an ideal type; in fact, the discretion held by implementing officials with specialized jobs is 'unavoidable'
>
> 5. Dependency relationships are minimal. There are few 'veto points' or links in a 'delivery chain'; the implementing agency does not rely on the cooperation of others.
> 6. Support from influential groups is maintained. The implementation process is long, and continuous support from key actors is crucial.
> 7. Conditions beyond the control of policymakers do not significantly undermine the process. Socioeconomic conditions can often be unpredictable (Sabatier, 1986, p. 25) and affect the costs of, or support for, implementation.
>
> (Cairney, 2019, pp. 28–29)

The bottom-up approach is the second main model and recognises that individuals at subordinate levels are likely to play an active part in implementation and may have some discretion to reshape objectives of the policy and change the way it is implemented. The bottom-up approach sees policy implementation as an interactive process involving policymakers, implementers from various levels of government and other actors. But taking such an approach presents two challenges: first, the evaluation of the effects of a policy becomes difficult, and second, it is also difficult to separate the influence of individuals and different levels on policy decisions and consequences.

In commenting on the development of implementation theory over time, Hupe and Sætren (2015) noted the historical tendency for researchers to coalesce into either top-down or bottom-up schools of thought, each with their own opposing ideas on empirical-methodological and normative issues related to the study of policy implementation. One notable contribution that attempts to overcome this duality comes from Matland (1995) who developed a two-by-two typology which attempted to illustrate how top-down and bottom-up approaches can vary according to policy areas. He proposes that the value of either approach depends on the degree of ambiguity in goals and means of a policy and the relative amount of conflict between stakeholders involved in policymaking and implementation. Traditional top-down approaches may present a relevant guide for the implementation process when a policy is clear and the conflict is low. However, some top-down models, such as the Mazmanian–Sabatier framework, are also relevant when conflict is high and ambiguity is low, which makes the structuring of the implementation process particularly important. In contrast, bottom-up models provide a more appropriate description of the implementation process when the policy is ambiguous and the conflict is low. When conflict as well as ambiguity is present, both models may have some relevance.

Ultimately, top-down and bottom-up perspectives have utility in drawing attention to the fact that both top and bottom play important roles in implementation processes, but there remains the danger that each can ignore the portion of the implementation reality explained by the other. The development of principal–agent theory emerged in political science in the 1970s as an attempt to give greater recognition to the complexities of implementing policy. It was particularly instrumental in influencing public administration and policy during the 1990s, also a time during which sport policy in the UK began to be shaped by a partnership approach to public policy.

The central tenet of principal–agent theory highlights the role of particular individuals or organisational entities as the key parties within the policy process, able to resolve conflicts, clarify expectations or monitor results. The principal–agent relationship, however, illustrates the challenges that occur when the 'agent,' a person or entity (which can be an organisation), takes action on behalf of another person or entity (the 'principal'). The principal–agent model may be employed to elucidate central problems in interaction between principals and agents in both policy implementation and public policymaking. The problems are potentially aggravated and/or exacerbated when there is an increased divergence of interests between the two parties. The principal–agent model was initially applied in private sector settings but acquired strength from those who advocated NPM modes of governance in public administration. NPM used tools such as short-term contracting of public services to augment the position of the principal in relation to public service provision. In UK Leisure services, such a tool was initially seen during the contracting out of services under Compulsory Competitive Tendering (CCT) in the late 1980s and early 1990s.

Principal–agent theory represented an alternative to top-down and bottom-up approaches which were each recognised to overemphasise particular directions in implementation processes. Further, there is merit in utilising the approach to understand the role of 'people' as actors and the source of action or inaction, rather than the bureaucracies of organisations as autonomous entities. Nevertheless, the amount of discretion given to the agents and the complexity of the principal–agent relationship are affected by two key contexts. First, the nature and dimensions of the policy problem, including the scale of change required, the size of affected group, the relative complexity of the intervention, the extent to which policy outcomes are clear or ill-defined, the number of causes, the degree of political sensitivity, and the length of time before changes become apparent. Challenges remain as the situational context as well as beliefs and priorities of implementing agents differ across policy areas and systems. Therefore, no 'one-size-fits-all' solution to the challenges of effective policy implementation exists. Sabatier and Mazmanian (1980, p. 553) proposed that it is also significant to keep in mind that different stages in the implementation process exist:

- The policy outputs (decisions) of implementing agencies
- The compliance of target groups with those decisions

- The actual impacts of decisions made and enacted by agents
- The perceived impacts of those decisions
- The political system's evaluation of a statute in terms of major revisions in its content

In summary, the practice of policy implementation involves three activities: first, interpretation which involves the translation of the policy into administrative directives; second, organisation which sees the establishment of administrative units and methods necessary to put a programme into effect; and third, application, the administering of the service. Lessons from implementation research indicate that the trend is towards a multi-theoretical approach, in which the direction of change is non-linear and systemic change happens due to dynamic interactive processes rather than a centrally determined design (Gornitzka et al., 2005).

The unproductive schism between top-down and bottom-up perspectives in implementation research seems to have dissipated, as recognition that both perspectives are valid and needed has gained more ground since the 1990s (Hupe & Saetren, 2015, p. 95). A synthesised integrative analytical framework (Winter, 2012a) has emerged as a heuristic device that guides investigators in the direction of a handful of clusters of variables that have repeatedly been illustrated to be important in explaining policy implementation (Hupe & Saetren, 2015, p. 95). Winter (2012b, p. 265) suggests that implementation research can be improved by '(first) accepting theoretical diversity rather than looking for one common theoretical framework, and second, developing and testing partial theories and hypotheses rather than trying to reach for utopia in constructing a general implementation theory.'

Policy change may not lead to anticipated outputs and outcomes if the process of implementation leads to an 'implementation gap.' Hogwood and Gunn (1984, p. 197) attribute the failure to implement to three factors: bad execution, when policy is not carried out as intended; bad policy, when it is implemented but fails to have an (intended) effect; and bad luck, when it is undermined by factors outside of the control of policymakers. Thus, the main question is: how can we explain the significance of implementation roles and processes on the ultimate outcomes of policy?

Implementation is complex and will fail or be seriously delayed if insufficiently prepared. A key point for the strategic direction of sports organisations is to ensure active engagement and support to adopter organisations – in other words, to build adequate capacity within the processes involved in implementation. Implementation equals change in procedures and practices, which typically require the development of both individual and organisational capabilities. To speed up implementation, practitioners need support to understand and apply new practices in local settings. This has given rise to the notion of capacity building as a way of designing implementation processes. By definition, organisational capacity refers to 'the overall capacity of a non-profit and voluntary organisation to produce the outputs and outcomes it desires' (Hall et al., 2003, p. 4). Organisational capacity is generally regarded as a multidimensional concept, comprising a range of organisational attributes that are considered critical to an organisation's ability to achieve its goals and satisfy its stakeholders' expectations (Doherty & Cuskelly, 2020, p. 241). Sports organisations possess numerous resources that enable them to be active participants in the policy process and in being able to make a good deal of policy on their own. Further, these organisations generally want to use their expertise and ideas to shape policies. But these organisations confront a number of challenges when they attempt to utilise those resources to be effective within the policy process (Peters, 2015, p. 227). What organisations want or are required to implement is perceived differently and transformed differently by the various persons and organisations tasked with implementation. The capacity of organisations involved in policy implementation is also influenced by the nature of the staffing within those organisations (Peters, 2015, p. 226). Enacting policy requires organisations to build capacity to meet expectations, to communicate and to involve target groups to establish a process of interpretation and reflection among the stakeholders to reach conclusions on how to implement intended actions. Such considerations have been brought to the fore in recent theorising on policy enactment, as summarised in the following section.

Policy Enactment

For Ball et al. (2012), to evaluate policy implementation is to assess how well policies are realised in practice, to which they contend that it is very difficult – and sometimes, impossible – to determine which implementation practices will lead to desired or other outcomes. Ball et al. (2012) state that policies do not normally outline exactly what must be done in order for them to work in practice and that policies are seldom delivered on the ground by those who make them; so they cannot simply be implemented. Instead, policies are interpreted from text and translated into practice by diverse policy actors according to the dynamics of the contexts in which they are negotiated, contested, resisted and struggled over within institutions (Braun et al., 2011; Ozga, 2000). To this effect, Ball et al. (2012) and Braun et al. (2011) speak to processes of policy enactment as opposed to policy implementation.

From a policy enactment perspective then, practitioners are not viewed as homogenous nor as 'passive recipients or mere implementers of top-down policy decisions' but rather that they actively interpret and translate policy to fit their own context (O'Gorman, 2011; Tan, 2017, p. 589). Ball and colleagues differentiate between the constituent processes of interpretation and translation that occur in policy enactment. Policy enactment begins as policy actors, both individually and collectively, make situated interpretations of a policy text and discourse which are inflected and nuanced according to their own values and the culture of their institution, and through which they consider the implications of a policy, how to respond to it and the consequences if they do not (Ball et al., 2012). Policy is then recontextualised in line with an organisation's priorities, needs and resources as policy actors translate it 'into materials, practices, concepts, procedures and orientations' through which it can be put into action (Ball et al., 2012; Ball et al., 2011, p. 620). Policies can be formulated by or externally to an organisation, and where prescribed externally, Braun et al. (2011) have shown that delivery organisations (e.g. schools) produce their own 'take' on policy as they seek to understand and translate it in keeping with their situated reality.

The enactment of policy takes place under material conditions of varying resources and therefore is constrained or enabled by specific contextual factors which Ball and colleagues (2012) consolidate into a typology of the following four overlapping contextual dimensions: situated contexts (e.g. locality, membership base, organisational history); professional and occupational cultures (e.g. values, workers' positioning, biographies, experiences in, and commitment to an organisation); material contexts (e.g. budgets, infrastructure, technology, and staffing) and external contexts (e.g. broader policy contexts and agendas). Ball et al. (2012) thus present this framework as a heuristic device for policy scholars to use to illuminate the complex, dynamic, non-linear and sometimes contradictory ways in which policies are enacted by policy actors in practice in and across heterogeneous, if not always or altogether dissimilar, organisations characterised by differing resource environments.

To place policy enactment into a wider context through which higher-level objectives are rendered into action by those organisations and actors delivering 'on the ground,' Ball (2003) uses his research on the education system to unpack the advanced liberal way that the state drives policy change and reform. Whilst espousing the rhetoric of devolved authority and decentralised power that shifts control from the state to organisations, what is argued to be taking place instead is a re-regulation of state control wherein new modes of invisible social control have become embedded – a more '"hands-off," self-regulating regulation' of the wider policy delivery apparatus (Ball, 2003; Singh, 2018; Singh et al., 2014, p. 828; Solomon & Lewin, 2016). To this effect, Ball et al. (2012) and Braun and Maguire (2020) speak of technologies that drive the machinery of policy delivery – the machinery encompassing the many and often minor processes that unfold across the 'delivery chain' as policies are translated into organisational practices.

Ball (2003) articulated a triumvirate of key policy technologies: performativity, the market and managerialism. Together, such technologies support a shift to a devolved environment wherein central management bodies set an overall operating framework for the system that steps away from more bureaucratic relations. Such a framework is characterised by, and rests upon, measures and monitoring systems of productivity (targets, indicators, audits, evaluations, inspections), which have re-aligned the culture and practices of public sector organisations to those long associated with the private sector. This environment thus drives performances of individuals and organisations to measure up to and fulfil requisites necessary for job security, promotion, funding, etc. The notion of performativity is prominent within policy enactment research in education, and Ball describes it as 'a technology, a culture and a mode of regulation that employs judgements, comparisons and displays as means of incentive, control, attrition and change – based on rewards and sanctions (both material and symbolic)' (2003, p. 216). The technology of performance therefore serves to steer, directly or indirectly, the practice and policy commitment of delivery organisations and policy actors from a distance, as the performance culture it feeds generates 'a set of pressures which work "downwards"' through the system (Ball et al., 2012, p. 74; Singh et al., 2014). However, it may be the case that organisations, whilst acknowledging a policy, might use strategic fabrications via official reporting systems to represent themselves and their practice in policy-compliant ways (Ball, 2003; O'Gorman et al., 2021). Thus, such creative acts of non-implementation or performative implementation only superficially reflect practice or commitment to organisational change (Ball et al., 2012).

Indeed, as processes of government have shifted towards such processes of governance, Ball explains that such transformations can lead to a complex and convoluted terrain of government that will bring about 'problems of coordination and accountability and transparency' in the policy process (2009, p. 537). Against this backdrop, there is a fertile ground for analysis of the 'different sorts of roles, actions, and engagements embedded in the processes of interpretation and translation' in the enactment of sport policy by policy actors, in conjunction with the intersecting contextual dimensions and discourses that affect it (Ball et al., 2011, p. 625).

Ball stressed that policy is open to 'the embodied agency of those people who are its object' (Ball, 1994, pp. 10–11), and to further illustrate the peopled nature of policy enactment, Ball et al. (2011, 2012) present a typology of policy actors to identify and examine the different roles, actions and engagements (policy work) of stakeholders embedded within policy enactment processes. Ball et al. (2012) offer eight categories of 'policy actor' (see Table 1.1) that are fluid – in the sense that people may combine different aspects of such policy work or transition between roles.

This typology of policy actors facilitates the study of how policies are enacted, and how policy work is undertaken at the local level (Ball et al., 2012). However, not only is a policy actor's freedom to interpret and translate policy restricted or enabled according to contextual factors, but it is also influenced via situated power relations and constrained by established discourses (Ball et al., 2012, 2011). What is more, Ball et al. (2012) suggest a policy enactment approach allows researchers to consider how policy actors make sense of policy and how various policies and discourses have shaped their own knowledge and subjectivities over time. Ball and colleagues highlight here that implementation studies demonstrate a tendency to focus their attention on current or recent policies and typically overlook what Ball et al. (2012, p. 6) refer to as a policy actor's 'discursive archive' from which they can draw on 'over and against contemporary policy.'

Policy enactment therefore provides an analytic framework by which to understand how delivery organisations and policy actors creatively respond to policy demands in practice and against the reality of the material conditions, diverse variables and dynamic contexts that shape the enactment of policy – and which will likely differ from organisation to organisation (Ball et al., 2012; Singh et al., 2014).

Introduction   15

Table 1.1 Policy actors and policy work

Policy actors	Policy work
Narrators	Interpret, select and enforce meanings of policies
Entrepreneurs	Advocate/champion particular policies and are creative as policies can originate with them
Outsiders	Entrepreneurship and partnership: external consultants or partners who introduce policies or policy ideas and support translation and monitoring
Transactors	Report when policy is done and can be accounted for, and this way policy responses are made calculable enabling their monitoring and enforcement
Enthusiasts	Can be encouraged to support policy agendas and influence others to do so too; they translate policy in creative ways through their practice and are invested in and gain satisfaction from their policy work
Translators	Plan and produce institutional policy texts, processes, artefacts and events
Critics	Engage in the monitoring of management, maintaining counter-discourses (e.g. Union representatives) and become particularly active when policies or policy translations threaten the interests of members
Receivers	Are often junior staff who are compliant due to their dependence on policy for the guidance and direction it offers them – some cope with policy, whilst others defend policy as they struggle through their experience of it

Source: Adapted and synthesised from Ball et al. (2011, pp. 626–634) and Ball, Maguire and Braun (2012, pp. 49–66).

Orientation and Structure of the Book

The preceding sections have emphasised the complexities of sport policy and of approaches to understanding implementation processes, as well as the importance of different types of organisations and actors in these processes. The intention throughout the remainder of the book is to draw out the complexity of and varying perspectives on sport policy implementation through focusing each of the chapters on specific types of organisations. Represented organisations have roles and positioning in sport policy implementation that varies significantly across, and in some cases within, the different chapters. The overall selection of the specific types of organisations included in the book sought to encompass those that have consistently had significant involvement in sport policy implementation over time, even if the specific nature of this involvement may have fluctuated with shifts in the orientation of sport policy and implementation approaches.

The spread of the organisations that is covered spans those such as Sport England and UK Sport (Chapter 2) that may be considered to have had substantive roles in crafting sport policy implementation, to those such as schools or voluntary sports clubs (Chapters 9 and 10) that tend to react to enact and/or deliver sport policy implementation. Other chapters focus on types of organisations that fulfil more intermediary roles, with national governing bodies (Chapter 3), Active Partnerships (Chapter 4), local authorities (Chapter 5) and national sport equity agencies (Chapter 7) having responsibilities both for shaping policies for particular areas or sports and for implementing national sport policies. These different roles have a degree of necessarily imperfect alignment with the scale and scope of the different types of organisations covered across the book. In this regard, there is a range from the first chapter which covers two specific national agencies to those that operate in specific localities. The size of the set of organisations covered in any one chapter also varies considerably in number, up to and around a hundred thousand in the case of voluntary sport clubs for example, which also means that there is substantial variation amongst particular types of organisations covered in some chapters. The set of chapters also spans organisations that represent public, private and voluntary sectors, with public health agencies (Chapter 6), sporting charities (Chapter 8) and professional football clubs (Chapter 11) being examples which represent each of these sectors in turn. Finally, and pertinently, the organisations covered vary considerably in the extent to which they focus on or span different sport policy areas related to PE and school sport, community sport and physical activity, and elite sport, respectively.

As editors seeking to bring together chapters that spanned this diversity of organisations, we wished to develop a book that both encompassed different perspectives and had a shared focus in order to draw collective learning on sport policy implementation. The structure of each chapter, comprising both academic and professional practitioner contributions, is intended to contribute to these aims by offering both overarching analysis and specific insider accounts from individuals who have worked as different types of 'policy actors' on behalf of the organisations that the book covers. In this regard, academic contributors were all asked to provide an explanation of the characteristics of the organisations or type of organisation that their chapter covers, together with substantive content on these organisations' involvement in sport policy over time, their contributions and responses to implementation of sport policy, and resulting consequences and outcomes. Professional practitioners were then asked to respond to the key issues raised in the academic contributions though considering their own perspectives and experiences in or with these types of organisations and in the practice of sport policy implementation. In bringing together academic and professional practitioner contributions in this way, we hope the book will provide readers with a rare opportunity to consider an integrated dialogue between different viewpoints that can often be unnecessarily and detrimentally separated. Furthermore, in seeking to draw together themes identified and discussed across the book in a concluding chapter, our intention is to help readers identify central issues in implementing sport policy in the UK, consider their wider theoretical relevance and suggest potential developments for future policy, practice and research.

References

Baker, C., El Ansari, W., & Crone, D. (2016). Partnership working in sport and physical activity promotion: An assessment of processes and outcomes in community sports networks. *Public Policy and Administration*, *32*(2), 87–109. http://doi.org/10.1177/0952076715625104

Ball, S. J. (1994). *Education reform: A critical and post-structural approach.* Open University Press.

Ball, S. J. (2003). The teacher's soul and the terrors of performativity. *Journal of Education Policy*, *18*(2), 215–228. https://doi.org/10.1080/0268093022000043065

Ball, S. J. (2009). Editorial: The governance turn! *Journal of Education Policy*, *24*(5), 537–538. https://doi.org/10.1080/02680930903239904

Ball, S. J., Maguire, M., & Braun, A. (2012). *How schools do policy: Policy enactments in secondary schools.* Routledge.

Ball, S. J., Maguire, M., Braun, A., & Hoskins, K. (2011). Policy actors: Doing policy work in schools. *Discourse: Studies in the Cultural Politics of Education*, *32*(4), 625–639. http://doi.org/10.1080/01596306.2011.601565

Braun, A., Ball, S. J., Maguire, M., & Hoskins, K. (2011). Taking context seriously: Towards explaining policy enactments in the secondary school. *Discourse: Studies in the Cultural Politics of Education*, *32*(4), 585–596. http://doi.org/10.1080/01596306.2011.601555

Braun, A., & Maguire, M. (2020). Doing without believing – Enacting policy in the English primary school. *Critical Studies in Education*, *61*(4), 433–447. http://doi.org/10.1080/17508487.2018.1500384

Cairney, P. (2009). Implementation and the governance problem: A pressure participant perspective. *Public Policy and Administration*, *24*(4), 355–377. http://doi.org/10.1177/0952076709340508

Cairney, P. (2019). *Understanding public policy* (2nd ed.). Macmillan.

Coaffee, J., & Johnston, L. (2005). The management of local government modernisation: Area decentralisation and pragmatic localism. *International Journal of Public Sector Management*, *18*(2), 166–174. http://doi.org/10.1108/09513550510584982

Coalter, F. (2017). Sport and social inclusion: Evidence-based policy and practice. *Social Inclusion*, *5*(2), 141–149. http://doi.org/10.17645/si.v5i2.852

Collins, M. (2010). From "sport for good" to "sport for sport's sake"-not a good move for sports development in England? *International Journal of Sport Policy and Politics*, *2*(3), 367–379. http://doi.org/10.1080/19406940.2010.519342

Department for Culture, Media and Sport. (2000). *A sporting future for all.* DCMS.

Department for Culture, Media and Sport. (2001). *The government's plan for sport.* Her Majesty's Stationary Office.

Department for Culture, Media and Sport/Strategy Unit. (2002). *Game plan: A strategy for delivering government's sport and physical activity objectives.* DCMS/Strategy Unit.

Department of National Heritage. (1995). *Sport: Raising the game.* DNH.

Diamond, J. (2006). Au revoir to partnerships: what's next? *International Journal of Public Sector Management*, *19*(3), 278–286. https://doi.org/10.1108/09513550610658231

Doherty, A., & Cuskelly, G. (2020). Organizational capacity and performance of community sport clubs. *Journal of Sport Management*, *34*(3), 240–259. http://doi.org/10.1123/jsm.2019-0098

Gornitzka, A., Kogan, M., & Amaral, A. (Eds.). (2005). *Reform and change in higher education: Analysing policy implementation.* Springer.

18 Iain Lindsey et al.

Green, M., & Houlihan, B. (2006). Governmentality, modernization, and the "disciplining" of national sporting organizations – Athletics in Australia and the United Kingdom. *Sociology of Sport Journal, 23*(1), 47–71. http://doi.org/10.1123/ssj.23.1.47

Hall, M., Andrukow, A., Barr, C., Brock, K., Wit, M., Embuldeniya, D., Jolin, L., Lasby, D., Lévesque, B., Malinsky, E., Stowe, S., & Vaillancourt, Y. (2003). *A qualitative study of the challenges facing Canada's nonprofit and voluntary organizations*. Canadian Centre for Philanthropy.

Harris, T., Hodge, L., & Phillips, D. (2019). *English local government funding: Trends and challenges in 2019 and beyond*. Institute for Fiscal Studies.

Hill, M., & Hupe, P. (2015). *Implementing public policy* (3rd ed.). Sage.

HM Government. (2015). *Sporting future: A new strategy for an active nation*. Cabinet Office.

Hogwood, B., & Gunn, L. (1984). *Policy analysis for the real world*. Oxford University Press.

Hood, C. (1976). *The limits of administration*. Wiley.

Houlihan, B., & Green, M. (2009). Modernisation and sport: The reform of sport England and UK sport. *Public Administration, 87*(3), 678–698. https://doi.org/10.1111/j.1467 -9299.2008.01733.x

Houlihan, B., & Lindsey, I. (2013). *Sport policy in Britain*. Routledge.

Hupe, P., & Sætren, H. (2015). Comparative implementation research: Directions and dualities. *Journal of Comparative Policy Analysis: Research and Practice, 17*(2), 93–102. http://doi.org/10.1080/13876988.2015.1015360

Keech, M., & Nauright, J. (2018). Sports industry and policy in the United Kingdom. In J. J. Zhang, R. H. Huang, & J. Nauright (Eds.), *Global expansion of the sports industry* (pp. 427–460). Emerald.

Kurunmäki, L., & Miller, P. (2006). Modernising government: The calculating self, hybridisation and performance measurement. *Financial Accountability and Management, 22*(1), 87–106. http://doi.org/10.1111/j.0267-4424.2006.00394.x

Lindsey, I. (2009). Collaboration in local sport services in England: Issues emerging from case studies of two local authority areas. *International Journal of Sport Policy, 1*(1), 71–88. http://doi.org/10.1080/19406940802681210

Lindsey, I. (2011). Partnership working and sports development. In B. Houlihan & M. Green (Eds.), *Routledge handbook of sports development* (pp. 517–529). Routledge.

Lindsey, I. (2020). Analysing policy change and continuity: Physical education and school sport policy in England since 2010. *Sport, Education and Society, 25*(1), 27–42. http://doi.org/10.1080/13573322.2018.1547274

Matland, R. E. (1995). Synthesizing the implementation literature: The ambiguity-conflict model. *Journal of Public Administration Research and Theory, 5*(2), 145–174. https://doi.org/10.1093/oxfordjournals.jpart.a037242

Mazmanian, D. A., & Sabatier, P. A. (1983). *Implementation and public policy*. Foresman.

McDonald, I. (2005). Theorising partnerships: Governance, communicative action and sport policy. *Journal of Social Policy, 34*(4), 579–600. http://doi.org/10.1017/S0047279405009165

O'Gorman, J. (2011). Where is the implementation in sport policy and programme analysis? The English Football Association's Charter standard as an illustration. *International Journal of Sport Policy and Politics, 3*(1), 85–108. http://doi.org/10.1080/19406940 .2010.548339

O'Gorman, J., Partington, M., Potrac, P., & Nelson, L. (2021). Translation, intensification and fabrication: Professional football academy coaches' enactment of the elite player performance plan. *Sport, Education and Society, 26*(3), 309–325. http://doi.org/10.1080/13573322.2020.1726313

Ozga, J. (2000). *Policy research in educational settings: Contested terrain.* Open University Press.

Peters, B. G. (2015). Policy capacity in public administration. *Policy and Society, 34*(3–4), 219–228. http://doi.org/10.1016/j.polsoc.2015.09.005

Phillpots, L., Grix, J., & Quarmby, T. (2011). Centralized grassroots sport policy and 'new governance': A case study of county sports partnerships in the UK–unpacking the paradox. *International Review for the Sociology of Sport, 46*(3), 265–281. http://doi.org/10.1177/1012690210378461

Sabatier, P. (1986). Top-down and bottom-up approaches to implementation research: A critical analysis and suggested synthesis. *Journal of Public Policy, 6*(1), 21–48. http://doi.org/10.1017/S0143814X00003846

Sabatier, P., & Mazmanian, D. (1979). The conditions of effective implementation: A guide to accomplishing policy objectives. *Policy Analysis, 5*(4), 481–504.

Sabatier, P., & Mazmanian, D. (1980). The implementation of public policy: A framework of analysis. *Policy Studies Journal, 8*(4), 538–560. http://doi.org/10.1111/j.1541-0072.1980.tb01266.x

Singh, P. (2018). Performativity, affectivity and pedagogic identities. *European Educational Research Journal, 17*(4), 489–506. https://doi.org/10.1177/1474904117726181

Singh, P., Heimans, S., & Glasswell, K. (2014). Policy enactment, context and performativity: Ontological politics and researching Australian National Partnership policies. *Journal of Education Policy, 29*(6), 826–844. http://doi.org/10.1080/02680939.2014.891763

Solomon, Y., & Lewin, C. (2016). Measuring 'progress': Performativity as both driver and constraint in school innovation. *Journal of Education Policy, 31*(2), 226–238. http://doi.org/10.1080/02680939.2015.1062147

Sport England. (2010). *The English sports council grant in aid and national lottery distribution fund: Annual report and accounts, 2009–2010.* The Stationery Office.

Sport England. (2016). *Towards an active nation.* Sport England.

Sport England. (2020). *Annual report and accounts: The English sports council grant-in-aid and national lottery distribution fund.* https://assets.publishing.service.gov.uk/government/uploads/system/uploads/attachment_data/file/947605/Sport_England_2019-20_Annual_Report_and_Accounts.pdf

Sport England. (2021). *Uniting the movement.* Sport England.

Tan, C. (2017). The enactment of the policy initiative for critical thinking in Singapore schools. *Journal of Education Policy, 32*(5), 588–603. http://doi.org/10.1080/02680939.2017.1305452

UK Sport. (n.d.). *Historical funding figures.* https://www.uksport.gov.uk/our-work/investing-in-sport/historical-funding-figures.

Winter, S. (2012a). Implementation perspectives: Status and reconsideration. In B. G. Peters & J. Pierre (Eds.), *Handbook of public administration* (pp. 265–278). Sage.

Winter, S. (2012b). Implementation: Introduction to Part 5. In B. G. Peters & J. Pierre (Eds.), *Handbook of public administration* (pp. 255–263). Sage.

Chapter 2

National Sports Agencies

Pippa Chapman

Introduction

This chapter explores the role of the two sports councils who have responsibility for sport across England and the UK, respectively, Sport England and UK Sport. These organisations receive government funding from the exchequer and the National Lottery via the Department for Digital, Culture, Media and Sport (DCMS), and they interpret government policy through both their own internal activities but also through working with a range of partners who deliver programmes that ultimately implement policy. The sports councils are crucial organisations in the translation of Westminster government policies into strategies and practices through the distribution of public monies and through directing organisations with whom they work, creating a link between the government and the organisations responsible for implementing policy at a more local level. There are clear decision-making and monitoring mechanisms in place, with funding allocations guided by funding principle documents that are published on a cyclical basis and any funding granted being subject to regular reporting.

The other UK home nations, Scotland, Wales and Northern Ireland, all have their own sports councils that have their own policy priorities and funding arrangements working with devolved administrations, and their roles and responsibilities are generally similar to those of Sport England, with some additional responsibility for high-performance sport. With regard to home nation sports councils, this chapter will focus on Sport England only due to its policy direction and income coming from the Westminster government and its alignment with UK Sport in terms of implementing the overall Westminster government sport policy.

Historical Outline

The initial establishment of a sports council in the UK was the Advisory Sports Council in 1965, which was formed following the recommendations of the *Wolfenden Report*, published in 1960 (Coghlan, 1990). This first sports council was a non-executive body that was chaired by the then sports minister, Denis Howell. The establishment of a sports council was described by Green (2007, p. 935) as

DOI: 10.4324/9781003162728-2

'the first indication of serious government intervention into the sport and recreation sector.' Later, in 1972, an executive sports council, named the Great Britain Sports Council, was established by Royal Charter, and the primary focus of the Council was mass participation. Sports councils for Northern Ireland, Scotland and Wales were also established in the 1970s, and these organisations also took a lead role in developing mass participation sport in their respective home nations. At this time, the British government retained a 'hands off' approach to high-performance sport, though political interest in international sporting success increased initially in the 1980s and was then solidified from the 1990s onwards (McDonald, 2011). In the GB Sports Council's 1982 policy document, *Sport in the Community: The Next Ten Years*, there was an acknowledgement of the work of other nations' governments investing public funds in high-performance sport, but it was noted 'It is neither tradition nor policy to treat top level sport in this way in Britain' (The Sports Council, 1982, p. 40).

An increase in the overall political salience of sport in the mid-1990s, including the establishment of the Department of National Heritage (DNH) in 1992 and the publication of its first sport policy, *Sport: Raising the Game*, in 1995, with its explicit dual-focus on sport participation (particularly for young people through school sport) and international sporting success, brought about changes to the structure of the sports council. Furthermore, the establishment of the National Lottery in 1994 and the decision that some of the monies raised for good causes would be allocated to sport meant there was a clear income stream for sport that could be used to fulfil the government's policy objectives. The Sports Council was therefore divided into separate organisations in 1996: the United Kingdom Sport Council, responsible for elite sport across the UK, and the English Sport Council, responsible for mass participation and grassroots sport in England. The two organisations were then rebranded in 1999 and became UK Sport and Sport England, respectively.

Both UK Sport and Sport England are non-departmental public bodies, with their sponsoring department being DCMS, and both are National Lottery Distributors. Successive governments since the 1990s have tended to make clear statements about their priorities for sport and the role they see sport taking in society, but there is a good amount of discretion in the sports councils' interpretation of government policy. In this 'agent' role, the sports councils set out strategies to clearly state their responsibilities, priorities and decision-making, which includes specific funding principles to guide funding allocations to their partners. The sports councils report to government regularly, and as they are publicly funded organisations, their accounts have to be published and accessible to the public on an annual basis.

The nature of the two sports councils' work with their partners moves them from the role of 'agent' to being the 'principal' as they set the overall objectives, and it is the responsibility of their funded partners to be 'agents' and respond with the specifics of how policy will be implemented for their particular organisation, which may be sport-specific or cross-sport, and national or local. Organisations wishing to receive funding and support from UK Sport and Sport England have to make their case according to the relevant sports council's funding principles, and when decisions about funding are made, the relationships with funded partners are subject to contracts and regular monitoring.

Despite continuity in political interest in sport, how the sports councils have operated has changed over time in terms of how they are run. In particular, there were many changes in the 2000s due to the Labour government's wide-ranging policy of modernisation. As discussed by Houlihan and Green (2009), modernisation resulted in changes to not only UK Sport and Sport England themselves but also the partners with whom they work, and they note Lord Carter's terminology of a 'spine of accountability,' indicating the line of responsibility from the government through the sports councils and to the organisations in receipt of public funding. Houlihan and Green (2009, p. 689) further discuss the nature of the relationships between the sports councils and the organisations they fund as 'increasingly contractual' and note that the sports councils were ready and willing to involve themselves in other organisations' affairs, especially national governing bodies (NGBs). The work to modernise sport organisations in receipt of public funds led to wide-ranging change in how key areas of work in sport were addressed, including the governance of organisations (Tacon & Walters, 2016) and the more technical work of coaching and talent identification and development (Houlihan & Chapman, 2015). With specific reference to governance, the sports councils work together to set standards to which NGBs and other organisations in receipt of public money must adhere, with the most recent version of the Code for Sports Governance being published in December 2021 (Sport England, 2021a).

Despite ongoing support from successive governments over the past 25 years, UK Sport and Sport England are not without their critics. There have been specific criticisms of the two organisations, and these criticisms have led to reviews of their work (Houlihan & Green, 2009) and considerations of how the two organisations can be made more efficient, including suggestions of merging the two organisations. The high political salience of sport generally, including a sharp focus on delivering the Olympic and Paralympic Games in London in 2012, and the intended 'legacies' of those Games have meant that the organisations have been able to not only survive but thrive as cornerstones of policy implementation for successive Westminster governments since the 1990s. Policies published by successive governments and broader policy rhetoric have highlighted the government's position that sport is of value in the UK in terms of individual and societal benefits, plus broader economic and diplomatic advantages (HM Government, 2015; HM Government, 2021).

Priorities and Roles

UK Sport

Overall, UK Sport has benefitted from relatively stable policy objectives for high-performance sport since its establishment in the 1990s: namely, achieving medal success at international competitions, in particular the Olympic and Paralympic

Games. UK Sport has other responsibilities, including leading work on bidding for major events and work in the fields of international relations and development, but high-performance sport systems and funding athletes to prepare for international competitions account for the majority of its work and of the money it grants, with 67% of its spending in the 2019/2020 financial year going to NGBs and athletes (UK Sport, 2020a). The main changes UK Sport has experienced in its work to implement government policy since the late 1990s are changes to the scope of which sports it funds, changes to its responsibilities for funding and supporting the different levels of the World Class Programme and changes – primarily increases – in the levels of funding it receives and grants to partners.

UK Sport's focus has always been on high-performance sport, but the sports it has supported with National Lottery funding have fluctuated. In its early years, UK Sport funded a range of both Olympic and non-Olympic sports and disability sports including Paralympic sports and disciplines. A report by the National Audit Office in 2005 included recommendations that the number of athletes receiving funding should be reduced, with tighter eligibility criteria to enable this and that fewer sports should be supported by UK Sport (National Audit Office, 2005). From 2006, UK Sport's funding principles were informed by their 'No Compromise' approach, which entailed setting medal targets for NGBs and rewarding success and punishing failure when it came to whether or not the sports achieved these targets. This approach, while generally accepted as being successful, has been criticised at times. Following the 2012 Olympic and Paralympic Games, a Select Committee within the House of Lords was established to examine the legacy of the Games, and the subsequent report from this Committee recommended that UK Sport should take a more flexible approach to allocating funding, noting

> too strict an adherence to this approach, which is by its nature based largely on a retrospective assessment of performance, will develop a growing gap between the sports which already do well and those which have little realistic prospect of developing in the next few years.
>
> (House of Lords, 2013, p. 10)

However, this recommendation was rebuffed by the government in its response to the House of Lords report (Cabinet Office, 2014), and UK Sport did not fully explore revising the 'No Compromise' approach until 2019 (Ingle, 2019).

UK Sport's support and funding for NGBs and athletes are structured according to the World Class Programme (WCP) (previously known as the World Class Performance Programme – WCPP). The early version of this programme, the WCPP, had three levels: Talent Identification and Confirmation, Olympic Development Programme and Olympic Podium Programme (McDonald, 2011); with the highest level of funding for the Olympic Podium Programme. As McDonald (2011) outlined, NGBs were, and remain, crucial partners for UK Sport, and meeting medal targets was a key indicator of whether policy had been implemented successfully, along with specific processes and standards for governance and accountability. At present, UK Sport's WCP has two levels: 'Podium' and 'Podium Potential.' This programme structures funding according to the likelihood of athletes winning medals at the next Olympic and Paralympic Games or the Games that follow. The support that UK Sport then provides is a combination of funds to the NGB, funds directly to the athlete and other support services provided by UK Sport and the English Institute of Sport.

London winning the bid to host the 2012 Olympic and Paralympic Games during the International Olympic Committee (IOC) session in Singapore in 2005 led to a greater focus on Olympic and Paralympic sports and the development of systems to produce medal-winning performances amongst British athletes. The British government declared that its intention for the British team at the Olympic Games in 2012 was to have representation across all sports in the Olympic programme, which led to funding being granted to NGBs that had previously not been supported by UK Sport, with examples including Handball and Synchronised Swimming. At this time, the decision was also taken to move the full responsibility of the World Class Performance Programme to UK Sport, rather than the lower levels of the Programme being managed and funded through Sport England. Expanding the number of sports to receive public funding, the full responsibility of the WCPP moving to UK Sport and the greater sense of urgency around developing athletes to ensure a successful Games in 2012 led to a significant increase in government funding for UK Sport. At the beginning of the 2005–2008 funding cycle (to support preparations for the 2008 Olympic and Paralympic Games in Beijing), the total funding through UK Sport was approximately £75 million. However, this figure was revised in 2006 after London's bid was successful, and the final total spend for the cycle was in excess of £235 million.

In subsequent Olympic cycles, and across Olympic and Paralympic sports and summer and winter sports, funding has increased, but the number of NGBs that UK Sport works with and grants funds to has changed over time. Following London 2012, funding ceased to the sports that had been granted money to ensure there was British representation, which left these organisations with a resource gap (Bostock et al., 2018). Interest in, and therefore funding for, winter sports came later than the initial push for developing high-performance systems in summer sports, but there is now a similar growth in the amount of money and the expectations for medals being won at the Winter Olympic and Paralympic Games, though the figures remain modest compared with summer sports. The total funding for NGBs for the 2002 Winter Olympic Games was just under £2 million, while the funding for preparations for the 2022 Winter Olympic Games was over £22 million (UK Sport, n.d.a). Working more closely with winter sport NGBs means a more diverse set of partners for UK Sport, but the nature of those partners varies little compared with organisations with whom UK Sport has a longer history.

The responsibility that UK Sport has to grant, or indeed *not* to grant, funds to NGBs is a tool that shapes the implementation of government policy significantly as only those sports that can evidence their potential for success receive funds and therefore are part of the high-performance system that UK Sport oversees. Whether a sport receives funding in one cycle (Olympic quadrennial) tends to affect whether they receive funding in subsequent cycles as without funding, NGBs struggle to develop their systems sufficiently to then be able to demonstrate medal-winning potential, and therefore, they can be stuck in a loop of not receiving support from UK Sport. This approach, and the influence of the No Compromise principles, has softened in the recent past, and UK Sport now has smaller grants available for sports with less-developed high-performance systems, known as Progression Funding (UK Sport, 2020b).

As previously noted, granting funds to NGBs and supporting high-performance systems are the core of UK Sport's work and account for the majority of its spending, but it also has departments focused on bidding for and supporting the delivery of major events and international relations, whose work relates to building relationships with other countries and with international sport organisations. The government's policy focus on hosting of events has increased significantly in the past 20 years, with UK Sport as a key partner in implementing this work. When bidding for events, UK Sport works closely with relevant NGBs and local governments in cities and/or regions, as well as the central government, thus broadening the scope of partners with whom UK Sport works, albeit for relatively short periods of time.

Similarly, within UK Sport's international relations and international development work, the range of partners with whom the organisation works goes beyond British NGBs. This has included development work in partnership with national and international sports federations and sport- and youth-focused non-government organisations, a lot of which in more recent history have been linked with the hosting of major events in the UK. For example, as part of the bid to host the 2018 Hockey World Cup in England, UK Sport worked in partnership with national and international hockey organisations to help develop technical knowledge in coaching and officiating for hockey in Ghana and the broader West Africa region (UK Sport, n.d.b).

In the recent past, UK Sport's work has expanded to build teams that look to address issues that have arisen in high-performance sport in the UK and to add further to the evidence base that informs key decisions in relation to events. Specifically, there is now a team responsible for assessing NGBs' 'culture' to ensure the well-being of athletes and other professionals working in high-performance programmes, and there are new roles within the events team for monitoring the value of events. This could be viewed as 'mission creep' insomuch as the additional roles, and expansion of departments require additional resources, but it also supports UK Sport's status as a meaningful organisation if it can tackle key issues in the system and evidence the positive impact of its work, thereby securing future income and an ongoing role in the shaping and implementation of sport policy.

Sport England

Sport England's primary remit is to support opportunities for people to participate in sport and other forms of physical activity in England. The precise nature of this remit has fluctuated somewhat over time depending on government policy and various notions of the use of sport in society. The general objective of increasing sport participation was not a priority in the late 1990s, with *Sport: Raising the Game* focusing more on young people's involvement and sport in schools. However, the Labour governments through the 2000s focused more directly on increasing participation in sport and outlined the need for sport to be used as a tool for social development and addressing issues in society in *Game Plan*, which was published in 2002. The Labour government's later sport policy focus shifted to 'sport for sport's sake,' as outlined in the 2008 policy document, *Playing to Win: A New Era for Sport*, though this document references physical activity as well as more 'traditional' sport. The Conservative-led Coalition government (2010–2015) continued to focus on sport but highlighted the importance of engaging young people in their 2012 policy, *Creating a Sporting Habit for Life*. The most recent government policy for sport, *Sporting Future: A New Strategy for an Active Nation*, was published by the government in late 2015, and this policy focuses on the role that sport and physical activity can play in individual and social development. The shift to such a strong focus on physical activity represented a significant change for the British government, and Sport England had to adapt its work accordingly.

In terms of how Sport England implements government policy, working with a network of partners at national, regional and local levels is a constant feature of the organisation's work. This has included the establishment of networks of partners, including County Sport Partnerships, which were an ongoing feature of Sport England's policy implementation through the 2000s and have continued to be so in their rebranded guise as Active Partnerships. The nature of the partner organisations in terms of their scope and the number of organisations working with Sport England have fluctuated as Sport England has responded to changes in government policy and moved to work with the most appropriate partners to implement government policy according to the particular focus on sport, physical activity and specific populations. Additionally, Sport England has established programmes to address specific, and at times local, issues, for example, the Sport Action Zones programmes that ran in the 2000s (Houlihan & White, 2002).

A key aspect of Sport England's policy implementation work with these partners has been the contractual and reporting arrangements put in place that are a condition of funding being granted, which is an oft-noted feature in principal–agent arrangements for policy implementation. The most prolific version of these contracts was the Whole Sport Plan approach to planning for NGBs, which was first introduced in the *Game Plan* policy. In their Whole Sport Plans, NGBs had to provide details of how they would implement policy in line with Sport England's priorities, including targets for increasing participation levels (Collins, 2010). Phillpots et al. (2010) noted how problematic the contractual arrangements could be in the context of County Sport Partnerships, with target setting and reporting being prioritised over the establishment of sustainable change at a local level. In terms of monitoring, as well as reporting from organisations it funded, Sport England also collected national data on sport participation levels from 2005 onwards, first through the Active People

National Sports Agencies   27

Survey and latterly the revised version, Active Lives. Rowe (2009) noted that the Active People Survey provided far more detailed data on people's sporting activities than had been gathered previously, with data being collected and reported relating to, for example, demographics, location, the nature and frequency of activity.

However, in 2008, as the London 2012 Olympic and Paralympic Games approached, the government moved to focus on increased sport participation alongside aspirations for winning medals, especially at the home Games, so NGBs became the primary partners for Sport England (Houlihan & Lindsey, 2013; Keech, 2011). The *Playing to Win* strategy, published in 2008, outlined this focus on more of a 'sport for sport's sake' agenda in terms of increasing participation (in line with the government aspiration to use London 2012 as a catalyst for increasing mass participation) and supporting the broader high-performance sport system in terms of providing opportunities for talented people to progress in sport (DCMS, 2008).

In 2012, DCMS published *Creating a Sporting Habit for Life*, a policy that focused on increasing sport participation amongst young people aged 14–25 years. The government highlighted Sport England within this document as the government's key partner to achieve its objectives, and the government acknowledged the range of partners through whom Sport England would work to implement policy, which primarily incorporated sport and education organisations. In this document, the government set out clear high-level objectives for NGBs, including the centrality of Whole Sport Plans, and although young people were the primary focus of this policy, and subsequently the work of Sport England also had this focus, there remained a more general objective of 'a growth in participation across the adult population' (DCMS, 2012, p. 9).

The Westminster government's 2015 sport strategy, *Sporting Future*, re-shaped Sport England's remit to include physical activity, and this focus continues to date. Following the publication of *Sporting Future*, Sport England published a five-year strategy, *Sport England: Towards an Active Nation* (Sport England, 2016), that operationalised the government's aspirations focusing on increasing participation in physical activity as well as more traditional sport. The strategy also outlined the broader range of partners with whom Sport England would work and the importance of building a stronger understanding of why people do and do not participate in sport and physical activity. Although the government has not released a formal sport policy document since 2015, the general rhetoric in relation to sport and increasing participation has remained, as has the funding for Sport England. Despite the absence of a renewed government policy statement at the time of writing, Sport England published an updated strategy in 2021 titled *Uniting the Movement* (Sport England, 2021b). This ten-year strategy outlined the importance of increasing physical activity levels across the population of England, linking this with a range of issues including health, building communities and recovery from the Covid-19 pandemic, and noted the continuing importance of a range of partnerships to implement the strategy without providing details about who these partners will be. Dowling (2021, p. 2) referred to the overall content of the strategy as being 'characteristic of incremental rather than fundamental change' compared with the

2016 strategy and noted the risk of releasing a ten-year strategy when there could be a great amount of political change in that period.

Throughout these changes in policy focus, Sport England has consistently had to work with a more complex network of partners when compared with UK Sport. On a sport-specific basis, NGBs for sports representing either England only or Great Britain have been long-term partners of Sport England, and the breadth of NGBs that receive funding is greater than the number that receive funds from UK Sport. Before the publication of *Sporting Future* in 2015, Sport England's partners were primarily NGBs and organisations working at a local level (including local authorities and County Sport Partnerships). However, the mission to implement a broader set of policy objectives incorporating not only sport but physical activity has seen the number of organisations with whom Sport England works increase, and the networks they comprise become more complex. Indeed, during a conference speech in November 2021, the Minister for Sport, Tourism, Heritage and Civil Society, Nigel Huddleston, commented that in the period 2015–2021 Sport England 'has allocated over £1.5 billion to nearly 5,000 organisations across the UK' (DCMS, 2021, para 16). Furthermore, with the aim of monitoring progress not only in terms of the number of people participating but also considering the contribution to individual and population-level objectives linked to health and well-being, Sport England has a more challenging set of objectives to achieve than simply the number of people engaged in sport on a regular basis.

Case Study: The Positioning of Talent Programmes

Although Sport England and UK Sport's work is fundamentally separate, there are some aspects of their work in implementing government policy where they work together, where their work dovetails and their work overlaps. An area of work that has been subject to a lot of change with responsibility moving back and forth between the organisations is talent; that is identification, support and development of talented athletes. The Cunningham Report (Cunningham, 2001) highlighted the importance of specific efforts for improving talent identification and development and creating clear links and a pathway from initial participation in sport to international excellence for those who are talented. While this has been acknowledged and consistently acted upon by relevant organisations, the delineation of roles and responsibilities between UK Sport and Sport England has been somewhat problematic over the years.

Initially this level of the WCPP was situated with Sport England, and the organisation was funded accordingly and worked with NGBs to develop their talent work. Early talent-related work in this area for Sport England included the World Class Start and World Class Potential programmes (Houlihan & White, 2002). However, as noted previously, after London won the bid to host the 2012 Olympic and Paralympic Games, responsibility for the entirety of the World Class Performance Programme was passed to UK Sport. This meant that work, and funding, was moved away from Sport England, including funding for the lower levels of the World

Class Performance Programme, plus the Talented Athlete Scholarship Scheme and the English Institute of Sport, to UK Sport. From a funding perspective, this change represented an additional £32.5 million per annum for UK Sport, with that money mainly being derived from the National Lottery. Hosting the London 2012 Games became something of a mediating factor in terms of decision-making and the balance of power for implementing policy, placing more of that power, and indeed resource, in UK Sport's hands. The drive for success at London 2012 meant, as Bloyce and Smith (2010, p. 144) stated, '[Talent Identification and Development] has become a more obvious and central feature of [elite sport development] policy in the UK.' In terms of policy implementation, this meant that UK Sport held the funds for athletes on the first level of the WCPP, but there was also a new approach to talent introduced in 2007: Talent Transfer programmes.

Talent Transfer programmes focused on expanding the talent pools in specific sports by appealing to people with experience of high-level sport to consider transferring to another sport in order to increase their personal potential for success and to bolster that sport's athlete pool (Houlihan & Chapman, 2015). Each of the programme focused on specific demographics or physical characteristics and/or specific sports and resulted in success for some of the transferred athletes. The additional injection of money into the high-performance system and the impetus for national representation and success at the London 2012 Olympic and Paralympic Games meant that for sports where the likelihood of success, or in some cases of even being able to field competitive squads, was lower, there was a need to accelerate the process of development, and therefore have a better chance of implementing policy. The first Talent Transfer programme, named 'Sporting Giants,' was initiated in 2007, and the success of this and subsequent programmes means that they have become a long-term feature of UK Sport's work.

Sport England re-established its interest in talent work when it began a new programme called the England Talent Pathway in 2009. This work did not move any responsibility for talent away from UK Sport but rather UK Sport's focus moved more to the emerging Talent Transfer work. Sport England's efforts in relation to talent focused instead on working with NGBs to implement effective systems for developing young people's talent. Sport England's strategy document *The Talent Plan for England* (Sport England, 2018) indicates a dovetailing of the two organisations' work as an athlete in an Olympic or Paralympic sport moves from the 'Performance Foundations' to 'Podium Potential' levels of the pathway. While NGBs are Sport England's central partner for this work, the involvement of other organisations and institutions at both local and national levels is acknowledged, once again demonstrating a complex network of partners, or 'agents,' with whom Sport England works.

Conclusion

For reasons of scope and focus, and as noted in the Introduction, this chapter has considered the roles of UK Sport and Sport England in the implementation of

Westminster government policy and has not been able to explore the nuances of policy implementation by the other home country sports councils. While Sport England and UK Sport may initially appear to have similarities in terms of their having remits for specific aspects of sport, their processes around contracts and monitoring of their partners, and continued support and funding from successive governments since the 1990s, there are clear differences in their operations when it comes to implementation of policies. UK Sport has a much clearer and more consistent set of measures for success and a far smaller network of partners with whom the organisation works. The specifics of its remit have fluctuated a little with key turning points in the broader policy context, but there has been a high degree of stability in terms of the partners with whom UK Sport works and through whom policy is implemented. By comparison, Sport England's objectives and its network of partners have had far greater variance over time and are generally more complex than that of UK Sport, and although the fundamental question of numbers participating has remained, the focus on the nature of what activities people do, when, how, why, etc. has had to be adjusted repeatedly throughout its 25-year history.

Due to its more straightforward remit, it can be concluded that UK Sport's implementation of government policy has been successful. The results from successive Olympic and Paralympic Games over the past 20 years indicate that the implementation of government policies prioritising medal success has succeeded as the development of a system and the input of increasing funding has led to a significant increase in the number of medals being won. Furthermore, the government's interest in having major sports events hosted in the UK is another policy success for the government, implemented by a range of organisations with UK Sport as their key agency acting on behalf of the government.

However, not every sport is successful in meeting its targets at every Games, so successful implementation is not universal across the World Class Performance Programme and the No Compromise approach. That said, 'failure' at the Olympic or Paralympic Games could be a result of the natural ebb and flow of international competition, and in such cases broader indicators of the success of a NGB's performance programme can become important for that sport continuing to receive support from UK Sport. A key challenge that UK Sport could face going forward is increasing questions about the general value of medals and the system causing problems (for example, a number of examples of 'toxic culture' within high-performance programmes), so work being done around rhetoric regarding social value and attempts to evidence 'impact' may further develop.

It is more difficult to make a firm conclusion regarding the success or failure of Sport England's policy implementation. The biggest challenge that SE and its partners have faced is the moving targets of government policy in relation to increasing participation but also the value of sport in achieving other objectives. Sport England has adapted to each change of policy and maintained relationships with NGBs throughout, while also diversifying its portfolio of partners. Sport England has consistently done enough to protect its status as a meaningful organisation that bridges the gap between government policy and organisations that implement policy objectives at national and local levels. Additionally, while there has been a change in the overarching policy agenda in relation to participation and governments' foci that have shifted over time, there has remained a core objective of increasing participation, and NGBs have continued to be primary partners in implementing this policy for Sport England.

As discussed, Sport England has a more complex range of partners, and there is now a very open picture in terms regarding with whom the organisation will work as it continues to set priorities beyond simply sport, to sport and physical activity. These challenges may be mirrored to some extent in the other home nation sports councils, not least because the very issue of increasing sport participation and PA levels and understanding individuals' motivations and behaviours for doing so (or not) are not solely challenging issues in England. Questions also exist about Sport England's role, more specifically the role it may be seeking to carve for itself, especially in the absence of a firm directive from government at present. In the past, Phillpots et al. (2010, p. 269) described Sport England as 'a watchdog of public funds'; but more recently Dowling (2021) stated that the tone of *Uniting the Movement* (Sport England, 2021) suggests greater ambition from the organisation, including cross-departmental working.

PRACTITIONER REFLECTION AND INSIGHTS

Andy Reed, Founder of the Sports Think Tank and Chair of the Sport for Development Coalition

This is a timely chapter. It is good to reflect on the roles of Sport England and UK Sport once again. I have been fortunate to have spent much of the last 25 years close to these bodies and the decision-making in government as a Member of Parliament (MP) and part of the ministerial teams in the Department for Culture, Media and Sport and the Treasury. It is only thanks to these reflections in this chapter that I have time to look at what we have been trying to achieve over this period. Sometimes you can't see the wood for the trees at the heart of short-term thinking in government and the electoral cycle. It is right to be challenged as at the time decision-making is not always as analytical and deliberate as some academics would like to believe.

Much of the fluctuations in sport policy comes down to the various actors and individuals in leadership in the various stakeholders – in government and the chairs and chief executives of Sport England and UK Sport. If I reflect, each of these dynamics has changed considerably over time. I can't overemphasise the power of personalities and their motivations. Policy making, I have observed, is not always as rational and deliberate as we would all hope!

I have worked with around 20 secretaries of state and sports ministers. Their success or failure is often out of their control. When No10 and the Treasury have occupants who 'get sport' things happened. Otherwise, sport is so far down the policy priorities it can easily get overlooked. This is understandable. The challenges facing the country and constituents always seem far more pressing than sport policy – the economy, the NHS, foreign policy and education.

The average life span of a minister is about 2.4 years. Nobody arrives as a junior minister (the sports role is a Parliamentary Under Secretary of State in DCMS and usually alongside other duties like gambling, civil society or tourism) and wants to continue the work of the previous minister. Each minister and Secretary of State bring their own perspectives on sport and want to 'leave a legacy.' So their individual opinions carry a lot of weight. The advice from their civil servants in DCMS on the main priorities or issues that need dealing with often shapes their period in office.

Sport policy and the performance of Sport England and UK Sport have always been open to criticism, which has sometimes been justified. They are both established as bodies at 'arm's length' from government, but, as many have observed over the years, those arms can be very short. While ministers could never absolutely direct the spending of these bodies, 'requests' were always made! And unsurprisingly the bodies were able to accommodate shifts in spending or priorities!

Sport England's remit has fluctuated over the years as identified in Pippa's excellent chapter. In the early 2010s the relationship between the government and Sport England was often fractious. The government was keen to see participation figures going up with the investment and putting pressure on Sport England – with its future as a body questioned at several times. At the time, funding NGBs based on their 'Whole Sport Plans' seemed a sensible and proportionate approach for Sport England to distribute funding to the sector, but it quickly became about the numbers. This led to often calling out NGBs who were perceived to have 'failed' to help Sport England achieve the desired growth in participation. At the Sports Think Tank that I founded after my time as an MP, we have long argued participation figures were never going to be achieved in this contractual model and traditional setting.

The 2015 Sporting Future strategy was therefore a welcome change in direction and emphasis from government – focusing on the social outcomes not just the absolute participation numbers. To achieve these new outcomes, new partnerships are required. The traditional sport sector is not going to be able to deliver these outcomes. This has influenced an ongoing shift has continued into new Sport England strategies and funding approaches. The role of Sport England has, therefore, been changing – with many asking even if the name is relevant any longer as the body softens its sports-specific remit. Now, its Uniting the Movement strategy is being rolled out to the 'sector' and is fundamentally changing the way Sport England works and funds the sector. Now the emphasis is rightly on tackling the ongoing inequalities in access to sport and physical activity and ensuring that the biggest benefit is felt in the places and communities overlooked in the past.

As well as a need to work much more closely and consistently together inside government, there is now a growing understanding that getting the nation active requires a systems approach. Sport England is recognising it doesn't have the expertise to do this 'to the sector' – it must be done in genuine partnership. Increased walking and cycling won't be delivered through DCMS or Sport England but through the range of other stakeholders and government departments. We are thus learning a new approach and a new language. System, localism, place and new challenges around tackling inequalities and climate change will all be at the heart of the new Sport England working relationship.

At the same time the remit for UK Sport ostensibly remains the same since its focus was singularly focused on delivering success in the Olympic and Paralympic medals tables in 2012. When we won the right to host the Olympics in 2005, the profile of sport policy changed overnight. A powerful case was made to us in government that Team GB needed to do well at a home Games. This meant investing in the system identified by UK Sport to deliver success in and win medals. At my time in the Treasury, we approved the additional investment being asked for by UK Sport's leaders, Peter Keen, John Steele and Sue Campbell – they had worked out they needed £100m a year to get Team GB to fourth in the medals table in London with an estimated 65 medals. Five years later after this investment found it was into the system, we of course delivered 65 medals!

Medal success was specifically the remit of UK Sport and Sport England's role was to deliver the participation legacy. Levels of physical activity and participation in sport were expected to rise off the back of the inspiration of the Games. Of course, we now know that no Olympic Games has delivered a sustained participation legacy, but hope was placed on the sports agencies, primarily through the NGBs, that this time it could be different.

I had always understood that the increased funding for UK Sport and the NGBs at the 2012 Games would then be scaled back post London 2012. Several sports and the other home nations had seen 'temporary' cuts to their budgets on the understanding that by 2014 things would return to 'normal.' Some NGBs have letters confirming as much from the Chair of UK Sport. But the nation and ministers got hooked on the winning medals pathway. The shift in policy to focus on and target Olympics and Paralympics medals remained in place by default beyond the 2012 Games and heading into Rio in 2016. This became known as the No Compromise approach which, especially in the aftermath of 2012, placed even greater focus on solely winning medals in very specific sports.

Even when UK Sport has delivered its objectives for government, we now realise this has not been universally without problems. NGBs' funding has relied heavily on meeting targets and receiving their funding. However, the No Compromise environment has been linked to issues with safeguarding, bullying and the well-being of athletes. Some of the edges have thus been softened around the singular approach to medals and more sports included in the funding model. There does remain a massive focus on the medal table – but just getting there in a healthier way!

In a strange way I feel more certain about the roles of Sport England and UK Sport than I have for a long time. The two bodies have generally been able to work out where their remits sit and work closely together. UK Sport will continue to ensure we win medals but hopefully with means that avoid some of the problematic consequences that we have seen, and we will continue to bid for major events. We can all argue about the costs and merits of doing so, but politically I can see it remaining a priority for some time. The Sport England Uniting the Movement strategy is a ten-year strategy for the first time. If it can stay the course, I can see how it should shift the dial in the way we raise levels of activity with new partnerships. As chair of the Sport for Development Coalition – I can see the level of genuine commitment to do things differently from the leadership of Sport England.

However, I write this at a time when the country has no effective government and awaits a new prime minister (PM). As discussed, sports policy and direction depend on the sense of purpose from the top. An engaged PM and Treasury can make things happen. A sports minister or DCMS can shift policy and direction over time. I may be feeling confident in a long-term vision and strategy from the major stakeholders, but that could all change again! Whilst we love to think sports policy (or indeed any government policy) is developed seamlessly and with a long-term vision – we need to bear in mind how politics and short-termism still dominate our Westminster culture. People and big personalities can make an enormous difference.

Overall, it is easy to forget how much has changed in the last couple of decades. The sport policy-balanced scorecard would show a mixed set of results. We can but work to address the challenges that sport faces and that lie in the implementation of changing policies and ultimately hope that positive headway can be made.

References

Bloyce, D., & Smith, A. (2010). *Sport policy and development: An introduction.* Routledge.

Bostock, J., Crowther, P., Ridley-Duff, R., & Breese, R. (2018). No plan B: The Achilles heel of high performance sport management. *European Sport Management Quarterly, 18*(1), 25–46.

Coghlan, J. F. (1990). *Sport and British politics since 1960*. The Falmer Press.

Collins, M. (2010). 'From 'sport for good' to 'sport for sport's sake'–not a good move for sports development in England? *International Journal of Sport Policy and Politics*, *2*(3), 367–379.

Cunningham, J. (2001). *Elite sports funding review: A report to the prime minister and secretary of state for the department for culture, media and sport*. DCMS.

Department for Culture, Media and Sport (DCMS). (2008). *Playing to win: A new era for sport*. DCMS.

Department for Culture, Media and Sport (DCMS). (2012). *Creating a sporting habit for life*. DCMS.

Department for Digital, Culture, Media and Sport (DCMS). (2021). *Speech: Nigel Huddleston speech to sport for development conference*. Retrieved November 3, 2021, from https://www.gov.uk/government/speeches/nigel-huddleston-speech-to-sport-for-development-conference

Dowling, M. (2021). Uniting the movement? A critical commentary on Sport England's new strategy. *Managing Sport and Leisure*, 1–5. https://doi.org/10.1080/23750472.2021.1942170

Green, M. (2007). Olympic glory or grassroots development?: Sport policy priorities in Australia, Canada and the United Kingdom, 1960–2006. *International Journal of the History of Sport*, *24*(7), 921–953.

HM Government. (2015). *Sporting future: A new strategy for an active nation*. https://assets.publishing.service.gov.uk/government/uploads/system/uploads/attachment_data/file/486622/Sporting_Future_ACCESSIBLE.pdf

HM Government (2021). *Global Britain in a competitive age: The integrated review of security, defence, development and foreign policy*. https://assets.publishing.service.gov.uk/government/uploads/system/uploads/attachment_data/file/969402/The_Integrated_Review_of_Security__Defence__Development_and_Foreign_Policy.pdf

Houlihan, B., & Chapman, P. (2015). Modernisation and elite sport development in England and the United Kingdom: Talent identification and coach development. In S. S. Andersen, L. T. Ronglan, & B. Houlihan (Eds.), *Managing elite sport systems* (pp. 43–60). Routledge.

Houlihan, B., & Green, M. (2009). Modernization and sport: The reform of sport England and UK sport. *Public Administration*, *87*(3), 678–698.

Houlihan, B., & Lindsey, I. (2013). *Sport policy in Britain*. Routledge.

Houlihan, B., & White, A. (2002). *The politics of sports development: Development of sport or development through sport?* Routledge.

House of Lords. (2013). *Keeping the flame alive: The Olympic and Paralympic legacy* (HL Paper 78). https://publications.parliament.uk/pa/ld201314/ldselect/ldolympic/78/78.pdf

Ingle, S. (2019, February 12). UK Sport to relax 'no compromise' approach to funding after Tokyo 2020. *The Guardian*. https://www.theguardian.com/sport/2019/feb/12/uk-sport-no-compromise-funding-olympics

Keech, M. (2011). Sport and adult mass participation in England. In B. Houlihan & M. Green (Eds.), *Routledge handbook of sport development* (pp. 217–230). Routledge.

McDonald, I. (2011). High-performance sport policy in the UK. In B. Houlihan & M. Green (Eds.), *Routledge handbook of sport development* (pp. 371–385). Routledge.

National Audit Office. (2005). *UK sport: Supporting elite athletes*. The Stationery Office.

Phillpots, L., Grix, J., & Quarmby, T. (2010). Unpacking the paradox: Centralised grassroots sport policy and "new governance": A case study of county sports partnerships in the UK. *International Review for the Sociology of Sport*, *46*(3), 265–281.

Rowe, N. F. (2009). The active people survey: A catalyst for transforming evidence-based sport policy in England. *International Journal of Sport Policy and Politics, 1*(1), 89–98.

Sport England. (2016). *Sport England: Towards and active nation.* https://sportengland-production-files.s3.eu-west-2.amazonaws.com/s3fs-public/sport-england-towards-an-active-nation.pdf

Sport England. (2018). *The talent plan for England: Creating the world's best talent system.* https://sportengland-production-files.s3.eu-west-2.amazonaws.com/s3fs-public/the-talent-plan-for-england.pdf?VersionId=FMAAxsmgrkyJ0hXlJQl2aB7s9uIpV.uN

Sport England. (2021a). *Revised code for sports governance published.* https://www.sportengland.org/news/revised-code-sports-governance-published

Sport England. (2021b). *Uniting the movement: A 10-year vision to transform lives and communities through sport and physical activity.* https://sportengland-production-files.s3.eu-west-2.amazonaws.com/s3fs-public/2021-02/Sport%20England%20-%20Uniting%20the%20Movement%27.pdf?VersionId=7JxbS7dw40CN0g21_dL4VM3F4P1YJ5RW

Tacon, R., & Walters, G. (2016). Modernisation and governance in UK national governing bodies of sport: How modernisation influences the way board members perceive and enact their roles. *International Journal of Sport Policy and Politics, 8*(3), 363–381.

The Cabinet Office. (2014). *Government and Mayor of London response to the House of Lords Select Committee on Olympic and Paralympic legacy report of session 2013–14: 'Keeping the flame alive: The Olympic and Paralympic legacy'* (Cm8814). The Stationery Office. https://assets.publishing.service.gov.uk/government/uploads/system/uploads/attachment_data/file/279480/CM8814_Accessible.pdf

The Sports Council. (1982). *Sport in the community: The next ten years.* The Sports Council.

UK Sport. (2020a). *Grant-in-aid and national lottery distribution fund annual report and accounts for the year ended 31 March 2020.* https://www.uksport.gov.uk/-/media/files/annual-reports/uk-sport-annual-report-and-accounts-2019-2020_web-accessible.ashx

UK Sport. (2020b). *UK sport outlines plans for £352million investment in Olympic and Paralympic sport.* https://www.uksport.gov.uk/news/2020/12/18/paris-cycle-investment

UK Sport. (n.d.a). *Current funding figures.* https://www.uksport.gov.uk/our-work/investing-in-sport/current-funding-figures

UK Sport. (n.d.b). *International partnerships programme: Building and maximising the benefits of international sport partnerships.* https://www.uksport.gov.uk/-/media/files/international-relations/ipp-booklet.ashx?la=en&hash=7A3EB22DE7B59F5F4E485B500F887A6F

Chapter 3

National Governing Bodies of Sport

Mathew Dowling and Spencer Harris

Introduction

This chapter explores the changing nature and evolving roles and responsibilities of National Governing Bodies (NGBs) of sport particularly in relation to their role as interpreters and implementers of sport policy within the United Kingdom (UK). The chapter begins by discussing the key features and characteristics of NGBs, followed by a brief historical overview of their involvement within the sport policy process from the 1960s to the present day. Our attention to key events and policy milestones is deliberately selective rather than exhaustive in that we seek to identify key events and policies which have shaped the roles and responsibilities of NGBs within the UK context. Following this, we expand on our discussion of the role of NGBs to briefly consider their priorities and role in implementing policy before offering in-depth analysis of the NGB-led implementation of community sport policy in England.

Characterising NGBs of Sport

As not-for-profit organisations, NGBs typically maintain a private limited or charitable legal status.[1] They are primarily responsible for governing and regulating their respective sports at a national level. As we will argue throughout this chapter, the role of NGBs within the policy process has and continues to change over time. Nonetheless, their primary functions have remained consistent – to set sporting rules and regulations, distribute funding and support to its constituent membership (usually clubs), organise competitions, prepare national team programmes and grow and develop their sport. The five sports councils (Sport England, Sport Scotland, Sport Wales, Sport Northern Ireland and UK Sport), who ultimately certify or decertify NGBs, currently recognise over 100+ NGBs across the UK[2] making them one of the largest and most visible organisational entities within the sporting 'ecosystem.' Importantly, as central actors, NGBs play a critical role within the implementation of a range of policy objectives. It is this latter point on which this chapter will focus specifically.

As an important caveat to the discussion that follows, we recognise from the outset that not all NGBs are created equal. NGBs vary considerably in terms of

DOI: 10.4324/9781003162728-3

their size and scale. Some are well-established, powerful and wealthy entities that have substantial turnover often from income generated through commercial ventures, whilst others are much more modest entities with minimal turnover and limited commercial interest. The latter often means that some NGBs are resource dependent, heavily reliant upon the government funding (via grant and lottery funding allocation through the sport councils) to ensure their survival. As NGBs are a heterogeneous group of organisations, we find it more useful to discuss them in relation to particular subsets, e.g., well-funded Olympic sport NGBs; smaller, less-well-funded NGBs; non-Olympic NGBs and relatively independent or commercially viable NGBs that are not reliant upon public funding. Whilst this chapter encompasses all of these subsets, our emphasis is particularly focused on the former (i.e., Olympic sport NGBs) as these are most likely to be involved with the implementation and interpretation of public policy.

Finally, while the internal structure of NGBs differs from body to body, the majority of NGBs consist of a national organ (e.g., Football Association, England and Wales Cricket Board, Table Tennis England) employing a professional executive together with administrative and development (i.e., sport development) personnel, with more specific governance and strategic matters overseen by a number of (often voluntary) committees and/or working groups, with an overarching board of directors maintaining ultimate responsibility for the direction and fiscal health of the organisation. Additionally, integral to NGB structures is the nationwide network of regional or county associations that govern the sport at that spatial level and the many clubs (which may be voluntary run, public sector managed or offered through the private sector, depending on the sport) that organise and provide sport at the local community level. In short, while NGBs may not have sole responsibility for their sport, it is fair to argue that they are the guardian of it. Furthermore, while the nature and characteristics of the relationships between NGBs, and regional/sub-regional structures and clubs will vary significantly, it is this chain of structures and their governing arrangements that is dominant in the design and delivery of sport programmes across the UK.

Charting the Evolving Role of NGBs in UK Sport Policy, 1960–2021

Many NGBs were created in the late 19th and early 20th century in the midst of the industrial revolution and in response to the need for codification to enable sport teams to compete using a common set of laws. The initial role and function of NGBs were quite perfunctory, focusing on the creation and enforcement of rules and regulations (i.e., codification) and the organisation of sporting competitions. Most NGBs began as relatively small bodies, often through the bringing together of club representatives or committees. Most NGBs in their formative years, and some even today, can be characterised as being largely informal, volunteer-run and membership-focused entities which can be described as a 'kitchen table' archetype design (Kikulis et al., 1995; Parent et al., 2021).

Historically, NGBs have enjoyed relative independence and autonomy from the state (Houlihan, 1997). This is, in part, due to government traditionally viewing sport, and by extension the work of NGBs, as a 'gentlemanly pastime' and an 'amateur pursuit' and of little direct interest to the government (Houlihan & White, 2003). As a result, within their formative years, 'government policy had little influence on the operations and management of NGBs' (Green, 2007, p. 91). It was also due to the voluntary tradition and relative autonomy of NGBs that there was 'an uneasy and ambivalent relationship between some governing bodies and the sports councils' (Houlihan & White, 2003, p. 165). According to Houlihan (1997), it was not until 1960s that the UK government accepted sport as a 'legitimate responsibility,' and prior to this period, government interest and involvement in sport were ad hoc and piecemeal. Furthermore, it should also be noted that government interest in sport during the post-war period should be understood as part of broader expansion of the welfare state (Houlihan & White, 2003) insofar as the government viewed sport as a means to achieve wider social objectives. This theme of instrumentalism has remained a consistent feature of the NGB–government relationship and continues to have ongoing implications for the sport policy process, as discussed below.

The policy arrangements for sport in the UK began to change due to increasing governmental intervention in sport which occurred post-1960s, the establishment of the Wolfenden committee and its subsequent recommendations, most notably of which for NGBs included the direct investment of taxpayer monies into sport and the creation of the English Sport Council (established in 1965; given Royal Charter status in 1972) (Coghlan & Webb, 1990). For Houlihan and White (2003), the Wolfenden report was significant 'not only in raising the profile of sport within government, but also, and more importantly, in shaping the context within which public involvement in sport was to be considered for the next generation' (p. 18). The Wolfenden report would also be important in setting the regulatory and funding framework for how government would support NGBs. First, the report set a precedent regarding the relationship between NGBs and the government in that the latter would not have direct involvement with NGBs, but rather provides 'grant aid' funding (exchequer) and support via the sport councils (which remain a persistent feature of UK sport policy to this day). Second, the assumption that underpinned government ministers and many of those working within sport, particularly throughout these formative years, was that NGBs were the most appropriate and legitimate body for carrying out and realising elite sport policy-related objectives.

Despite the 1980s being characterised as a period of relative neglect for sport in general (Houlihan & White, 2003), the period was significant for NGBs for two, closely related, reasons. First, a range of New Public Management (NPM) practices were introduced, largely in response to Thatcher's government demanding that sport councils hold NGBs to account for public monies. Although it should be acknowledged that these reforms were not directly aimed at NGBs, they nonetheless had significant consequences for them as many of these NPM practices, such as performance targets, performance plans and annual monitoring processes remain a key feature of the sport policy landscape to this day. Second, the 1980s

40 Mathew Dowling and Spencer Harris

witnessed a changing relationship between the state and society, with a shift away from conventional government towards the contemporary notion of governance (Rhodes, 1997). This macro-level change would have profound consequences for sport (Grix, 2010; Grix & Phillpots, 2011) which led to, amongst other things, a proliferation of organisations to deliver objectives determined by the state.

The period from the 1990s onwards was notable for increased government investment in elite sport (Bloyce & Smith, 2009; Green & Houlihan, 2005). Central to this was the 1994 creation of the National Lottery that would enable the sports councils to distribute funding directly to NGBs to grow and develop their sport. The additional funding provided by the National Lottery would provide a significant boost for Olympic sport NGBs, although this increased funding was matched with a new, revised set of NPM requirements. Hence, whilst funding, most notably for the development and support of elite sport, became more readily available throughout the 1990s, this funding was granted with 'strings attached' (Green, 2007). Consequently, this increased investment was tempered with an equal and parallel decrease in autonomy for NGBs (Green, 2007; Green & Houlihan, 2005). NGBs became subject to the government rhetoric of *'earned autonomy'*[3] whereby government would provide conditional funding – via arms-length agencies – if NGBs achieved performance goals (Houlihan & Green, 2009). The establishment of the Youth Sport Trust (YST) in 1995 and UK Sport in 1997 would eventually lead to a clearer separation and division of investment portfolios. At this point, from the mid-2000s onwards, the YST worked with NGBs on school sport, the home country sport councils worked with NGBs on community sport, and UK Sport collaborated with NGBs on high-performance sport.

Towards the end of the century, the 1997 change of government from Conservative to Labour brought with it a fundamental change in the direction of sport policy as articulated in the Department of Culture, Media and Sport's (DCMS) *Sporting Future for All* strategy (DCMS, 2000). NGBs maintained their lead role for international sporting success and continued to grow the role of NGBs in supporting school–club links and satellite clubs and leading the coordination of sport-specific development pathways in order to give the sport the best chance of success on the world stage. *A Sporting Future for All* recognised

> that a closer partnership with the governing bodies of sport [NGBs] is crucial if we are to deliver our ambitious plans for English sport. We believe that governing bodies [NGBs] must be responsible for setting the strategic vision for their sport and that resources should be behind these strategies to give them every chance of success.
>
> (DCMS, 2000, p. 47)

Devolution of power and *'earned autonomy'* remained consistent features in government rhetoric, stating that 'we will offer partnerships to the governing bodies of sport [NGBs], giving them greater devolved power over the deployment of funds, in return for a number of commitments' (DCMS, 2000, p. 27). These commitments reinforced and reiterated the government's view that NGBs should play an important role in achieving international sporting success and provide strategic direction for sport more generally. More specifically, the policy stated that NGBs should involve elite athletes in community sport programmes, invest broadcasting revenue into community sport, tackle under-representation and inequalities in sport and continue to 'modernise' their administrative structures and processes.

Two years later, the government published *Game Plan* (DCMS/Strategy Unit, 2002), a jointly developed policy by the DCMS and the Strategy Unit that would set the administrative framework by which sport would be organised for the next 20 years. For NGBs, *Game Plan* would reinforce and reaffirm the government's desire to have NGBs at the centre of delivery for achieving international sporting success. The emphasis on NGBs by government is unquestionable in this period with the strategy giving attention to them no less than 216 times within the policy document. More specifically, *Game Plan* focused on four key areas of change that would impact NGB strategic and operational planning: a continued NGB modernisation programme, development of performance plans, a need to create a 'one-stop-shop' to streamline NGB funding allocations and an increasing emphasis on achieving high-performance sport objectives. Two major developments occurred directly as a result of Game Plan that would have significant implications for NGBs. First, in response to *Game Plan*, Sport England published a National Framework for Sport in England (Sport England, 2004), which in turn initiated a regional planning process and the creation of Whole Sport Plans. Second, was the implementation of UK Sport's '*No Compromise*' funding approach in 2006, whereby grant-aid funding to NGBs was contingent on past success and the assessed strength of the talent pool.

In 2008, the then Secretary of State for Culture, Media and Sport, James Purnell, introduced a dramatic shift in sport policy, repositioning the DCMS to focus on and invest in sport for its own sake rather than instrumentally. This change was driven by Purnell's desire to build a world-class sport development system and his unwavering belief that the spillover benefits of sport – in particular, education, crime prevention and health promotion – should be paid for by other government departments. Accompanying this shift in policy, Purnell promoted NGBs as the lead agency for community sport, significantly enhancing the investment of public monies into NGBs and affording them the opportunity to further develop and increased investment in integrated Whole Sport Plans. These plans would evolve and become a compulsory requirement for demonstrating how NGBs planned to address the twin challenge of growing mass sport participation and improving elite sport success (i.e., medal wins). For some sports, the evidence suggests that the increased investment did increase medal success,[4] although some have questioned at what cost (Houlihan & Zheng, 2013). The post 2012 era exposed the challenges and perhaps (un)intended consequences associated with implementing both community sport and elite sport policy. While some NGBs received significant investment to increase mass participation in community sport during this period (i.e., 2008–2015), many organised sports experienced actual decreases in participation rates – an area of focus to which we will return in the section below. At the elite level, while some NGBs experienced an increase in medal success, others (e.g., basketball, handball, table tennis, weightlifting) lost substantial amounts of funding as they were not deemed capable of producing medals.

From 2015 onwards, DCMS sport policy, *Sporting Future: An Active Nation* (DCMS, 2015), shifted yet again back towards a focus on sport for development or sport for good, with sport agencies such as Sport England being required to demonstrate their wider social impact in order to justify taxpayer investment. For NGBs, this has resulted in a targeted investment portfolio into high-performance sport with government (via UK Sport) investing in fewer sports with a larger share of funding. This approach can be seen to align with sport for good outcomes insofar as elite sport success is perceived to enhance national pride and feed the national feel-good factor. However, while this funding model did appear to support impressive medal hauls for several NGBs at the Rio and Tokyo summer games, it has also exacerbated the funding challenge for small or less successful NGBs, reinforcing the so-called *Matthew Effect* whereby rich and successful sports have greater potential for future success and poorer, less successful sports have limited resources to invest in their future development and therefore questionable prospects regarding future success.

For community sport, the policy pendulum shifted back to sport for good signalling the governments continued reliance upon, but shift away from, the 'core sport market' (i.e., NGBs) by allocating increased funding to non-traditional service providers such as charities and trusts, as long as they could demonstrate attainment towards one of the five outcomes of the new policy (physical well-being, mental well-being, individual development, social and community development, economic development). More recently, the ever-changing funding arrangements and requirements from both UK Sport and Sport England have led NGBs to compete amongst each other and other non-traditional service providers for funding. This policy, along with the subsequent strategies published by Sport England and UK Sport, respectively, also reaffirmed government's desire to move away from the safe confines of sport, towards the importance of achieving broader social outcomes with an increasing emphasis on health and well-being.

In the next section, we attempt to conceptualise the role of NGBs both as key conduits and potential sites for policy formulation and implementation. Consistent with the aim of this book, the discussion draws upon the policy implementation literature – utilising both top-down and bottom-up approaches – to investigate the extent to which NGBs have (or have not) been able to implement sport policy.

NGBs' Priorities and Role as Policy Implementers

Commercialisation, globalisation and governmentalisation have had a major combined effect on the range and diversity of challenges that NGBs must respond to. Commercially, NGBs are challenged to broker partnerships with marketing and media entities to maximise revenues to reinvest in the development of their organisation and/or sport. Globally, they are required to respond to an increasing array of demands and collaborate with a diverse network of national, continental and international stakeholders to promote their sport, participate in competitions and contribute to the networked governance of their sport at national, continental and international levels. And, the increasing government interest in, and funding of, sport has brought about a clearer focus on specific targets for sporting outcomes in school, community and elite sport settings. Furthermore, these government-derived and -driven policies have required NGBs to collaborate on projects to pursue social outcomes such as health and wellness, education and community development (Green, 2006). These are the additional challenges faced by the modern NGB in addition to their traditional roles in setting down the rules of competition, agreeing and reviewing the constitutional rules of the governing body, organising competitions and taking care of their membership (Katwala, 2000).

While the wide range of issues presented above represents a fuller account of the diversity of priorities facing NGBs, we wish to consider how NGBs respond to and implement public policy. Given the scope of this chapter, we will focus specifically on the role and responsibilities of NGBs in interpreting and implementing community sport policy (e.g., to increase the number of people taking part in sport and physical activity) as this represents a more recent innovation in public policy when compared against the role of NGBs in elite sport policy and reflects an area of public policy where substantial public monies were invested in NGBs for the purpose of leveraging a mass sport participation legacy from hosting the Olympic Games (Harris & Dowling, 2021).

On the one hand, it is possible to present a convincing argument that community sport policy represents top-down policy processes. Policy is laid down and defined by a government department (i.e., DCMS). Funding is allocated by the same department alongside key non-departmental governing bodies (i.e., UK Sport and Sport England). Policy directives and resources are then allocated to NGBs in order that they may translate the policy – through varied technical and practical arrangements – into practice. Alongside this, tools and guidance documents are created to set down how policy will be evaluated. From this vantage point, it is clear to see a hierarchical chain of command dictating the core focus, resources and means for evaluating policy. On the other hand, when considering policy from the bottom-up perspective, we can clearly see the work of street-level actors to improvise and to do what they can do, ultimately implementing what Lipsky referred to as 'agency policy' (Lipsky, 2010, p. 221).

For community sport policy, the top-down, bottom-up perspectives reveal the central role of NGBs. During the period 2008–2016, NGBs were, at their various levels of operation, the chief translator and transactor of policy. They were responsible for selecting and enforcing meanings of policy for their sport, creating plans to articulate their activities, targets and funding requirements for their sport and providing routine reports on progress. Additionally, alongside developing the strategy for their sport (through Whole Sport Plans), NGBs were responsible for operationalising the strategy – either directly through their own workforce or more commonly in collaboration with the wider sport network including their regional and/or county structures, County Sport Partnership (CSP) networks and local clubs and schools. NGBs had vigorously campaigned and championed their cause and key role in leading on and strategising across community sport, not only because they argued that as the guardians of sport, it was their role to lead on mass sport participation, but because this work was seen to be an integral part of the sport development pyramid.

The section below provides a more detailed discussion of the NGB implementing of community sport policy, pulling on theoretical ideas highlighted in the introduction of this book (c.f. Cairney, 2011; Winter, 2012) to examine policy outputs and outcomes, and the critical factors that influence them.

NGB-Led Implementation of Community Sport Policy

This section applies a framework to examine the policy standards, resources, key actors, performance outcomes and outputs/implementer behaviours in relation to the implementation of community sport policy in England between 2008 and 2016. This period has been selected as substantial public monies were invested in NGBs to address the twin challenges of elite-level success in international sports competitions and increasing mass community sports participation – this latter challenge forming part of the pre- and post-games legacy of the London 2012 Games.

Policy standards: The 2008–2016 period witnessed the significant investment of public monies into NGBs of sport in England for the purpose of implementing community sport policy. We separate developments within community sport policy into two periods with similar policy goals (i.e., getting more people to participate in sport more frequently) but different targets. The first period (2009–2012) focused on a specific target of getting at least two million more people in England to be more active by 2012. The second period (2013–2016) focused on increasing the number of people participating in sport by 1% per annum.

Resources: Over the two periods, a total investment of £736 million was made into NGBs for the purpose of implementing an increase in mass sport participation. Additionally public monies were invested in CSPs and other partners to support NGB implementation efforts. Importantly, over the two phases of policy, each eligible NGB was required to apply for funding, submitting a detailed Whole Sport Plan including details of the growth target for the NGB (i.e., how many more people the NGB thought it could get to play their sport). Sport England then allocated funding to each NGB based on its assessment of three key criteria: (a) the growth potential of each sport, (b) the stated growth target of each sport as stated by the NGB and (c) the clarity of the NGB Whole Sport

Plans in detailing how they would deliver increased participation. The total invested in each sport for each phase is detailed in Table 3.1.

Key actors: Policy standards and funding were agreed upon by DCMS and Sport England. Policy planning and translation were led by NGBs of sport. Policy implementation was led by NGBs collaborating with CSPs, national partner organisations (e.g., Street Games, Sports Coach UK), local authorities, schools, higher/further education, coaches and clubs. Policy evaluation was completed by Sport England using the Active People annual survey instrument.

Outcomes/performance: For the period from 2009 to 2012, the changes in participation were predicated on the benchmark data collected in 2008. Table 3.1 shows that participation in 7 of 28 sports had increased with the most significant gain in athletics (0.58% change), attributed largely to informal running and jogging rather than formal athletics. More notable was the pattern of decline across several organised sports. For example, participation in swimming in 2012 decreased by 1.21% when compared to 2008, football fell by 0.20%, rugby union by 0.14%, cycling by 0.13%, basketball by 0.09% and rugby league by 0.08%. Less surprising given the global economic crises of 2008 were the decreases in relatively 'expensive' sports such as golf (0.33%), snowsports (0.04%) and sailing (0.10%). The net effect of these changes in individual sports participation over the 2008–2012 period was that despite significant investment of public monies (~£360 million), participation in sport declined.

From 2013 onwards, the UK had the benefit of riding the 'feel-good factor' wave associated with the 2012 summer games, and NGBs had the opportunity to revise plans for 2013–2016 and to take account of, and learn from, their experiences implementing community sport policy during 2009–2012. Importantly, NGBs also received an additional £370 million investment of public monies for the period 2013–2016. Despite these opportunities, sport participation remained stubbornly fixed in a downward trend, with a small number of exceptions (see Table 3.1). For example, the informal possibilities associated with athletics and cycling likely buoyed these sports, enabling them to record 1.40 and 0.26 percentage point (pp) increases in 2016 compared to 2008. Interestingly, netball (0.07 pp) was the only team sport, alongside other sports such as boxing (0.12 pp) and table tennis (0.03 pp) to record any increase in participation over the period. In contrast, participation in swimming decreased by 2.13 pp in 2016 compared to 2008, football decreased by 1.01 pp, golf by 0.61 pp, with several other sports experiencing declines, albeit less significant in percentage terms. In short, the overall participation data reveal that despite the excitement of the 2012 games, the detailed vision and plan associated with the sports participation legacy simply was not achieved.

Outputs and implementer behaviours: The community sport policy process between 2008 and 2016 reveals a number of outputs and implementer behaviours that directly or indirectly influenced the implementation of policy and changes

Table 3.1 National Governing Body of sport funding 2008–2016

Sport	Investment £M (1st phase) (2009–2012)	% 1 × 30pw (2008)	% 1 × 30pw (2012)	Change (2008–2012)	Investment £M (2nd phase) (2013–2016)	% 1 × 30pw (2016)	Change (2012–2016)	Change in participation (1 × 30) (2008–2016)	Total Investment £M (2008–2016)
Cricket	37.8	0.49	0.51	0.02	27.5	0.41	-0.10	-0.08	65.3
Cycling	24.2	4.37	4.24	-0.13	32.0	4.63	0.39	0.26	56.2
Football	25.6	5.18	4.98	-0.20	30.0	4.17	-0.81	-1.01	55.6
Rugby Union	28.8	0.56	0.42	-0.14	20.0	0.44	0.02	-0.12	48.8
Rugby League	30.7	0.20	0.12	-0.08	17.5	0.12	0.00	-0.08	48.2
Netball	17.3	0.29	0.31	0.02	25.3	0.36	0.05	0.07	42.6
Athletics	20.4	3.89	4.47	0.58	22.0	5.29	0.82	1.40	42.4
Tennis	26.8	1.18	0.88	-0.30	17.4	1.02	0.14	-0.16	44.2
Swimming	20.9	7.83	6.62	-1.21	20.0	5.70	-0.92	-2.13	40.9
Badminton	20.8	1.29	1.20	-0.09	18.0	0.98	-0.22	-0.31	38.8
Squash and racquetball	12.6	0.71	0.67	-0.04	13.5	0.51	-0.16	-0.20	26.1
Golf	12.8	2.29	1.96	-0.33	13.0	1.68	-0.28	-0.61	25.8
Hockey	11.5	0.24	0.19	-0.05	12.0	0.20	0.01	-0.04	23.5
Table Tennis	9.3	0.18	0.32	0.14	11.0	0.21	-0.11	0.03	20.3
Sailing	9.6	0.22	0.12	-0.10	9.3	0.13	0.01	-0.09	18.9
Canoeing	8.5	0.10	0.11	0.01	10.2	0.08	-0.03	-0.02	18.7
Rowing	9.1	0.21	0.19	-0.02	8.2	0.20	0.01	-0.01	17.3
Judo	10.2	0.05	0.03	-0.02	6.1	0.03	0.00	-0.02	16.3
Basketball	8.2	0.45	0.36	-0.09	6.8	0.38	0.02	-0.07	15.0
Boxing	4.7	0.26	0.35	0.09	5.8	0.38	0.03	0.12	15.0
Volleyball	5.6	0.12	0.07	-0.05	4.6	0.06	-0.01	-0.06	10.2
Mountaineering	1.3	0.21	0.26	0.05	3.0	0.19	-0.07	-0.02	4.3
Rounders	2.2	0.06	0.04	-0.02	2.2	0.03	-0.01	-0.03	4.4
Bowls	0.8	0.86	0.58	-0.28	2.0	0.50	-0.08	-0.36	2.8

Fencing	1.0	0.04	0.03	−0.01	1.6	0.03	0.00	−0.01	2.6
Snowsport	1.0	0.29	0.25	−0.04	1.5	0.26	0.01	−0.03	2.5
Taekwondo	0.8	0.06	0.06	0.00	1.2	0.05	−0.01	−0.01	2.0
Weightlifting	0.6	0.29	0.17	−0.12	1.0	0.22	0.05	−0.07	1.6

Whilst the following sports received Whole Sport Plan funding to grow participation (see figure in parenthesis), the sample size for the sport was insufficient for a once a week participation result: Angling (1.4), Archery (0.9), Baseball/Softball (2.7), Boccia (0.8), Goalball (0.4), Gymnastics (10.8), Handball (0.6), Lacrosse (2.2), Modern Pentathlon (0.9), Movement/Dance (0.9), Orienteering (2.3), Shooting (0.8), Triathlon (4.7), Water-skiing (1.0), Wrestling (0.3).

in mass sport participation. These outputs and behaviours are summarised, below:

(1) A deviant and fragmented policy system: Community sport represents both a deviant and fragmented policy system. It may be considered deviant insofar as it fails to genuinely reflect the central government rhetoric of 'decentralisation' where power is ostensibly taken from the centre and given to cities, towns and local communities. This is problematic as key decisions are taken by NGBs at a national level, and many of these decisions fail to reflect local circumstances and/or secure consensus from local-level agencies such as local schools, colleges and voluntary run sports clubs. It is fragmented due to the disjointed structure of community sport, the reliance on NGB-CSP cooperation and the deep, complex structures of power between NGBs and CSPs, and the inability of NGBs to identify and deliver against the different needs of local communities up and down the country.

(2) Priority diffusion: Whilst NGBs and CSPs are engaged in the delivery of community sport, they each have differing values and beliefs regarding sport. NGBs prioritise elite sport and traditional sport development activities (athlete, coach, club, competition development), whereas other local-level agencies such as CSPs or local authorities focus attention on broader physical activity and the social outcomes attached to sport. Thus, local-level collaboration can be complex with one partner (NGBs) emphasising specific sport-related priorities and others focusing attention on broader social or physical activity outcomes. Ultimately, this policy diffusion makes the process of increasing sports participation more complex than it otherwise might be.

(3) The initial focus and emphasis of work: At the start of this new policy period (2008), the focus was very much on achieving the 1 million target or the numbers associated with the 1% increase in participation. As a result, much of the early evaluation was fixated on who will take on what specific growth target (i.e., apportioning the target to different NGBs) rather than focusing on the detail of their plans, the robustness of the implementation plan (what will happen, when, by whom, how will this be evaluated, how will changes be implemented, etc.) and the realism of the targets apportioned to each NGB.

(4) Lack of local reach: There exists a major gap in the implementation of community sport policy. NGBs and CSPs are referred to as implementation agents, but they reside at the national and sub-regional levels and do not have the resources or reach to deliver policies at the local community level. However, community sport takes place at the local community level – in schools, colleges, clubs, community centres, playing fields, multi-use games areas and so on. Thus, NGBs and CSPs rely upon a range of volunteer workers. This relationship is made more complex due to the range and diverse nature of the agencies involved in delivering sport at the local level, the fact that NGBs and CSPs have no direct authority over local-level deliverers, the historic

National Governing Bodies of Sport   49

relationship and storylines that exist between these agencies (in particular NGBs and local voluntary run clubs) and the differing motives and priorities of professionals pursuing policy goals and volunteers managing their sports club.

(5) Funding bottleneck: The problem of implementing community sport policy is further hindered by the lack of funding that makes its way down to the street level. The majority of funding invested in NGBs is taken up by building its infrastructure and employing more staff. While this may be viewed as a critical investment for NGBs to manage policy implementation, the lack of balance in resource allocation, specifically the lack of monies left over to support programme development and delivery is a fundamental flaw. These funding arrangements leave community sport with limited funding to invest in local deliverers or the design and delivery of local initiatives. This is essentially a problem of too many strategists, managers and enablers and not enough doers. The problem is further exacerbated by the austerity cuts to local authority budgets and the trickle-down effect that such cuts have had on the provision of local sports facilities, the development of outreach sports programmes and grants/support offered to local clubs and associations.

(6) Self-preservation above all else: The community sport policy system is made up of several individual units rather than truly representing a collective or communal system. While individual units may attempt to cooperate and collaborative, the structure of the system – with a clear reliance on public funding – is set up in such a way as to prioritise self-preservation and thus promote competition among actors for public monies. Concerns for community sport outcomes, while important, come second when pitted against survival. Consequently, in a challenging policy environment full of varied priorities, the need to survive and maintain the credibility and reputation of one's organisation can dilute effective collaboration and the ability of agents to coalesce and formalise a genuine epistemic community focused on the interests of policy community.

(7) Skills shortage: The sport workforce is recognised as being replete with sport enthusiasts – people who are passionate and highly invested in sport. At the same time there is evidence to suggest that some NGBs lack the softer skills needed to operate effectively. For example, the community sports workforce has lots of knowledge of the system, the structures and tools of the system, but they lack leadership experience and, need to develop communication, brokering, negotiation and conflict resolution skills to operate effectively in the multi-faceted community sport environment and – in order to grow participation – to step outside the institutional norms of NGBs to better understand the reality of the non-sports enthusiast. This is partly about marketing expertise and how NGBs go about understanding consumers and growing their sport. It is also about having strategic intent and a skilled workforce that are able and willing to think more innovatively about how they might be able to grow their sport.

50   Mathew Dowling and Spencer Harris

To be clear, the focus of this case is not intended as simply criticism of government or Sport England's lack of oversight or the NGBs' lack of concern about the realities of implementation. That said, over £700 million of public money was invested in NGBs for the purpose of increasing mass sport participation. While it is possible that the investment stymied societal trends and lessened the decrease in mass sport participation, we argue that it is important to analyse the case based on accurate accounts of what was intended and what happened so that we may be able to identify lessons to improve the implementation of sport policy in the years ahead.

Summary

This chapter has sought to explore the role of NGBs in implementing sport policy. In doing so, we have provided a historical overview of NGBs and their changing role within the sport policy process and begun to theorise NGBs as both sites for interpreting and implementing sport policy through an in-depth discussion of NGBs implementing community sport policy from 2008 to 2016. As the chapter has highlighted, the challenge for the modern NGB is both the internal negotiation and external navigation of multiple, often competing and contradictory policy objectives which are often enforced upon them as a result of their funding/resource dependencies. This is further compounded by the fact that government policies and objectives have changed over time and will likely continue to do so in the future.

Within the UK, there still remains substantial variation in the size and scale of NGBs. Some are very large, wealthy and influential and do not require government funding, whilst others still remain small entities with limited commercial interest and income. Arguably with the increasingly targeted approach adopted by government (via Sport England and UK Sport) and the revenue generated from television exposure for a select few 'commercially viable' sports, NGBs have become even more disparate and varied in terms of their size and scale in recent years. As a result, NGBs often find themselves stuck between a proverbial 'rock and a hard place,' 'pushed and pulled' in different directions due to the competing and changing demands of their funding partners (i.e., paymasters) on the one hand, versus their membership or customer base (i.e., clubs and athletes) on the other.

These structural conditions and challenges are compounded by the problems of coordination, transparency and accountability that are broadly associated with the shift from government to governance (Rhodes, 1997). The problem of coordination can be seen in the fragmentation of the community sport system, the capacity of key actors to create and sustain meaningful collaboration, the difference in values, beliefs and priorities across the community sport system, and the complex patterns of power between different actors in the system. The problem of transparency (or lack thereof) is evident in NGBs prioritising elite sport over community sport, despite the rhetoric of the Whole Sport Plans and the attempt to portray community sport as a genuine priority as evidenced in the inflated growth targets that NGBs presented.

In short, we argue that for many NGBs, these targets were primarily set to leverage a higher investment from Sport England, rather than any genuine calculus of potential growth. Further concerns regarding transparency can be seen in the funding bottleneck and, in particular, the clear prioritisation of funding the growth of the NGB empire – leaving little, if any resource, to be invested in grassroots programme development and delivery. As for the problem of accountability – despite the data demonstrating the clear failure of community sport policy implementation between 2008 and 2015 – we have yet to see evidence of the DCMS, Sport England or NGBs taking responsibility for these failures. Instead, we have witnessed the DCMS and Sport England managing the politics of perception, crafting a narrative that highlights the successes of community sport policy with no attention to the problems and policy learning that, if made available, could help to greatly enhance future policy implementation.

PRACTITIONER REFLECTION AND INSIGHTS

Ian Freeman, Former Coaching Systems Officer and Athlete Development (Technical Lead), Swim England

National Governing Bodies (NGBs) of sport continuously face key challenges based around community sport participation, especially in socio-economically challenging times. Here, I discuss my experiences of working within Swim England (one of the larger NGBs) in relation to policy implementation. Swim England has seen, through data gathered in 2019, 14 million adults (31.3% of the nation) going swimming (Sport England, Active Lives Adult Survey) and 1.18 million children went through their Learn to Swim programme. Swim England also had 188,499 club members (as of December 2018), 1,045 affiliated clubs and 40,000 'Just Swim' members. Swim England's responsibility is based primarily in areas of health and well-being, community participation, competition programmes, codes and rules, memberships, the National Curriculum and Learn to Swim programmes. In conjunction with this, the Institute of Swimming and its awarding body are the profit-making arms responsible for the education and certification of teachers and coaches across all aquatic disciplines (Swimming, Diving, Water Polo, Artistic Swimming and Marathon Swimming). Finally, British Swimming is the high-performance division responsible for elite-level competitive performances and the Olympic and Paralympic successes funded by UK Sport.

Swim England's infrastructure is very well developed; it is mainly leisure centre based for recreational participants, school curriculum swimming, the Learn to Swim programme and swimming clubs which provide talent development and high-performance environments, so is not as fragmented in comparison to many sports at street level.

From 2009 to 2013, Swim England's Senior Leadership Team set out a series of simple outcomes in their National Strategy with four aims:

1. To set a culture change agenda to increase participation in the sport
2. To drive quality into the voluntary sector through affiliated clubs to strengthen the talent pathway
3. To revitalise the training of swimming teachers, coaches and officials with a programme, supported by the industry, to challenge the best in the world
4. To deliver swimming pool programmes which reflect not only the need for income but also the necessity of pool designers to design pools which meet world-class environmental standards whilst still meeting the needs of customers

Swimming participation numbers, however, still declined, despite the 2008 Olympic and Paralympic Games medal successes in Beijing and the intended legacy from the London 2012 Games. Swimming was not seen as a viable activity for many people, and the decline was also attributed to some degree to national austerity at that time. It was also noted that swimming had some key challenges in comparison to some other sports, and a number of areas were highlighted through Swim England's Research and Insight Team customer survey that included (but was not limited to) travelling time and distance to the pool, pool temperature, getting changed, issues with hair, those concerned with body image and aesthetic appearance and those with a lack of confidence in the water and whether to use certain lanes. It was through these issues that Sport England felt that Swim England should primarily look to provide a Whole Sport Plan which looked at long-term initiatives designed to increase participation over time. The setting up of the Research and Insight Team was based primarily to work closely with Sport England and to investigate and attempt to exert more influence in the key areas listed above (amongst many others including swimming values, ethnicity and inclusion, water well-being and non-swimmers). In relation to the Research and Insight staff, the importance of this task was huge as Swim England continued to receive bad press following almost every Active People Survey report. However, Swim England's 'participation focused' approach was adopted across the whole NGB with ideas coming from all departments. My personal focus was on developing more self-aware teachers and coaches and providing a more inviting and fun environment for all potential swimmers whether recreational or competitive.

It is important to understand that large NGBs and the nature of sport evolves over time due to socio-economic changes, shifts in domestic priorities and Olympic/Paralympic performances, which makes the environment very transient in nature. Swim England often had a rapid turnover of key staff which left them often seeing fragmented progress in relation to effective long-term policy implementation taking place. One principal factor was Swim England's multidisciplinary range of priorities and its traditional 'top-down' approach to policy implementation, which was Senior Leadership Team and Departmental Heads led, with very little consultation with relevant employees with key expertise in specific fields, all of which can lead to divergent viewpoints.

This divergence, I feel, was due to Senior Leadership meetings with Government and Sports Council level staff where key decisions were made. On reflection, this made any input from the bottom-up (e.g., researchers and sport policy innovators) very difficult to be heard at the developmental 'ideas stage' and left little room for others to play a role in any initial policy decisions and subsequent implementation processes. This was especially relative to areas where ongoing research into key areas impact swimming participation, such as family/social values, teacher and coach education, and athletic/ skill development. Research and insight into participatory practices were of key relevance, and there was possibly a failure to utilise the relevant, expert staff who had more lateral, innovative and embedded thought processes based around self-awareness, participant awareness and environment awareness. Improved softer skill practices which more effectively engage all swimmers were not fully explored as the 'top-down,' 'agency policy approach' continued to dominate and adhered to the hierarchical norm.

Also overlooked was the subsequent culture change that takes place across sport and, especially within larger NGBs (e.g., new teacher/coach learning and development practices, practitioner learning materials and new athletic development methods), which takes place over time. It is due to this transitory nature of NGBs that agency policy and practice, alongside continued staff turnover, often lead to the failure to notice any longitudinal changes in already embedded policies, but also the opportunity to monitor, modify and re-embed these issues where necessary.

For example, Swim England took almost ten years to fully embed their Long-Term Athlete Development (LTAD) framework into their coach education programme, which, in 2014, was developed into the more innovative and swimmer-specific Athlete Development Support Pathway (ADSP). Although the framework was primarily implemented 'top-down,' the process also involved a lot of 'bottom-up' research and development but was embedded into the coach education programme in an almost subliminal manner in order to minimise any top-down intervention. As a result, the framework was widely accepted across the NGB, as well as being well-received by teachers and coaches and published in key texts, which demonstrates that non-traditional, cost-effective implementation approaches can work if allowed to do so by Senior Leaders.

Another issue that arose was when key staff came in from different (non-sporting) industry sectors. For example, Swim England looked to bring in staff from such fields as product retail. Many of these employees were experts in their field, but they had no real experience of working on complex matters based around sport-specific policies, human behaviours and increasing participation. There appeared to be a shift within the NGBs' terminology where the 'organisation' was referred constantly to as 'the business' or 'the company' and started to move down a more corporate route. From the NGBs' standpoint, this could be seen as a more professional and commercial outlook, but it may have generated an even greater divide between Senior Leaders and staff regarding policy implementation. As discussed, this approach also resulted in large staff turnover as the NGB still failed to raise participation figures. Policy implementation-wise it also created a greater divide and a more siloed feel to working practice – a good number of staff with a wide knowledge of key sporting practices felt there was a disconnect with their corporate counterparts. This resulted in many of the former group leaving, with a gap emerging for personnel with a high investment in and passion for sport. Personally, there was also a feeling of self-preservation due to possible under-utilisation of my skills, coupled with an enthusiasm and desire to make a difference in key teaching and coaching outcomes. Although it did not affect my ability to collaborate with others, there appeared to be an element of competitive self-interest in others which definitely diluted effective collaboration and any agreed policy outcomes.

The case study in this chapter certainly touches on many of the experiences and challenges I encountered. Whilst most decisions were centralised through the Swim England Senior Leadership Team and Departmental Heads, many messages were construed as 'deviant and fragmented' when delivered to staff members. However, in relation to priority diffusion, Swim England's messaging to the regions has always been very effective and professional. Relating that directly to the Research and Insight Team's participation values has yielded excellent responses to specific policies across the country. This suggests that there is an ability to communicate key messages, but more work is still required here, especially with Active Partnerships, to work even more closely at regional and local levels. In addition, more needs to be understood as to how decisions at a national level are not always 'bought into' at the regional level and are hard to implement fully unless there is an excellent regional staff system (which Swim England has), which potentially allows for more effective policy implementation processes to take place. However, I agree that this is also reflective of differing regional communities and their socio-cultural and economic status. The funding bottleneck question is also key and one where we see many 'top heavy' NGB business models (many are registered charities) focusing on profit making and increasing managerial staff numbers, leaving very little to fund key NGB officers and initiatives, thereby leading to the disconnect from community sport and local authorities in relation to the funding of these key initiatives.

Notes

1 There is no single recognised legal structure for NGBs within the United Kingdom. NGBs can be unincorporated associations, trusts, limited companies, community interest companies or charitable incorporated organisations (https://www.sportandrecreation.org.uk/pages/governance-library-organisational-structure).

2 See Sport England (n.d.) for a list of recognised NGBs (accurate as of March 2021). The issue of NGB recognition is further complicated due to the peculiarities of the home nations and the administrative structure of sport within the United Kingdom. In most cases a single governing agency is recognised; however, in some cases multiple organisations are recognised by sports councils across the home nations (England, Scotland, Wales and Northern Ireland). In the case of some sports, there is no recognised governing body across any home nation (Australian rules football, Biathlon), or there is an absence of a recognised governing body in particular home nations (e.g., Curling and Northern Ireland). Some countries are governed by a UK-wide governing entity (e.g., British American Football Association – governs Scotland, England and Wales). There are also some governing bodies that operate both within a home nation and also have a UK-wide remit (e.g., British Judo).

3 We recognise the problematic concept of earned autonomy (from government) insofar as Principle 5 of the Olympic Charter reinforces that sport should remain autonomous (i.e., autonomous and free from government involvement). However, this is a messy issue as the governments of numerous nations directly or indirectly fund NGBs and are thus 'involved' in the NGB. The concept of earned autonomy used in this context means greater freedoms from government steering or oversight on general NGB governance matters to more specific issues concerning the allocation of public monies.

4 In Atlanta 1996, Team GB ranked 36th overall (just ahead of Belarus), with a total of 15 medals (1 Gold, 8 Silver and 6 Bronze). This is compared to London 2012 whereby Team GB came 3rd overall (beating Russia), with a total of 65 medals (29 Gold, 17 Silver and 19 Bronze).

References

Bloyce, D., & Smith, A. (2009). *Sport policy and development: An introduction*. Routledge.

Cairney, P. (2011). The new British policy style: From a British to a Scottish political tradition? *Political Studies Review*, *9*(2), 208–220. https://doi.org/10.1111/j.1478-9302.2011.00233.x

Coghlan, J. F., & Webb, I. (1990). *Sport and British politics since 1960*. Routledge.

DCMS. (2015). *Sporting future: A new strategy for an active nation*. Author.

Department for Culture Media & Sport [DCMS]. (2000). *A sporting future for all*. DCMS.

Department for Culture, Media and Sport/Strategy Unit. (2002). *Game plan: A strategy for delivering government's sport and physical activity objectives*. Author.

Green, M. (2006). From 'sport for all' to not about 'sport' at all? Interrogating sport policy interventions in the United Kingdom. *European Sport Management Quarterly*, *6*(3), 217–238. https://doi.org/10.1080/16184740601094936

Green, M. (2007). Olympic glory or grassroots development? Sport policy priorities in Australia, Canada and the United Kingdom, 1960–2006. *International Journal of the History of Sport*, *24*(7), 921–953. https://doi.org/10.1080/09523360701311810

Green, M., & Houlihan, B. (2005). *Elite sport development: Policy learning and political priorities*. Routledge.

Grix, J. (2010). The 'governance debate' and the study of sport policy. *International Journal of Sport Policy and Politics*, *2*(2), 159–171. https://doi.org/10.1080/19406940.2010.488061

Grix, J., & Phillpots, L. (2011). Revisiting the 'governance narrative' 'asymmetrical network governance' and the deviant case of the sports policy sector. *Public Policy and Administration*, *26*(1), 3–19. https://doi.org/10.1177/0952076710365423

Harris, S., & Dowling, M. (Eds.). (2021). *Sport participation and Olympic legacies: A comparative study*. Routledge.

Houlihan, B. (1997). *Sport, policy and politics: A comparative analysis*. Routledge.

Houlihan, B., & Green, M. (2009). Modernization and sport: The reform of sport England and UK sport. *Public Administration*, *87*(3), 678–698. https://doi.org/10.1111/j.1467-9299.2008.01733.x

Houlihan, B., & White, A. (2003). *The politics of sports development: Development of sport or development through sport?* Routledge.

Houlihan, B., & Zheng, J. (2013). The Olympics and elite sport policy: Where will it all end? *International Journal of the History of Sport*, *30*(4), 338–355. https://doi.org/10.1080/09523367.2013.765726

Katwala, S. (2000). *Democratising global sport*. The Foreign Policy Centre.

Kikulis, L. M., Slack, T., & Hinings, C. R. (1995). Sector-specific patterns of organizational design change. *Journal of Management Studies*, *32*(1), 67–100.

Lipsky, M. (2010). *Street-level bureaucracy: Dilemmas of the individual in public service*. Russell Sage Foundation.

Parent, M. M., Hoye, R., Taks, M., Thompson, A., Naraine, M. L., Lachance, E. L., & Séguin, B. (2021). National sport organization governance design archetypes for the twenty-first century. *European Sport Management Quarterly*. Advanced online publication. https://doi.org/10.1080/16184742.2021.1963801

Rhodes, R. A. (1997). *Understanding governance: Policy networks, governance, reflexivity and accountability*. Open University.

Sport England (2004). *The framework for sport in England: Marking England an active and successful sporting nation: A vision for 2020*. Sport England.

Winter, S. C. (2012). Implementation perspectives: Status and reconsideration. In J. Pierre & G. Peters (Eds.), *The SAGE handbook of public administration* (pp. 265–278). Sage.

Chapter 4

The Active Partnerships

Marc Keech and Jack Wilkinson

Introduction

This chapter explores the evolving roles and responsibilities of the organisations now known as Active Partnerships since their inception in 1999. The Partnerships have become a significant part of the sport and physical activity landscape across England and were established by Sport England in 1999–2000 as a nationwide network of local partnerships, originally designed to lead the local delivery of national programmes (the period of Active Sports, 1999–2004). Their initial remit was to create partnerships across sports organisations, support National Governing Bodies (NGBs) locally and to coordinate sports activities within their area with the primary role of driving up participation in sport. Generally, they were created as hosted organisations, i.e. established as semi-autonomous organisations embedded within county councils, local authorities or universities and funded primarily by Sport England (SE) but also through local partner funding. Some Partnerships map onto one or more geographical counties or metropolitan areas, and some work across aggregated unitary authorities. They evolved into County Sports Partnerships (CSPs) in response to the 2004 *Framework for Sport in England* (Sport England, 2004) establishing a key role up until 2016 as interpreters and implementers of sport policy. CSPs became networks of local agencies and local representatives of NGBs, supported by Sport England, that worked together to increase participation in sport and physical activity. Finally, as Active Partnerships (since 2019), the rebranded name that better reflects the collaborative nature of its work, the 43 Partnerships are now all locally-led organisations and embedded within their communities. In a typical Active Partnership area, there will be around 2,000 sports clubs, 500 schools and hundreds of facilities and providers, not to mention many more informal opportunities (Mason, 2021, p. 1). Still funded by Sport England, they are tasked with identifying the best opportunities for increasing sport and physical activity in their communities. The Active Partnerships national team is the network's charity organisation, representing all 43 Partnerships to deliver high-impact programmes, builds strong local networks and has adopted the 'highest levels' of governance. However, the needs of its partners and communities are changing, with levels of physical activity worryingly low and affected by a

DOI: 10.4324/9781003162728-4

complex system of influences, meaning that no single organisation can create 'sustainable change at scale.'

Partnership working has been presented as a critique of both market- and state-led forms of governance, while in policy discourse partnerships are presented as offering the potential for a more resource-efficient, outcome-effective and inclusive-progressive form of policy delivery. Partnerships have been interpreted either in normative terms as inherently progressive or as discursive constructs designed to nullify opposition to dominant interests via processes of incorporation and interpellation (McDonald, 2005). Partnerships in sport policy emerged to become the key mechanism of service delivery in the UK and around the world (Babiak & Thibault, 2008, 2009; Miller & Ahmed, 2000) which reflects the key influence that central government exerts over the strategic development of sport policy. But multi-agency partnerships in the public sector became increasingly important following the election of the 'New' Labour government in 1997. Enlarging managerial power sits at odds with devolving power to local communities but ideologically and in terms of implementing policy, partnerships were advanced across many areas of public policy as a tool of 'joining up' policy areas and as a response to organisational fragmentation. Structurally, partnership working was seen as a potential solution to ongoing social problems. Wilson (2003, p. 336) stated 'local governance involves multi-agency working, partnerships and policy networks,' but Skelcher (2000, p. 9) suggested that 'partnership bodies are being created to manage the complexities of policy networks.' The political importance of partnerships rests on the claim that they represent a more effective, democratic and participatory form of service delivery (McDonald, 2005, p. 580).

Origins

The origins of partnership working in sport can be found in the 1982 publication *Sport in the Community: The Next Ten Years* (Sports Council, 1982), but 'the Partnerships,' a colloquial and collective term often used to identify the organisations identified in this chapter lie, like many other aspects of sport policy in England, in the paper *Sport: Raising the Game* (Department of National Heritage, 1995), a justified landmark in the history of sport in the UK, not for the depth of its analysis but for the priority and commitment of the prime minister who sought to back his aspiration with resources to be generated by the instigation of the National Lottery. Structural changes in the policy landscape ensued (augmented in the course of successive Labour governments from 1997 through to 2010), accompanied by a torrent of policies and systems through which to invest Lottery funds. The attribution of the effect of new facilities and international success to the Lottery's good causes is simplistic. It overlooks the policy base established in the preceding years. From its inception in the 1960s to the mid-1990s, public sport policy developed on a rather ad hoc basis, with little involvement or leadership from central government (Houlihan, 1997). Much was developed more through engagement at regional and county levels between 1975 and 1995. Swathes of policy were produced and supported by programmes of interaction and investment (e.g. with Sport Development Officers). Further dimensions of interaction were the amount of technical support (publications and advice) and research (evidence and evaluation) produced by the Sports Council/Sport England (especially from 1990 to 1995) and the national frameworks and networks by which sport was already developing before *Raising the Game*. Arguably, the first half of the 1990s saw the origins of a multi-disciplinary, engaged and integrated period of sport policy from top-down and from grassroots-up. Furthermore, some of the most significant policy developments for sport were in the statutory field of Land Use Planning such as the production of Planning Policy Guidance for Sport and Recreation. It was a key area of Sports Council/Sport England expertise, perhaps reflecting the influence of the previous generation of geographers and town planners.

The Partnerships are now twenty-first century agencies, but most of the policy issues they had to initially address had already been defined in the 1990s. Chief Leisure Officers and Sports Development Officers had been working collaboratively out of common interest for years, in partnership long before partnership became the requisite means of operation across all services and another cliché in management-speak. There were also antecedents and, thus, alternative models of coordination and support such as County Sports Development Units, rooted in local sport and anchored in local government and through the development of Local Government Acts which encouraged the adoption of private sector management approaches through processes such as Compulsory Competitive Tendering (CCT) of Local Authority services. Any fair assessment of CSPs needs not only to nod in recognition of previous development but also consider how they may have fared in the system that preceded them.

Active Sports Partnerships

The inception of the Partnerships was as a national network of Active Sports Partnerships. *Active Sports* was initially designed as a five-year development programme and an element of the Sport England's More People programme (ESC, 1997). A 1998 survey (cited in Sport England, 2002, p. 3) revealed that 90% of respondents agreed that Lottery grants should be available to improve coaching opportunities for young people and that 89% agreed on the need for funding to identify and develop young people with talent in sport. The recommendations formed the basis of Sport England's approach to establish the 45 Partnerships, initially through discussions with 45 county-based Chief Leisure Officers Groups (or their equivalent in metropolitan areas). In 1998/1999, the proposals for implementing the Active Sports programme were considered and the access criteria worked out. Nine sports were included: athletics, basketball, cricket, girl's football, hockey, netball, rugby union, swimming and tennis, plus a tenth sport, rugby league, to be promoted in particular areas. Sport England worked closely with the Chief Leisure/Culture Officers Associations at national level to obtain views and support which

60 Marc Keech and Jack Wilkinson

grew and culminated with the formal programme launched at the latter's AGM on June 25, 1999 (Sport England, 2002, p. 3). Agreed in June 1998, the programme intended to

> support partnerships between local authorities, governing bodies of sport and other key local, regional and national organisations ... [whilst aiming] ... to ensure that young people are given the chance to further their interest in sport and realise their full sporting potential.

> (Sport England, 2002, p. 3)

The first phase of Active Sports Managers received their induction training in October 1999. A nationally agreed Development Framework was produced for each sport to guide local delivery. The production of these frameworks involved national experts, suppliers, local delivery agencies and Partnerships to ensure they were both challenging and realistic. The Active Sports Guide, which included all ten frameworks, set quality standards and parameters for local delivery. Both authors of the chapter were involved in the inception of the partnership in Sussex with Wilkinson specifically acting as a policy broker in his role as a senior regional manager for Sport England, and the following extract outlines the initial approach and priorities in this partnership:

> The Partnership was established in October 2000 after it was identified that a co-ordinated approach to enhance the provision of sport across Sussex was required. From the outset the partners established the Partnership as a co-ordinating body that operated at both a strategic and delivery level and the *Active Sports* programme has been the catalyst for this to happen. The partnership approach is based on identifying the needs of the key stakeholders and formulating a 'consensus' approach to delivery. The Partnership Management Group have established the following priorities:

- Successful planning and implementation of the Active Sports programme
- Identifying and developing best practice to support the work of partner agencies
- Interpreting and responding to political priorities of partner agencies
- Strategic responsiveness developed through co-ordinated delivery
- Promoting sport as a tool to address cross cutting issues
- Aligning the partnership work to the Best Value process
- Facilitating joined up approaches
- Procuring external resources for sports development and physical activity initiatives
- Co-ordinating programmes with a proactive approach
- Raising standards and demonstrating impact/value for money

> Sussex Sport Partnership annual report (2001, pp. 4–5)

It was vital from the outset that the Partnerships utilised and supported existing structures wherever they were seen to be relevant and were an important part of the overall structure of sport across the respective areas. With initial enthusiasm, a number of new groups were also formed, particularly at sport-specific level, to add to the existing groups to create a communication structure for the Partnerships that theoretically permitted them to function across their whole range of objectives. In 2001 Sport England developed a Monitoring and Evaluation Framework for the Partnerships with reviews of performance being undertaken annually, and performance indicators linked to programme objectives, in order to monitor the quality of Partnership development plans submitted for Lottery funding and the impact of achievements against targets set. These moves were intended to promote the culture of continuous improvement and encourage innovative policies and strategies to be used. Overall, by 2002, £73.7m was allocated for the initial rollout of implementing nine sports in every Active Sports Partnership and rugby league in its 'heartlands.' Indicative budget planning figures were set for each Partnership and each sport to achieve nationwide delivery of Active Sports. A further £3m was allocated for the staging of nine Active Sports Talent Camps in 2002 and £2m for strengthening the NGB infrastructure to be able to support the Sports Partnerships and Regions to deliver these programmes (Sport England, 2002). Consequently, an estimated 50,000 young people were involved in Active Sports coaching events, a further 50,000 competitors involved in the Partnership Youth Games annually, whilst 10,000 young people and 3,000 coaches and volunteers were involved in the Active Sports Talent Camps in 2002 (Sport England, Sport England, 2002, p. 3).

Despite these numbers, the implementation of Active Sports and the establishment of the Partnerships as key organisations within local landscapes were mixed. For many, Active Sports was the 'trigger' and 'development tool' for local authorities and NGBs to work effectively together, many for the first time. The relative success of the approach generated discussion on the wider role of the Partnerships. But key problems needed to be addressed. Amongst a number of local authorities, dissent and dissatisfaction often focused upon contributing a proportion of often meagre budgets to the collective funding of the Partnerships at the expense of investing in bespoke projects directly with their own local areas. Further, many of the Active Sports Managers were on short-term contracts which risked losing the initial knowledge and experience acquired by those staff. The expanding programmes of the Sports Partnerships were also making increasing demands on their members, some of which had limited capacity to respond, whilst some of the Partnerships themselves were at an embryonic stage and are still vulnerable to shifts in organisational and policy change.

County Sports Partnerships

Following its 'modernisation' in 2003, Sport England responded to the government's *Game Plan* policy (DCMS/Strategy Unit, 2002) by producing the *National Framework for Sport in England* (Sport England 2004). The Framework reflected an attempt to address the concerns of *Game Plan* by situating sport within a series of social policy concerns such as improving community safety and reducing crime, as first recommended by the PAT 10 report (Coalter et al., 2000). As sub-regional agencies were responsible, in effect, for what Sport England's regional offices had previously undertaken, there was recognition of the need for sub-regional areas to have both the strategic and operational capacity to address *Game Plan* and the *National Framework for Sport*. CSPs were formalised between 2003 and 2005, an evolution of the previous Active Sport Partnerships that existed in each county across England. Subsequently, the role of CSPs was revised in 2008. Each CSP received core funding of £240,000 from Sport England and in return was expected to deliver on four key business objectives, as set out in the CSP core specification: (i) to deliver cross-sport services to meet NGB priorities, (ii) to develop and maintain the strategic alliances and local networks the NGBs and Sport England need to drive, deliver and secure resources, (iii) to deliver cross-sport coaching services to meet local need and (iv) to manage and operate the CSP and ensure sound governance (Harris & Houlihan, 2016, p. 434).

The development of effective CSPs was the most immediate and important organisational challenge facing Sport England in 2005–2006 for two reasons: first, there was a need to articulate a clear understanding of the role of CSPs and how partnership working would benefit all stakeholders involved in sub-regional structures, and second, Sport England had to support CSPs so that the latter could build the capacity to have the strategic overview for sport in their respective geographical areas. CSPs, therefore, had to show that they were distinctive in order to match the local needs and be fully inclusive and representative of all the key stakeholders involved in sport; e.g. from local authorities, voluntary sector, private sector to other wider policy areas such as health, crime, community safety and regeneration. CSPs were charged with bringing together all the key agencies responsible for sport in each area and needed to be cognisant of issues of governance within their respective areas. The challenge then, as it is now, was to continue the debate about the functions of community sport in order to address and effectively implement the new ways of working required by national policy.

By the mid-2000s, CSPs occupied a pivotal position, due to the responsibility for applying national policy to local situations and locations. Sport England's role in their new, post-2005 strategy of focusing on sport was to 'ensure that key parties act in partnership' with one another. Here the reference is to NGBs, local authorities and CSPs. There was not much choice whether these parties wished to cooperate; indeed, CSPs represented the opposite of autonomous actors, free from state interference (Grix, 2010, p. 169). Nevertheless, no sooner had they metamorphosed from Active Sports Partnerships into CSPs, their purpose was being questioned. The CSPs were in an exposed and vulnerable position, subject to national direction and funding yet nominally representative of their counties. *The Review of National Sport Effort and Resources*, led by Lord Patrick Carter, articulated that whilst in school sport and elite

The Active Partnerships 63

sport, government had clearly defined the policy and invested in the infrastructure required to achieve its key targets,

> in community sport, delivery is more complex and diverse: a range of public, private and voluntary sector providers operate within locally determined structures. The lack of a 'joined up' approach to community delivery risks not achieving the key policy objective of increasing and widening the base of participation, which would lead to a healthier nation; not fully realising the substantial investment in school sport; and not sufficiently developing the pool of talented participants which form the bedrock of elite success.
>
> (Carter, 2005, p. 6)

Carter's proposal to address the shortcomings was to establish, develop, communicate and embed a 'single system' for sport in the community from government to grassroots by investing in clubs, coaches and volunteers, strengthening school–community links and integrating talent pathways for aspiring performers. If the agreed national policy objectives for sport were to be realised, Carter argued that a 'spine of accountability' needed to be embedded throughout the sector:

- Ensure that there is a common purpose and shared set of performance targets from local level up through the system to Government, with clearly defined roles and responsibilities at each level
- Establish around 400 CSNs [Community Sport Networks] to oversee local projects and interventions, to include improved collaboration with SSPs [School Sport Partnerships] on strengthening school-community links
- Equip 45 CSPs as a key 'building block' in the system and channel for investment – alongside LAs [Local Authorities] and NGBs – in club development, coaches and volunteers. The three core functions of the CSP should be strategic co-ordination, so that the efforts of local deliverers are optimised; marketing and communications, so that sport is advocated to key decision makers and investment partners; performance measurement, so that progress is clearly tracked
- Task 9 RSBs [Regional Sport Boards] with overseeing CSPs, playing a strategic role at regional level in terms of influencing policy, championing sport for the achievement of social objectives and leveraging partnership funds

(Carter, 2005, p. 28)

By 2007, however, especially in light of London being awarded the 2012 Olympic and Paralympic Games, NGBs were arguing strongly and loudly for increased funding and a redefined role for sporting organisations. Chief Executive of the Amateur Swimming Association, David Sparkes, and Ed Warner, Chair of UK Athletics, gave evidence to the DCMS Select Committee in which they criticised Sport England's remit as one which was too broad (Keech, 2011). The government agreed announcing what many considered to be a serious 'u-turn' in policy (Revill, 2007).

> We will never build a world class community sports infrastructure unless we are clear that sport is a good thing and competition is a good thing. There is an old management axiom that the man who has five priorities has none. That is why I am categorically sure that the purpose of Sport England is to deliver sport in England. That means creating excellent national governing bodies, clubs, coaches and volunteers.
>
> (Purnell, 2007)

As a result of the aggressive lobbying by NGBs and Purnell's belief in their arguments, policy swung again with the emphasis shifting away from sport's role in broader social outcomes to a narrower focus to what has been commonly termed 'sport for sport's sake.' The strategy reflected a shift in emphasis and role of national governing bodies.

> The governing bodies in English sport command only some 6 million members, not all playing. Without exception they argue they need more volunteers to cope with the growing roles government expects of them … *The Secretary of State's action will almost certainly slow down the uncertain process of increasing mass participation.*
>
> (Collins, 2008, p. 82, italics added)

From 2009, CSPs were directed to agree on core services that they would make available to all 46 Sport England 2009–2013 funded NGBs and the services that CSPs will provide locally for Sport England. Whilst there was an expectation that there would be a consistency in the services delivered, the format in which they were delivered would vary between CSPs. Nevertheless, CSPs were expected to develop and maintain the strategic alliances and local networks that NGBs and Sport England required to implement policy and secure resources, in addition to promoting access and utilisation with all LAs and related stakeholders within their area. As MacDonald (2005, p. 595) argued, 'a more detailed empirical examination [was] necessary to tease out the nuances, complexities and contradictions of CSPs.' This view was echoed by Houlihan and Lindsey (2008), Mackintosh (2011) and Grix (2010) who noted that CSPs offered an excellent example of changing governance structures and policy delivery. CSPs only appeared to resemble 'real' partnerships in name. Although, in the period from 2004 onwards, CSPs consisted of a number of multi-agency members, resource dependency, primarily due to funding, towards Sport England ensured policy was essentially still centrally controlled. Unsurprisingly, the purpose, role and responsibilities of CSP kept changing, and over time many were forced to steer themselves in a different direction to the one they were originally established to achieve. What is very clear now is that many different versions of CSPs have evolved, all with different management models and all carrying out different roles and responsibilities according to where their sources of income. The structure of CSPs was simplified by defining the meaning or representation of the partnership at three distinct levels:

> the core team (a team of professionals, e.g. CSP Director, NGB Lead Officer, who are employed by the CSP to develop and deliver against the CSP's strategy and Core Specification); (ii) the board (selected representatives or individuals), whose primary role is to advise the CSP core team, provide guidance, and make decisions on matters of strategic importance; and (iii) the broader partnership (a network of organisations that have an association with the area served by the CSP, usually involving, but not limited to, local authorities, health and well-being agencies, NGBs, clubs, and schools). Whilst this articulation of CSPs is relatively consistent, the structure, size, and representation of each vary from partnership to partnership.
>
> (Harris & Houlihan, 2016, p. 436)

From CSPs to Active Partnerships

In 2015 the government shifted its strategic approach to focus on wider outcomes potentially deriving from sport and physical activity. It published a new cross-government sporting strategy, *Sporting Future*, in 2015. This strategy stated that future funding decisions would be based on achieving five key outcomes: physical well-being, mental well-being, individual development, social and community development and economic development. The government expanded Sport England's remit to include not only sport but also certain kinds of physical activity such as walking. Sport England reflected these changes in its 2016–2021 strategy, *Towards an Active Nation*. It aimed to understand and address the barriers to activity for the least active by working with a broader range of partners than the NGBs of traditional sports, and by encouraging local collaboration. Yet during this same period, particularly from 2010 onward, CSPs were the only possible agencies which could bridge the gaps across the landscape of grassroots and community sport. By 2016, and after the publication of *Sporting Future* (DCMS, 2015), CSPs were clearly established as key organisations for policy implementation, but there was a variable track record of delivering successfully at a local level across the network. However, Sport England did not, perhaps, focus sufficiently clearly on the redefinition of the core purpose of CSPs which, over time, raised questions regarding their purpose amongst partner organisations. With NGBs having failed to deliver on participation increases after the London 2012 Olympic and Paralympic Games, it was reasonable to suggest that CSPs should be Sport England's main delivery partner or agencies for growing participation in sport and physical activity whilst NGBs should focus on sustaining participation in sport.

Former Loughborough MP and Sports Think Tank Director, Andy Reed OBE, was asked by the Sports Minister Tracey Crouch MP in the Summer of 2016 to carry out the appraisal of the County Sport Partnerships (CSPs) as outlined in the

Sporting Future strategy. The appraisal concluded that CSPs and the collective CSP network remained vital to achieving the government's and Sport England's objectives, with key roles to play including:

- Facilitating and brokering collaboration and creating the conditions for effective locality approaches.
- Supporting the sector and shaping local provision to better meet customer needs
- Supporting and influencing local government and emerging structures
- Collectively delivering national programmes, partnering and scaling up best practice whilst celebrating local innovation.

(Reed, 2016, p. 3)

Following the appraisal, Sport England reconfirmed the value they placed on CSPs, emphasising the need to retain a nationwide network across England. The report itself highlighted the need for greater consistency of service delivery, accountability and transparency for Sport England investment in the CSP network. It called for a new 'core purpose and specification' for CSPs and for this to be made widely known and available. A key recommendation was that

All CSPs should have a clear understanding of what the support needs are of local authorities in their area and have a rationale for how they are working with them. They should develop and agree plans in partnership with strategic local bodies including all local authorities in their areas and should not be in competition where there is no consensus amongst the partnership. It is expected that genuine collaboration and partnership with local authorities will be the norm alongside their Trust and other Leisure providers. Local authorities, despite increasing financial pressures will have a massive impact on sport, leisure and active lifestyles through all of their services.

(Reed, 2016, p. 7)

The focus of CSPs, after the Reed-led appraisal increasingly reflected Sport England's focus on inactive people and under-represented groups in physical activity and sport, so much so that in March 2019 the national network of CSPs was rebranded as Active Partnerships. Then chief executive of the new Active Partnerships national network, Lee Mason, said this meant that Active Partnerships, as local organisations, needed to think and act differently.

Over the last year we have been changing to strengthen our approach to better tackle these issues … This has included confirming our long-term future partnership with Sport England to help deliver the national strategy, *Towards an Active Nation*, and a shift from programme delivery to a whole system, place-based approach … The term Active highlights the broad spectrum of

The Active Partnerships 67

sports and physical activities we embrace, the dynamic and agile way that we approach our work and our mission to increase levels of engagement in sport and physical activity.

(Knaggs, 2019)

The vision of the network became to make active lifestyles the social norm for everyone through working in partnership to create the conditions for this in every locality. But, following ten years of austerity policies, the Covid pandemic and the exceptional pressures on public finances, the capacity of local authorities was severely reduced, and partners such as education, youth, health and police services were all under pressure to deliver on core targets. Yet it was and is these partners whose Active Partnerships were tasked with addressing what were seen as, at best, stagnant levels of participation and working to tackle the inequality at the heart of inactivity.

The Partnerships and the Implementation of Community Sport Policy

Despite widespread policy impetus, more critical literature has highlighted the potential weaknesses of partnership working and has challenged the likelihood of partnerships being able to simultaneously achieve efficient and effective responses to complex issues (Lindsey, 2011, 2014). While widely accepted by policymakers as possessing the capacity to leverage fragmented systems and produce increased efficiency and innovation, there is a view that proposes that partnerships are adopted not because they are proven to be effective, but because a number of key organisations stipulate their use to provide legitimacy to development projects or, more likely, specify partnership working as a condition of funding and means of ensuring accountability (Morgan & Baker, 2021, p. 717). Consequently, a 'culture of partnership' (Mansfield, 2016, p. 715) has been created where the necessity to work in partnership becomes an end in itself, as opposed to a means to an end. Partnership working does not always benefit users of welfare significantly – in some cases it makes it worse. Partnerships reinforce power inequalities that are already in existence, at times diverting resources away from the core business of welfare service delivery and doing relatively little to empower service users (Rummery, 2002, p. 243). Yet who could possibly object to partnership as a concept?

In practice the Active Sports Partnerships were an unwieldy structure with variations in the circumstances and capacity (including funding) of different sports. At a time of significant structural changes and dissolution of the old order – not least in local government (where leisure services were absorbed into wider briefs) and in Sport England (which after 2003 retreated into a more strategic role) – the Active Sports model did not seem to be what was most needed to develop sport at local levels. The transition to a wider remit of County Sport Partnerships and to community sport was more appropriate although the change to support NGBs in 2008 and more recent changes from 2019 extended to an even wider remit. There was a diligent and conscientious attempt to resolve the latent conflict of identity and interest, including exercises such as TAES (Towards an Excellent Service), but fundamentally CSPs have been answerable to Sport England. This can be seen as wider tendencies to centralise authority at the expense of local autonomy.

Although one can draw a line between the solar sources of policy to the remotest spaces of action, there are usually various intermediate staging posts. Equally, the nearest and probably most influential point of reference for those working for the Active Partnerships is a line manager and the employer. Thus, the source, rationale, key messages and chapter-and-verse of policy may be unknown at the point of delivery. As Moore (2021, p. 180) has noted a particularly striking aspect of conventional approaches to policy making and implementation is an omission of the people who constitute the sport system (policymakers, practitioners, volunteers, etc.) and their immanent dynamics. Limited attention has been devoted to the daily working practices of the individuals who constitute key stakeholder organisations in relation to policy formation and execution. This is a generic policy challenge but not always recognised. Grix and Phillpots (2011) observed the paradox that while County Sport Partnerships were established to facilitate the delivery of sport policy at regional/local level by responding and adapting to local conditions, this resulted in a hierarchical mode of partnership that rests on resource dependency and asymmetrical network governance between the government and stakeholders in the sport policy network. The 2018 Performance Management and Improvement Framework was designed to provide an objective, transparent and proportionate reflection of their performance and create a learning environment to support the delivery of the objectives contained in the *Towards an Active Nation* strategy. But it also reinforced much of the resource dependency at a time when the complex environment of community sport was increasingly fraught with restraints and challenges that Active Partnerships faced at the local level (Beacom & Ziakas, 2022, p. 4) – and that was before the Covid-19 pandemic hit in 2020.

As key actors in the implementation of community sport policy in England, these Partnerships have been subject(ed) to a range of changes in policy direction and implementation over the 20 years of their existence. They have been funded through Sport England, and the standards, funding arrangements and performance measurement frameworks have continuously evolved in the context of a challenging, ever-changing landscape in which policy evaluation has been predominantly, but not exclusively, defined by the results of the Active People (2005–2016) and then Active Lives (2016 onward) surveys. Miller and Ahmed (2000) recognised that the construction of partnerships to meet specific funding requirements was often problematic, and so it has been for the Partnerships. The timescales afforded to building new partnerships have, in certain cases, resulted in processes that Painter with Clarence (2001) notably described as 'cobbling together alliances.'

The work of the Partnerships, over the course of their organisational iterations, has been affected by the fragmented and disjointed nature of community sport policy. These organisations have been assigned a range of strategic functions and yet, with regard to implementation, have never ultimately been assigned the responsibility, nor developed the capacity for policy delivery at the community level. Hatcher and Leblond (2003) were one of the first to note that public policy 'partnerships are characterised by processes of inclusion and exclusion' (p.42) and so became sites for expressions of frustration and tensions. Collaboration and cooperation between the Partnerships and especially NGBs, but also local authorities, schools, public health agencies and many others, complex enough as they were, became more difficult when subjected to a range of power dynamics and policy priorities which at times mirrored magnets meeting rather than evidence of sustained partnership working. As independent organisations in their own right, each Active Partnership has been affected by the local circumstances with which it has engaged and the differing values and beliefs regarding the purpose of community sport as, for example, a public health policy, a community safety policy or a support mechanism for a wide range of other examples across the spectrum of social policy. Since their inception, the Partnerships have had to consider the sport development actions of NGBs but also the broader social outcomes that many local agencies have to address. Ultimately, the primary goal of increasing sport participation requires a multi-agency approach yet has become significantly more complex because of the multiple agencies involved (NAO, 2022).

However, community sport is at the heart of communities in schools, colleges, clubs, charities, community centres, village halls, playing fields, the natural environment and so on, often run and sustained by volunteers. The complexity of delivering participation targets for sport and physical activity requires a substantial workforce, most of whom are unpaid and, often but not exclusively, and uninterested in policy priorities. Over the years the relatively small amount of Lottery and Exchequer funding available to Sport England is not enough to implement social change at population level, and yet the Partnerships have been incredibly resilient, adaptable and, now, focal to policy priorities despite the substantial loss of funding previously allocated to local authorities and schools. There is no single answer, policy, organisation or programme to address the complex challenge of increasing participation, tackling inactivity, addressing the inequalities within this and the multiple factors that affect people's activity levels.

Conclusion

Since the inception of the Partnerships, running sport and governing through various types of partnerships has become increasingly common. In each of the three main eras of policy and organisational formation, the specific priorities and issues have shaped and framed the conception and practice of the Partnerships and their ways of working in different ways. Common denominators do exist: throughout their existence, the Partnerships have illustrated consensus and cooperation, adaptation and flexibility, entrepreneurship and development, and also acted as recipients of top-down policy whilst also, at other times, acting as sites for local development and relationships as core values and also mechanisms for implementation. In advocating for the value and benefit of sport and physical activity, the Partnerships have often formed complex organisational coalitions involving a range of sporting and nonsporting agencies to address given purposes and priorities. Contrarily, as service providers, they have always relied on others, to some extent, in terms of funding their programmes. As Grix (2010) previously noted, they have acted as organisations 'commissioned' to meet objectives, with little or no chance for input from stakeholders to change priorities already set higher up the policymaking chain. More recently, in terms of their relationships with government, they have become involved in a more active role, one in which they work alongside government agencies and other stakeholders in new systems and arrangements for forms of collaborations.

Notwithstanding efforts to minimise resource dependency on public subsidies and find alternative funding streams, Active Partnerships are essentially government-funded organisations. Given this reliance, government policy for sport is essential to the strategies of Active Partnerships. The *Sporting Future* strategy (DCMS, 2015) and the subsequent refocus of government policy and investment into sport and physical activity were generally applauded, but the implementation of the policy has been uneven. The Active Partnerships are still subject to the ebbs and flow of policies. These ebbs and flows emanate from the fundamentally centralised nature of the British state but also from a lack of clarity in local purpose and the ongoing tension between delivering against policy outcomes aimed at social change whilst, concomitantly, ensuring the local infrastructure and capacity for increased numbers of participants is sufficiently robust. Whilst Active Partnerships and local partners require national strategy to provide guidance and direction, a common, shared purpose is likely only if decisions can be made at local levels of policy implementation. Any such national strategy requires lessons to be learnt from community development policy and a whole system, place-based approach rather than a 'top-down' strategy. In 2021, Sport England launched a new ten-year strategy, *Uniting the Movement*, cautiously welcomed as fulfilling this purpose. Whether it will enable Active Partnerships to be more effective remains to be seen.

PRACTITIONER REFLECTION AND INSIGHTS

Maxine Rhodes, Managing Director, County Durham Sport

County Durham seen from the outside is a university county, a cathedral county, a rural county: famed for the beauty of its surroundings and synonymous with the cultural capital of the city of Durham. With this comes a set of assumptions about its health and wealth. But it is a county of stark inequalities. For example, there is a 19-year difference in the number of years residents can expect to live in good health, depending on where in the county they live, and 24% of the population report a limiting illness or disability which affects their day-to-day activities. In terms of physical activity, one in five people in the county do nothing (County Durham Sport, 2022).

County Durham Sport (CDS), the Active Partnership for the County and one of the first County Sport Partnerships, delivers some of the priorities of English sport policy. Looking at the data, you could say we have failed – population level inequalities have widened and physical activity levels have not improved. However, we are just one piece of the jigsaw and as sport policy has shifted to realise the complexity of the task, so have we. A small organisation of ten staff (only eight full-time employees), CDS has moved from a local authority-hosted organisation to an independent charity. With new leadership and a new staff team, we have (since the first lockdown in March 2020) rebuilt the organisation. As a small organisation how can we inform, influence and encourage change across a vast system that has been blighted by austerity for a decade? How can we encourage people to be more active when they have a range of other more pressing matters to address? This is where the changes in sport policy support our endeavour. And whilst change takes time (and is often be at odds with political cycles), Sport England's new ten-year strategy, *Uniting the Movement*, gives us stability and focus and shows commitment to the Active Partnership network through a recognition of the importance of place-based working.

Changes in sport policy, associated with *Uniting the Movement*, have emphasised the way that patterns of inequality can impact sport culture in the UK and how that is less the responsibility of individuals and more the responsibility of the sector and its partners, society and, to some lesser, extent social policy. The move towards proportionate universalism (highlighted in *Uniting the Movement*) in funding approaches is very new in England, and we are learning much from Local Delivery Pilots and Active Places (both of which are planks of recent policy). These changes have encouraged greater awareness of interactions between class and cultural inequalities. Thus Active Partnerships reflect more on the ways in which whole systems operate, wittingly or unwittingly, to impact on activity patterns.

Whilst this is to be welcomed (as it aims to support a less siloed approach to local policy and strategy), it does give Active Partnerships a number of challenges. For a small Active Partnership such as County Durham Sport, the encouragement to reach widely challenges us to think carefully about how we prioritise work, partnerships and engagement. Active Partnerships vary in size and funding and Sport England allocate resource – which for us is our sole source of income – and so, whilst we recognise that everything is interconnected, we cannot do everything. Now with encouragement to think about the principles of proportionate universalism, we can legitimately focus on the most deprived areas of the County.

As a small, independent charity, you could be forgiven for wondering how we can have anything but a limited impact. In County Dunham we are fortunate to have good relationships with both the local authority and Public

Health Department and to share a number of key priorities. There is local authority commitment to local devolution and citizen participation (through Area Action Partnerships) and a general appreciation of the power of sport and physical activity to change lives, improve health outcomes and create better connected and happier communities. These high-level partnerships give us more power to influence change than our size would suggest. To maintain these, we need to bring value to everything we do with county-wide partners, and this demands an ability to build genuine relationships with colleagues. It is not a given that we are at the table and we aim to ensure that we do add value to the conversation.

Another challenge is to reach a wider constituency beyond sport and physical activity (public or third sector). We are unlikely to engage people in movement from the very sector that is currently not appealing to them. This has been helped (during the pandemic and beyond) by Sport England and the Tackling Inequalities Fund (now Together Fund) which utilised Active Partnerships' local knowledge, connections and infrastructure to help reduce the negative impact of coronavirus and the widening inequalities in sport and physical activity.

The challenge for organisations like ours, as we move through this policy change, is clearly not just in how far and wide we reach or how we maintain key strategic partnerships but also in how we prepare staff to do the work. Staff have had to operate differently (and not just because of Covid-19) and with a more focused appreciation (in varying levels of depth) of the politics of society and culture at the neighbourhood, local, regional and national levels. The skills we need from staff are less about sport and more about understanding inequalities and influencing others to work to address them. This requires staff to be adept at long-term partnership working (with a range of social actors, each of whom comes with their own 'brand' of knowledge and power); curious about the world around them and committed to developing the skills and ability to influence for long-term change. Whilst partnership work has always been central to the work of CDS, it is now everyone's business to understand the reason, and skills required for, effective partnership working, change management, learning and communication. This has been made somewhat easier by the five-year investment from Sport England and from the support of our national network as well as from the local research culture. Nonetheless, this is a challenge for the sector and one that makes us, at CDS, think and work more politically. We now attract a different kind of candidate with a deep connection to people and place and how to operate in the wider system, and this has required us to invest in our recruitment practices, staff development, induction and line management support.

Partnership working across complex systems is neither straightforward nor easy. We operate in the public and voluntary sector in County Durham where there are (as in all areas of the UK) varying degrees of understanding

The Active Partnerships 73

of system working. The voluntary sector provides us with friendly challenges as we develop our organisation, our understanding of asset-based community development and the implications of words we tend to use interchangeably in sport: consultation, cocreation and coproduction. There is still much more for us to learn at CDS, and our new learning culture helps us improve – drawing as it does from a range of disciplines including education theory and practice, community development approaches and the international development community rather than just sport. Such a change – to a broader understanding of social inequality and ways to challenge this – requires a deep shift in our thinking to give authority to experience, local context and consideration of the politics and power relations in places and spaces. However, sport policy alone cannot be used to remove inequalities. Whilst Sport England are committed to equity, it is not clear how far other national policymakers and government departments are. Indeed the recent levelling-up agenda appears to lack coherence, detail and funded support. Without policy connect, commitment to work that removes structural inequalities that perpetuate poverty, exclusion and inequality, physical activity patterns are unlikely to change.

Change in sport policy is to be welcomed as is Sport England's own philosophical movement. Time will tell if these changes are reflected in government's national sport strategy. But, as we approach (at the time of writing) the winter of 2022, I am mindful that the daily focus of people who we regard as inactive and who are the focus of sport policy will be food, shelter and fuel rather than engaging with leisure and sporting activities: 'By January 2023, it is estimated that 66 per cent, or 18 million households, in the UK will be in fuel poverty' (Lee et al., 2022, p. 4). Cold homes mean more ill health and death.

The current set of challenging economic circumstances has come on the back of over a decade of austerity. To transform national trends in well-being, physical activity, happiness and sporting excellence will require a national sports policy that deeply appreciates the ways in which place and policy mesh and can be harnessed to address inequalities and make physical activity an easier choice – especially for those communities identified in *Uniting the Movement*. Further investment to build upon and extend pilots that have sought to coproduce place-based approaches will no doubt help. But without policy connect across government departments and an appreciation of the way policy can work to reinforce structural inequalities that perpetuate poverty, exclusion and inequality, it may not be enough.

References

Babiak, K. M., & Thibault, L. (2008). Managing inter-organisational relationships: The art of plate spinning. *International Journal of Sport Management and Marketing*, *3*(3), 281–302. https://doi.org/10.1504/IJSMM.2008.017193

Babiak, K. M., & Thibault, L. (2009). Challenges in multiple cross-sector partnerships. *Non Profit and Voluntary Sector Quarterly*, *38*(1), 117–143. https://doi.org/10.1177/0899764008316054

Beacom, A., & Ziakas, V. (2022). Managing grassroots sport development: The role of UK active partnerships in policy implementation. In V. Ziakas (Ed.), *Trends and advances in sport and leisure management: Expanding the frontiers* (pp. 1–19). Cambridge Scholars.

Carter, P. (2005). *Review of national sport effort and resources*. Department of Culture, Media and Sport.

Coalter, F., Allison, M., & Taylor, J. (2000). *The role of sport in regenerating deprived urban areas*. Scottish Executive.

Collins, M. F. (2008). Public policies on sports development: Can mass and elite sport hold together? In V. Girginov (Ed.), *Management of sports development* (pp. 59–88). Butterworth-Heinemann.

County Durham Sport. (2022). Insight Hub. https://countydurhamsport.com/insight-hub/

Department for Culture, Media and Sport/Strategy Unit. (2002). *Game plan: A strategy for delivering Government's sport and physical activity objectives*. DCMS/Strategy Unit.

Department for Culture, Media and Sport. (2015). *Sporting future: A new strategy for an active nation*. DCMS.

Department of National Heritage. (1995), *Sport: Raising the game*. HMSO.

English Sports Council. (1997). *England: A sporting nation*. English Sports Council.

Grix, J. (2010). The 'governance debate' and the study of sport policy. *International Journal of Sport Policy and Politics*, *2*(2), 159–171. https://doi.org/10.1080/19406940.2010.488061

Harris, S., & Houlihan, B. (2016). Implementing the community sport legacy: The limits of partnerships, contracts and performance management. *European Sport Management Quarterly*, *16*(4), 433–458. https://doi.org/10.1080/16184742.2016.1178315

Hatcher, R., & Leblond, D. (2003). Education action zones and zones d'education prioritaires. *Education, social justice and inter-agency working: Joined up or fractured policy?* (pp. 29–57). https://doi.org/10.4324/9780203471975

Houlihan, B. (1997). *Sport, policy, and politics: A comparative analysis*. Routledge.

Houlihan, B., & Lindsey, I. (2008). Networks and partnerships in sports development. In V. Girginov (Ed.), *Management of sports development* (pp. 225–242). Butterworth-Heinemann.

Keech, M. (2011). Sport and adult participation in the UK. In B. Houlihan & M. Green (Eds.), *The Routledge handbook of sports development* (pp. 217–231). Routledge.

Knaggs, A. (2019). Rebrand sees CSPs become active partnerships. *Leisure Opportunities* [Online], March 13. https://www.leisureopportunities.co.uk/news/Rebrand-sees-CSP-become-Active-Partnerships/341140

Lee, A., Sinha, I., Boyce, T., Allen, J., & Goldblatt, P. (2022). *Fuel poverty, cold homes and health inequalities*. Institute of Health Inequality. https://www.instituteofhealthequity.org/resources-reports/fuel-poverty-cold-homes-and-health-inequalities-in-the-uk/read-the-report.pdf

Lindsey, I. (2011). Partnership working and sports development. In B. Houlihan (Ed.), *Routledge handbook of sports development* (pp. 517–529). Routledge.

Lindsey, I. (2014). Prospects for local collaboration into an uncertain future: Learning from practice within labour's partnership paradigm. *Local Government Studies*, *40*(2), 312–330. https://doi.org/10.1080/03003930.2013.805690

Mackintosh, C. (2011). An analysis of county sports partnerships in England: The fragility, challenges and complexity of partnership working in sports development. *International*

Journal of Sport Policy and Politics, *3*(1), 45–64. https://doi.org/10.1080/19406940.2010.524809

Mansfield, L. (2016). Resourcefulness, reciprocity and reflexivity: The three Rs of partnership in sport for public health research. *International Journal of Sport Policy and Politics*, *8*(4), 713–729. https://doi.org/10.1080/19406940.2016.1220409

Mason, L. (2021). Active partnerships: Supplementary written evidence (NPS 0098), written evidence to the house of lords inquiry into sport. https://committees.parliament.uk/writtenevidence/22038/pdf/

McDonald, I. (2005). Theorising partnerships: Governance, communicative action and sport policy. *Journal of Social Policy*, *34*(4), 579–600. https://doi.org/10.1017/S0047279405009165

Miller, C., & Ahmad, Y. (2000). Collaboration and partnership: An effective response to complexity and fragmentation or solution built on sand? *International Journal of Sociology and Social Policy*, *20*(5/6), 1–38. https://doi.org/10.1108/01443330010789151

Moore, L. (2021). Inside out: Understanding professional practice and policy making in UK high-performance sport. A process sociological approach. *International Journal of Sport Policy and Politics*, *13*(1), 179–185. https://doi.org/10.1080/19406940.2020.1844274

Morgan, H., & Baker, C. (2021). Strategic or communicative partnerships? insights from sports programmes in the criminal justice sector. *International Journal of Sport Policy and Politics*, *13*(4), 715–732. https://doi.org/10.1080/19406940.2021.1951328

National Audit Office. (2022). *Grassroots participation in sport and physical activity.* Session 2022–23, July 8, 2022 HC72. https://www.nao.org.uk/reports/grassroots-participation-in-sport-and-physical-activity/

Painter, C., & Clarence, E. (2001). UK local action zones and changing urban governance. *Urban Studies (Edinburgh, Scotland)*, *38*(8), 1215–1232. https://doi.org/10.1080/00420980120060990

Purnell, J. (2007). 'World class community sport', a speech to the annual youth sport trust school sport partnership conference, Telford, November 28.

Reed, A. (2016). *#cspfuture: Appraisal of the future role of CSPs*. https://data.londonsport.org/dataset/vdk04/appraisal-of-the-future-role-of-csps

Revill, J. (2007). U-turn on 'sport-for-all' pledge. *The Observer*, November 25. http://www.guardian.co.uk/uk/2007/nov/25/olympics2012.london

Rummery, K. (2002). Towards a theory of welfare partnerships. In C. Glendinning, M. Powell, & K. Rummery (Eds.), *Partnerships, new labour and the governance of welfare* (pp. 229–245). Policy Press.

Skelcher, C. (2000). Changing images of the state: Overloaded, hollowed-out, congested. *Public Policy and Administration*, *15*(3), 3–19. https://doi.org/10.1177/095207670001500302

Sport England. (2002). *Active sports mid term report*. Sport England

Sport England. (2004). *The framework for sport in England*. Sport England

Sports Council. (1982). *The next ten years: Sport in the community*. Sports Council.

Sussex Sports Partnership. (2001). The Sussex sports partnership annual report, 2001 [Unpublished].

Wilson, D. (2003). Unravelling control freakery: Redefining central-local government relations. *British Journal of Politics and International Relations*, *5*(3), 317–346. https://doi.org/10.1111/1467-856X.00109

Chapter 5

Local Authorities and the Implementation of Sport Policy

Janine Partington, Stephen Robson and Louise Morby

Introduction

Local authorities make a significant contribution to the implementation of national sport policy through the delivery of sporting opportunities. Sport England (2015) estimates they are the largest investor within the broader sporting landscape, contributing over £1bn per year for facility development and management, sport development programmes, sport events and outdoor recreation. Many authorities also provide essential support (including small funding grants) to voluntary organisations such as sports clubs and community groups, who in turn provide crucial opportunities for local residents to engage in sport and recreation. However, despite this investment, the provision of sport and recreation by local authorities remains non-statutory and is therefore provided at the discretion of individual local authorities (Houlihan & White, 2002; King, 2009; Harris & Houlihan, 2014). Consequently, sport and recreation policy and provision can be described as 'inconsistent' (Harris, 2013, p. 85) and 'ambiguous' (Harris & Houlihan, 2014, p. 114), often depending on the political support and buy-in from locally elected politicians as to the quality, scope and level of investment in provision across different authorities. Furthermore, the discretionary nature of provision means that whilst central government and national stakeholders 'can set out policies for local authorities to follow ... [they] only have limited powers to see that they are carried out' (Bell, 2009, p. 79). As this chapter will illustrate, this has resulted in a complex relationship between local authorities and key stakeholders within the sporting landscape. Whilst traditionally viewed as significant players in the implementation of national sport policy, Houlihan and Lindsey (2013) argue that local authorities had become the 'forgotten partner' with their contribution being under-valued in relation to other stakeholders.

The fluctuating position of local authorities within the sporting landscape is reflective of the turbulent relationship that exists between local and central government. This has involved attempts by central government to exert control over local government and influence how public services, such as sport and recreation, are delivered. This ongoing 'institutional tinkering' (Painter, 2012, p. 6) by successive administrations has involved changes to the structural configurations of local

DOI: 10.4324/9781003162728-5

authorities and to their financial arrangements with central government, with the austerity measures implemented by the Coalition government in 2010 having particularly significant repercussions for local authority sport and recreation provision. For the majority of authorities, the culmination of top-down pressure from central government has been a shift from being direct deliverers of services to 'enablers,' with many outsourcing delivery of sport and recreation provision to external organisations such as leisure trusts. Continuing financial pressures on local authorities, not helped by 'shocks' such as the 2008 financial crash and the Covid-19 pandemic, place discretionary services such as sport and recreation under continuous pressure to demonstrate their 'value.' This chapter will explore how and why local government sport and recreation provision has changed from the Conservative government of the 1980s through subsequent administrations. The chapter will highlight those aspects of policy change we feel are particularly significant to the current position of local authorities and will finish by commenting on the challenges facing local authorities in the provision of sport and recreation in the future. Before this, however, we start by providing a broad overview of local government, specifically, the basics about its statutory role and relationship with central government.

What Is Local Government?

Local government is a system of elected representation, based on the division of a country into geographically defined jurisdictions, that provides services to the local populace. In the United Kingdom, local branches of government are generally referred to as *local authorities*, whilst in many other territories the term 'municipality' is more commonly used. The publication of the Wolfenden Report on Sport in 1960 proved significant for local authorities. The report made several recommendations about the role of organisations including local authorities and established the need for greater state involvement and investment in sport as part of broader welfare policy (Coghlan, 1990; Houlihan & White, 2002; Bergsgard et al., 2007; Jeffreys, 2012). The recommendations of the Wolfenden Report were still implemented slowly, although there were indications that local authorities had become more proactive in the provision of sport and recreation opportunities. The publication of the Local Government Act in 1972 initiated a reorganisation of local authorities (establishing a uniform, two-tier system of local government at county and district level), creating larger authorities with additional financial resources which thereby enabled the development of new public leisure facilities (Bloyce & Smith, 2010). Combined with additional funding from the Sports Council for capital development projects, this resulted in the number of indoor facilities trebling between 1973 and 1977 (Houlihan & White, 2002; Jackson, 2008; Bloyce & Smith, 2010).

Further structural changes have led to a less consistent approach in England with many *unitary* authorities being established in another reformation exercise in 1996. Unitary authorities are often seen in bigger cities such as Birmingham and Liverpool, with some disaggregated counties such as the former Cleveland

(Hartlepool, Middlesbrough, Redcar & Cleveland, and Stockton-on-Tees) also operating on this basis. Two-tier local government is still present in many areas, with responsibility for service provision distributed between the county council (e.g., Nottinghamshire) and district authorities (e.g., Bassetlaw District Council) and, in the case of Nottinghamshire, a single unitary body (Nottingham City Council). Some areas additionally have a smaller, third tier in the form of parish or town councils, which may also have responsibility for localised sport and recreation provision. Each unit of local government has a four-yearly electoral process to determine the political make-up of the council, with paid employees carrying out the wishes of the local electorate under the scrutiny of the elected council members. This is an obvious cause of tension when the controlling political party at local level is not the same as that of the national government, such that local authorities are expected to contribute to the delivery of national policy objectives but without the existence of a codified constitution that outlines the specifics of this relationship. The complexity of these structural and political arrangements can make service provision challenging, and it is therefore unsurprising that sport and recreation provision as a discretionary service can vary significantly from one area to another.

Regardless of the structure of local government in a given area, the local authority(ies) is/are responsible for a range of statutory (compulsory) public services such as social care, schools, housing and planning and waste collection. In all, more than 800 different services are provided by more than one million members of staff working in English local government (Local Government Association, 2021). Local authorities are funded from a range of sources. As well as central government grants, they impose local taxes known as council tax (paid by households) and business rates. In the first five years of the UK austerity era, commencing in 2010, English local authorities cut spending by 27% in real terms due to reductions in the central government grant, yet were still expected to deliver core services. Unsurprisingly, discretionary services are particularly vulnerable during periods of financial strain with services such as sport and recreation often being realigned, restructured or reduced, directly impacting most local authorities' ability to implement national sport policy. The remainder of this chapter deals with this challenge, examining the history of local authorities' connections to national sport policy from the late 1970s to the present day.

Local Authorities under Threat (the Conservative Government, 1979–1997)

Reform of local government was a recurring policy objective throughout this period justified by the perception that local government was financially inefficient and outdated with measures such as the Poll Tax and later the Council Tax introduced to control local government finances (Atkinson & Wilks-Heeg, 2000; Stoker, 2004; Chandler, 2007; Wilson & Game, 2011). So-called 'market forces' were deployed to drive efficiency and to improve quality in public services via the requirement for services to be put out to tender as part of a Compulsory Competitive Tendering (CCT) process (Stoker, 2004) – with sport and recreation services becoming available for tender in 1988. This approach aimed to 'cap, limit and control local democracy' by breaking local authorities' monopoly on local service delivery (Murray, 2015, p. 4). CCT marked a shift towards the marketisation of leisure services with external companies invited to bid for contracts to deliver these services on behalf of local authorities. Pressure to cut costs and increase income levels meant that many local users were priced out of local facilities whilst capital investment in the refurbishment and general upkeep of facilities reduced (Jackson, 2008; Jeffreys, 2012). Subsequent government investment into sport development programmes such as Action Sport with its emphasis on social outcomes therefore appeared somewhat contradictory to broader policy objectives (King, 2009).

Partly influenced by inner city riots in the early 1980s, triggered by a dissatisfaction with social, political, and economic conditions (Scarman Report, 1981), the Action Sport programmes aimed to engage unemployed young people in sport leadership activities. Although marketed as social welfare programmes, the programme emphasised notions of social control and illustrated the utility of sport as a relatively cheap way of engaging disaffected youth in urban areas (Houlihan & White, 2002, Collins, 2010). The programme was mainly delivered by Sport Development Officers (SDOs) employed within local authorities, which not only acted as a catalyst for the creation of specific teams of SDOs within authorities but also emphasised the value of undertaking outreach work within communities to extend sport and recreation opportunities (Lentell, 1993; Houlihan & White, 2002; Collins, 2010). This approach was captured in the Sports Council (1982) strategy 'Sport in the Community: The Next Ten Years' which signalled a shift from the facility development strategies of the 1970s towards mass participation and the targeting of under-represented groups (Houlihan & White, 2002; King, 2009; Collins, 2010).

However, following the publication of 'Sport: Raising the Game' (DNH, 1995), the focus of development work within local authorities shifted towards sport-specific development and away from community recreation and concerns with equity. Concurrently, increased emphasis was being placed on local government to act as 'enabling authorities' as opposed to service deliverers. CCT was extended, and the Private Finance Initiative introduced to encourage public–private sector partnerships and further contracting out of public service delivery (Atkinson & Wilks-Heeg, 2000; Chandler, 2007). Local government finances remained tight, with Jackson (2008) noting that many sports facilities were becoming increasingly dilapidated and in desperate need of investment. The creation of the National Lottery in 1994 plus funding opportunities via the European Union provided welcome opportunities for local authorities to bid for additional funding. The inclusion of sport as one of the five 'good causes' to be supported by the National Lottery generated (by 1999) an additional £200–250m per annum to be spent in support of sport policy and provided an opportunity for cash-strapped authorities to access much-needed capital and revenue investment (Jackson, 2008; King, 2009). This,

80 Janine Partington et al.

for Houlihan and White (2002), meant a more positive policy environment for local authority sport despite the ongoing challenge of CCT.

New Beginnings for Local Authorities? (New Labour, 1997–2010)

The election of the New Labour government in 1997 marked further attempts by central government to reform and modernise public services. The passing of Local Government Acts in 2000 and 2001 outlined the government's Local Government Modernisation Agenda (LGMA) which proposed significant reform to improve the effectiveness of service delivery. This marked a shift away from cost-effectiveness to concerns about the impact of services particularly in relation to New Labour's focus on social inclusion. The agenda promised a 'joined-up' approach to tackling social and community issues with partnership working as the preferred method of service delivery (Lowndes & Pratchett, 2012; Painter, 2012; Lindsey, 2014). Collaborative working was further endorsed in New Labour's sport policies, 'A Sporting Future for All' (DCMS, 2000) and 'Game Plan' (DCMS/Strategy Unit, 2002), and also featured in accompanying strategies from Sport England, such as the 'Framework for Sport in England' (Sport England, 2004). This unveiled a new delivery system for sport predicated on joined-up working between agencies, both vertically and horizontally. Local government was identified as the 'preferred delivery partner' for the creation of sporting opportunities and the extrinsic benefits of sport, particularly in relation to the potential contribution of sporting activities in tackling social exclusion (Harris & Houlihan, 2014, p. 114). SDOs in local government seized the opportunity to integrate sport across wider policy objectives such as community safety and neighbourhood renewal. In addition, partnership working coupled with access to external funding such as the Single Regeneration Budget and Sport Action Zone funding led to the growth in the staffing levels and scope of sport development teams.

Whilst New Labour elevated the role and status of local authorities, Atkinson and Wilks-Heeg (2000) argue that authorities effectively became a partner in the delivery of national policy rather than an autonomous actor. Local authorities were expected to fully embrace the role of 'enabling authorities' – albeit not in the sense of tendering service delivery as under the previous Conservative administrations but by coordinating delivery across a range of stakeholders (Wilson, 2003; Stoker, 2004; Chandler, 2007; Blanco et al., 2011; Stewart, 2014). Although central government claimed that 'what matters is what works,' the introduction of performance management tools such as Best Value and the Comprehensive Performance Assessment enabled the comparison of performance across authorities –an approach that was argued to be contradictory to the rhetoric of localism and which extended centralised control over the activities of local government (Atkinson & Wilks-Heeg, 2000; John, 2014). Sport England also adopted a more interventionist, top-down approach with the creation of the 'Active' Programme – a series of national schemes such as Active Sports designed to create pathways for young people to progress in sport (Houlihan & White, 2002, Houlihan & Lindsey, 2013). Active Sports was implemented via Active Sport Partnerships (later known as County Sports Partnerships, now Active Partnerships) who filtered programme funding to local authorities against agreed outcomes but with limited flexibility to adapt programme delivery to local needs (Charlton, 2010). Local authorities were also encouraged (via the promise of additional funding from Sport England) to develop Community Sport Networks (CSNs) that were tasked with undertaking strategic coordination of sport and physical activity across a local area. This was a further attempt to force closer working relationships between the different stakeholders involved in sport locally and to emphasise local authorities' role as strategic leaders, not service deliverers (Houlihan & Lindsey, 2013; Baker et al., 2016).

The removal of CCT legislation in the Local Government Act of 1999 and its replacement with Best Value which emphasised the need for continuous service improvement was largely viewed positively. Sport England (1999, p. 2) suggested that Best Value in sport and recreation services could be demonstrated 'through sport' by both promoting its value in other policy areas, and 'in sport' by evaluating the effectiveness of current service models. This triggered increasing numbers of local authorities to outsource delivery of sport and recreation services to leisure trusts, with some so-called 'super' or 'mega' trusts such as Everyone Active and Greenwich Leisure Limited, operating across local authority boundaries, winning contracts to take over the management of facilities in geographically diverse areas from Preston to Cornwall (Pamben, 2016, 2017). For many authorities, this model was considered to offer 'better value' than in-house delivery due to the ability of trusts to access additional external funding denied to local authorities and their eligibility to receive tax breaks due to their charitable status (ASPE, 2012; King 2013). Whilst financially attractive, adopting the trust model often created a separation between sport development services (which often remained in-house) and facility management (undertaken by the trust), the latter emphasising cost-effectiveness rather than 'sport for all' and widening participation – which, at that time, were key aspects of government sport policy (ASPE, 2012). However, such was the perceived success of the leisure trust model that by 2012 it was estimated that it had been adopted by over a quarter of English local authorities (King, 2012).

Although the availability of external funding for local authority sport increased under New Labour, King (2011 cited in Houlihan & Lindsey, 2013) argues that core budgets did not, highlighting the relatively precarious position of sport services within local government. The Carter (2005) report commissioned by the Department of Culture Media and Sport (DCMS) also provided a somewhat damning verdict on local authority sport arguing that it had been de-prioritised politically within authorities, whilst also highlighting inefficiency with the estimated average local authority subsidy per facility being cited as £262,000. Furthermore, the report also raised significant concerns about the lack of coordination and alignment of central and local sport policy, suggesting the local delivery system was not best placed to drive up participation levels. Continued governmental dissatisfaction with a lack of control over local sport policy led to local government falling 'out of favour' as primary deliverers of local sport services (Harris and Houlihan, 2014, p. 114). Responsibility for mass participation was instead passed to national governing bodies (NGBs) via the funding of Whole Sport Plans. This represented a shift from 'sport for good' to 'sports for sport's sake' (Collins, 2010) and was cemented in the new 'Playing to Win' (DCMS, 2008) strategy which outlined how the government aimed to seize the opportunities offered by the successful London bid to host the 2012 Olympic and Paralympic Games. As such, external financial resources such as National Lottery funding, available to local government sport, were reduced. For discretionary services such as local government sport, the omens were not good.

The Marginalisation of Local Government (the Coalition Administration, 2010–2015)

John (2014, p. 697) argues that the election of a Conservative-Liberal Democrat Coalition government marked 'a new era for local government,' highlighting election promises to decentralise and increase the accountability of public services. Further, the 2011 Localism Act sought to grant increased flexibility and freedom to local authorities, whilst 'lifting the burden of bureaucracy' on them (HM Government, 2010, p. 2). However, although the Act contained powers for local authorities to shape their own service priorities, it also contained over 100 powers for central over local government, suggesting that this was decentralisation within centrally imposed limits and restrictions (Lowndes & Pratchett, 2012; Stewart, 2014). The Coalition government also retained elements of New Labour's target-driven culture by continuing to publish comparative data across local authorities, holding local authorities to account for the success and failure of services of which they were not always directly in control (Painter, 2012; John, 2014).

Local authorities continued to be marginalised within national sport policy. There was little mention of them in 'Creating a Sporting Habit for Life' (DCMS, 2012) with NGBs being retained to lead on driving mass participation and community sport until 2017. In addition, the Comprehensive Spending Review in 2010 (triggered by the global economic crisis) was to prove significant for local government sport and recreation provision. Local authorities were faced with core budget cuts of 27% (amounting to £81bn of cuts by 2014/2015) (BBC, 2010; Parnell et al., 2015). In addition, Sport England was faced with a 33% cut in funding with repercussions for its funding programmes (Guardian, 2010). The Coalition's localism agenda, built on the principle that increased community involvement reduces the need for state involvement, was thus viewed as a 'convenient rationale for fiscal retrenchment' and an underhanded attack on local government (Painter, 2012, p. 11). Inman (2014, p. np) suggests that the impact of cuts amounted to a 'fundamental re-imaging of the state.' Discretionary services within local government such as sport and recreation were severely affected. In 2019, Harris et al. estimated that spending on sport and recreation by local authorities had reduced by 70% compared to 2009–2010 whilst spending on the maintenance and provision of open spaces was estimated to have reduced by 40%. In many authorities, reductions in funding for sport and recreation resulted in the closure of sports centres or reductions in opening hours, staff redundancies, and withdrawal of sports programmes, often in the most deprived communities (King, 2013; Parnell et al., 2015; Conn, 2015). Grant aid provided by local authorities to voluntary sector organisations reduced, whilst reductions in external funding for community sport outreach work created an increasing dependency on central government funding streams to support 'sport for all' activities. Only 20% of local authorities were able to support this provision through their core budgets (Chief Leisure Officers Association, 2012; King, 2013). In addition, declining capacity within local authorities meant there was often little support available to community groups undertaking asset transfer (taking on responsibility for the management of a facility) or taking on responsibility for service delivery – a somewhat unanticipated consequence of the localism agenda which had aimed to enable community involvement in service delivery (King, 2013; Finlay-King et al., 2017).

New Challenges for Local Authorities (the Conservative Administration, 2015 Onwards)

Despite the eroding of local government capacity through continued austerity measures, there remained an expectation from the Conservative government that local authorities would 'spend less, but deliver more' (Lowndes & Gardner, 2016, p. 358). It therefore appeared ironic that after being largely ignored in previous government sport polices, the new government strategy for sport, 'Sporting Future: A New Strategy for an Active Nation' (DDCMS, 2015) emphasised a more prominent role for local government as a deliverer and strategic coordinator of services (Allison et al., 2016; Ives, 2016). Local authorities were to encourage mass participation, facilitate partnership working, provide multi-use open green spaces for physical activity and seek to integrate physical activity into public health systems. The policy also promoted the potential economic impact of sport on local areas stemming from the hosting of mega events. Government ambitions to secure a 'decade of sport' following on from the London 2012 Olympic and Paralympic Games provided opportunities for local authorities in large cities to benefit from this investment, with many events lined up for future delivery, e.g. the 2019 Netball World Cup in Liverpool and the 2022 Commonwealth Games in Birmingham.

The tonal shift in policy represented by 'Sporting Future,' with its emphasis on 'sport for good,' proved unexpectedly prescient due to the social issues brought to the fore during the second half of the 2010s and beyond. Despite local authorities having been identified in 'Sporting Future' as a key partner in its delivery, austerity measures were not reversed and in some ways hardened, thus authorities' ability to contribute to the delivery of 'Sporting Future' continued to be compromised. The onset of the global Covid-19 pandemic created further challenges for local authorities. Lockdowns during 2020 and parts of 2021 led to the extended, and in some cases permanent, closure of public sports facilities. In addition, many facilities were repurposed as vaccination centres, whilst sport development staff were often re-deployed to provide support to individuals deemed in need. There was also a significant impact on the finances of leisure trusts, with many in danger of becoming insolvent and requiring additional financial support from local authorities to 'bail them out.' Community Leisure UK, the national umbrella organisation for leisure trusts, estimated that 50% of its members were experiencing severe cash flow problems (Hill, 2020). Indeed, some trusts, such as Inspiring Healthy Lifestyles (which managed leisure provision in Wigan and Selby), were taken back in-house ('insourced') to protect services and staff employment. Against a backdrop of ongoing austerity measures, the challenges brought about by the pandemic proved almost insurmountable, with the delivery of national sport policy far from the minds of local authorities' elected members and senior managers who were simply trying to maintain essential services to the most vulnerable.

A further trend in this period was a shift towards 'whole-systems change,' a process intended to 'align and connect' physical activity with a range of other systems and services aimed at tackling obesity and other health issues across defined geographical areas (Public Health England, 2020, p. 6). This was exemplified by Sport England's funding of 12 Local Delivery Pilots (LDPs) to pilot the development of whole-systems approaches to physical activity, some targeted at individual local authorities (e.g. Calderdale) and some (e.g. Essex) operating across partnerships of local authorities. The LDP programme represented an investment of £130m in local physical activity and sport with the funding awarded via a competitive bidding process. Whilst this was undoubtedly welcomed by the recipient authorities and provided a direct opportunity to implement national sport policy, it also signalled a fragmentation of the resources available to promote local authority sport and physical activity in general.

On the back of extensive consultation conducted during the pandemic, Sport England published a new strategy: *Uniting the Movement: Our 10-Year Vision to Transform Lives and Communities through Sport and Physical Activity* (Sport England, 2021). The explicit focus of this national strategy was not on mainstream sport participation but on the contribution of sport and physical activity to creating a 'nation of more equal, inclusive and connected communities ... a country where people live happier, healthier and more fulfilled lives' (Sport England, 2021, p. 7). The strategy was not accompanied by a new national sport policy document although there were indications that the government was working towards producing a refreshed strategy to update/replace 'Sporting Future' (DDCMS, 2021). The inquiry by the House of Commons Digital, Culture, Media and Sport Select Committee (UK Parliament, 2021) also attempted to identify how to secure the future of sport in the community, tacitly acknowledging the financial difficulties facing community sport providers, many of whom were facing extinction even before the pandemic. Covid-19 magnified the challenges and exacerbated the precarious position in which many local authorities found themselves. For example, Swim England (2021) reported a 'looming shortage[s]' of pools, emphasising the need for urgent replacements for those facilities built in the 1960s and 1970s that were coming to the end of their lifespan (Swim England, 2021). Furthermore, although the government had provided £100m in emergency funding to 'prop up' local authority sport and recreation facilities during the pandemic, rising energy prices led to a significant increase (estimated at 150%) in costs associated with operating public swimming pools with some authorities threatening pool closures without further support (Weaver, 2022).

Structural changes within Whitehall meant that the oversight of local authorities became the responsibility of a newly branded Department for Levelling Up, Housing and Communities. 'Levelling up' was a key Conservative manifesto promise in the 2019 election which outlined plans to tackle long-standing regional inequalities – the aforementioned Local Delivery Pilots could be said to be a manifestation of this. However, the ability of local authorities to continue providing facilities and sport and recreation opportunities for residents, particularly those from under-represented and disadvantaged groups, is likely to be hampered without further government investment. It remains to be seen whether this will be provided via the 'Levelling up' agenda or whether additional resources will be made available through the implementation of the promised new national sport policy. In the interim, relationships with organisations such as Active Partnerships, who saw their funding cemented in the ten-year Sport England vision, might become even more critical. The traditional variance in engagement between Active Partnerships and local authorities, in some areas working almost independently of each other (Keech, 2013; Grix & Harris, 2017), might be smoothed out by this distribution of resources. Arguably, the end of the Coalition government and the return to single-party control, rather than offering clarity and reassurance, signalled the greatest period of uncertainty for local authorities in what might be termed the 'national sport policy era.' In light of this, the final section of the chapter suggests enduring themes for practitioners and scholars alike to consider when assessing the status of local authorities as implementers of national sport policy.

Conclusion: Future Challenges and Opportunities in Implementing Sport Policy

Despite the reduced capacity and investment faced by many local authorities, there is a strong argument that they remain a crucial delivery agent of sport policy. The Department of Digital, Culture, Media and Sport Select Committee (2021) report on 'Sport in our Communities' outlined that local authorities were well positioned to provide facilities, support both formal and informal activities and ensure that they are accessible to everyone in the community. At the time of writing, local authorities had responsibility for 31% of grass pitches, 13% of sports halls and almost a fifth of all gyms. Additionally, when compared to the provision offered by schools and the private sector, public swimming pools owned by local authorities represent the majority of accessible water space. Local authorities are recognised as vital place-shapers; however, as the report acknowledges, demand was increasing for the limited available facilities, a situation which was set to be exacerbated by the expected closure of one in every three public facilities (LGA, 2021). The presumption is therefore that local authorities still have a crucial role to play in implementing national sport policy – the LGA urging the government to utilise future national Spending Reviews to put local government finances on a long-term, sustainable basis so that councils can repair ageing infrastructure and resume providing sport development support to clubs and communities. The implementation of sport policy by local authorities is unlikely to be straightforward at any point within the foreseeable future.

Whenever you are reading this, a number of things are likely to be the case: local authorities will be under-resourced relative to the demands placed upon them; local authorities will be asked to undertake an increasingly diverse and complex number of roles; local authorities will be essential to the well-being and sustainability of the communities they serve. As well as addressing inequalities that are likely to continue worsening, local authorities will be tackling the impacts of a population that continues to age, with an accompanying social care crisis to try and manage (Andrews & Dollery, 2021). Climate change will increasingly demand local authorities' attention, both in terms of operating more sustainably (upgrading ageing sport facilities is likely to be both challenging and expensive) and contributing to the fight against global warming through local awareness programmes and related interventions. The pull towards these agendas could present yet another threat to non-statutory provision such as sport and physical activity. There is, however, cause for optimism. As this chapter has shown through its history of local government's involvement in implementing national sport policy, local authority-led sport and physical activity can make a significant contribution in challenging domains such as care for older people. The army of council-based sport development professionals may be a thing of the past, but through strategic partnerships that engage diverse organisations and individuals, local authorities will remain favourably positioned to steer locally relevant services that interpret and implement national sport policy with the greatest impact.

PRACTITIONER REFLECTION AND INSIGHTS

Katy Bowden, Development Manager, Active Leeds

Leeds City Council serves the second largest local authority area in the United Kingdom, with a population in the region of 800,000. The Council has a long history of investing in and supporting sport and physical activity provision across the city via its Active Leeds service. At the time of writing, provision remains in-house after proposals to move into a leisure trust model were abandoned in 2008. The Council is therefore directly responsible for the management of 17 'dry' facilities, 14 swimming pools and 13 gyms plus an outdoor activity centre. In addition, the development team focuses on 'reducing inactivity and increasing the level of physical activity in Leeds' with an overarching focus on reducing health inequalities in the city's most disadvantaged communities. In recent years, the Council has also invested heavily in bringing major sports events to the city. The corporate plan 2020–2025 outlines support for residents to develop 'healthy, physically active lifestyles,' to 'support growth and investment' and to 'enhance the image of Leeds as a city.' A Council report estimated that physical activity generated an economic impact of £244.1m to Leeds economy and provided a total of over 7,000 jobs in Leeds, whilst volunteering in physical activity was worth £147.5m (information taken from Sport England local profile data). The Council takes a strategic approach towards the development of sport and physical activity and works closely with key partners to achieve its ambition for Leeds to be the most active big city in England.

The work undertaken across the city has been strongly influenced by national sport policy. During the 2012–2017 period, in which the national policy focus was on 14–25-year-olds, emphasis was placed on the implementation of NGB Whole Sport Plans including increasing levels of competition within schools and improving school–club links. Data and insight were used by national governing bodies to develop a largely product-based approach, such as Back to Netball, that local authorities could buy into and offer to local communities. This was a coached activity that provided females who had enjoyed netball at school an informal route back into the sport to build their confidence. Other sports also adopted this approach, with a multitude of branded products emerging as many NGBs targeted local authorities with large populations of 14–25-year-olds. Leeds, which has a higher than average proportion of young people, was therefore of interest to NGBs who had been encouraged by Sport England to engage with local authorities to coordinate these new opportunities across local areas.

The challenges associated with contributing to the delivery of national sport policy were amplified by the broader financial challenges facing the city council. In response to austerity measures implemented by the national government, a comprehensive service review was undertaken in 2011, with a subsequent reduction in the net operating budget for the sport and leisure service of £2m between 2010–2011 and 2011–2012. Centralised teams for facility programme management, aquatics and fitness were created to reduce duplication across leisure centres, whilst posts within the development team were deleted and a new structure implemented to create two clear functions: an Active Sports team who would work with NGBs and local clubs and an Active Lifestyles team who would focus on physical activity interventions. Further savings were generated through asset transfer of community sports facilities such as Armley Baths and the establishment of a social enterprise to run the City Performance Gymnastics programme. However, the need to balance increasingly challenging financial targets, whilst responding to the demands of key partners such as NGBs and trying to ensure access for vulnerable and disadvantaged groups to sport and physical activity, placed the service in a difficult position.

Indeed, the influx of NGBs working across the city created a number of operational challenges for the council. For example, NGBs representing different indoor sports all seeking to introduce their products in the same leisure centres at the same time stretched the capacity of the facility workforce, with some smaller NGBs relying on facilities to adopt their product, train staff and deliver the programmes themselves. In addition, the simultaneous introduction of so many new 'offers' and 'products' caused confusion in local communities. Some NGBs also required support from the development team to access their knowledge of local areas and guidance on where to target their new opportunities, whilst others required help in accessing facilities, contacting schools and engaging communities. In practice, adequate resources and capacity to support NGBs to implement their Whole Sport Plans in Leeds were not available, particularly when the target geographical areas that had been identified across the city by NGBs did not coincide with the priority areas for the Council – an example of a disconnect between national and local sport policy.

National participation data generated by the Active People Survey into the impact of Whole Sport Plans identified that although there were examples of good growth amongst some sports, most sports were primarily attracting already active participants, thus demonstrating an increase in the measure of the adults participating in 3×30 minutes of exercise per week but not altering those at 1×30 minutes per week, which remained relatively static. In addition, pressure on NGBs to demonstrate growth meant many focused their efforts into areas of the city where engagement required less effort, namely the more affluent areas. Attempts to address this with NGBs focused around the idea of a 'tale of two cities,' which highlighted the complexities of demographics of the city, namely the stark disparity in life expectancy between the north of the city and the south. The realities of what was needed – time and a substantial input of resources – to achieve systemic change in these areas caused a further conflict between the city council's priorities and the capacity of NGBs to respond to this challenge. This was partly resolved via Sport England funding for a 'Place Pilot,' which involved the commitment of additional resources to support NGBs to engage and deliver in areas of high priority as defined by the council. This funding was used to employ 'activators' to build connections in communities and develop appropriate activities in those areas such as community park tennis, Run Leeds and table tennis.

Subsequently, the five big issues outlined Sport England's (2021) *Uniting the Movement* strategy aligned well with local priorities in Leeds and reflected the challenges of the post-Covid environment. The Council was working towards a co-produced Physical Activity Ambition, a process that started with a city-wide consultation on physical activity which generated responses from over 4,000 residents. This revealed that there was motivation amongst residents to be physically active but that some social and environmental factors made this challenging for many individuals. A key focus moving forward for Active Leeds was to concentrate on 'system change' (to look at how factors which enable physical activity can be aligned, e.g. transport links, facility access, the physical environment) and to adopt community-led approaches to identify solutions. This represented a shift from the top-down approach utilised by NGBs towards an approach which embraces engaging with communities. For example, Leeds Girls Can (a local take on the successful national campaign) identified and supported volunteer ambassadors to drive opportunities within their local area or community. Elsewhere, Get Set Leeds Local (a Sport England-funded programme), based in four of the 1% most deprived neighbourhoods in the city, took a community-led approach to identifying, developing and implementing solutions to make it easier and more appealing to be active in a given place.

In addition to the strategic focus on physical activity, the Council has since 2013–2014 invested heavily in hosting major sports events such as the Tour De France Grand Depart in 2014, the 2015 Rugby World Cup, and between 2016 and 2022, the UK stage of the World Triathlon Series. Whilst such events contributed to the government's ambition to create a 'decade of sport' following the hosting of the 2012 London Olympic and Paralympic Games, the primary justification for the Council is economic impact (the World Triathlon Series is estimated to have brought in a cash boost to the local economy of £1.2m). Mega events also offer opportunities for spectator and volunteer engagement and the incorporation of mass participation races within the main programme. For example, development activities (including introductory programmes) that built towards the triathlon event weekend helped to generate new interest in swimming, cycling, and running in Leeds for a relatively small investment of resources.

Looking to the future, whilst there may be continued complementarity in national policies' focus on embedding long-term, systemic change by utilising community-led, asset-based community development approaches, Leeds City Council needs to continue being financially prudent as budgets remain stretched after more than a decade of austerity measures. The ability to generate income from facilities alongside accessing external funding opportunities is crucial, while investment is needed to support refurbishing and renewing existing facility stock. The challenge will be to fulfil these objectives whilst ensuring that facilities and activity programmes remain attuned to the needs of inactive and vulnerable groups across the city.

References

Allison, M., Cutforth, C., & Wood, S. (2016, September). Could the sentiment of Rio derail an active nation? *The Leisure Review*. http://www.theleisurereview.co.uk/articles16/rio_olympics.html

Andrews, R., & Dollery, B. (2021). Guest editors' introduction: The impact of ageing and demographic change on local government. *Local Government Studies*, *47*(3), 355–363. https://doi.org/10.1080/03003930.2021.1906231

Association for Public Service Excellence. (2012). *Local authority sport and recreation services in England: Where next?* ASPE.

Atkinson, H., & Wils-Heeg, S. (2000). *Local government from Thatcher to Blair: The politics of creative autonomy*. Polity Press.

Baker, C., El Ansari, W., & Crone, D. (2016). Partnership working in sport and physical activity: An assessment of processes and outcomes in community sports networks. *Public Policy and Administration*, *32*(2), 87–109. https://doi.org/10.1177/0952076715625104

BBC. (2010, October 21). Spending review 2010: Key points at a glance. *BBC News*. http://www.bbc.co.uk/news/uk-politics-11569160

Bell, B. (2009). *Sport studies*. Learning Matters.

Bergsgard, N. A., Houlihan, B., Mangset, P., Ingve Nødland, S., & Rommentvedt, H. (2007). *Sport policy: A comparative analysis of stability and change*. Butterworth-Heinemann.

Blanco, I., Lowndes, V., & Pratchett, L. (2011). Policy networks and governance networks: Towards greater conceptual clarity. *Political Studies Review*, *9*(3), 297–308. https://doi.org/10.1111/j.1478-9302.2011.00239.x

Bloyce, D., & Smith, A. (2010). *Sport policy and development: An introduction*. Routledge.

Carter, P. (2005). *Review of national sport effort and resources*. Sport England.

Chandler, J. (2007). *Explaining local government: Local government in Britain since 1800*. Manchester University Press.

Charlton, T. (2010). 'Grow and sustain': The role of community sports provision in promoting a participation legacy for the 2012 Olympic Games. *International Journal of Sport Policy*, *2*(3), 347–366. https://doi.org/10.1080/19406940.2010.519340

Chief Leisure Officers Association. (2012). *Financial settlements for culture & sport survey summary – June 12*. CLOA.

Coghlan, J. (1990). *Sport and British politics since 1960*. The Falmer Press.

Collins, M. (2010). From 'sport for good' to 'sport for sport's sake' – Not a good move for sports development in England? *International Journal of Sport Policy*, *2*(3), 367–379. https://doi.org/10.1080/19406940.2010.519342

Conn, D. (2015, July 5). Olympic legacy failure: Sports centres under assault by thousand council cuts. *Guardian*. https://www.theguardian.com/sport/2015/jul/05/olympic-legacy-failure-sports-centres-council-cuts

Department for Culture, Media & Sport. (2000). *A sporting future for all*. DCMS.

Department for Culture, Media & Sport. (2008). *Playing to win: A new era for sport*. DCMS.

Department for Culture, Media & Sport. (2012). *Creating a sporting habit for life*. DCMS.

Department for Culture Media and Sport/Strategy Unit. (2002). *Game plan: A strategy for delivering the government's sport and physical activity objectives*. DCMS.

Department for Digital, Culture, Media & Sport. (2015). *A sporting nation: A new strategy for an active nation*. DDCMS.

Department for Digital, Culture, Media & Sport Select Committee. (2021). *Sport in our communities: Government response to committee's fourth report* [Online]. October

21, 2021. Retrieved July 7, 2022, from https://publications.parliament.uk/pa/cm5802/cmselect/cmcumeds/761/76101.htm

Department of National Heritage. (1995). *Sport: Raising the game*. DNH.

Finlay-King, L., Nichols, G., Forbes, D., & Macfadyen, G. (2017). Localism and the big society: The asset transfer of leisure centres and libraries – Fighting closures or empowering communities? *Leisure Studies, 37*(2), 1–14. https://doi.org/10.1080/02614367.2017.1285954

Grix, J., & Harris, S. (2017). Government and governmentality of sport. In A. Bairner, J. Kelly, & J. W. Lee (Eds.), *The Routledge handbook of sport and politics* (pp. 3–15). Routledge.

Guardian. (2010, October 20). 2012 Olympics safe as spending review 2010 cuts sport funding by third. *Guardian*. https://www.theguardian.com/politics/2010/oct/20/spending-review-2010-olympics-sport

Harris, S. (2013). Reviewing the role of UK central government in sports development. In D. Hassan & J. Lusted (Eds.), *Managing sport: Social and cultural perspectives* (pp. 65–89). Routledge.

Harris, S., & Houlihan, B. (2014). Delivery networks and community sport in England. *International Journal of Public Sector Management, 27*(2), 113–127. https://doi.org/10.1108/IJPSM-07-2013-0095

Harris, T., Hodge, L., & Phillips, D. (2019). *English local government funding: Trends and challenges in 2019 and beyond*. Institute for Fiscal Studies.

Hill, J. (2020, April 14). Half of leisure trusts 'could collapse by June'. *Local Government Chronicle*. https://www.lgcplus.com/politics/coronavirus/half-of-leisure-trusts-could-collapse-by-june-14-04-2020/

HM Government. (2010). *Decentralisation and the localism bill: An essential guide*. DCLG.

Houlihan, B., & Lindsey, I. (2013). *Sport policy in Britain*. Routledge.

Houlihan, B., & White, A. (2002). *The politics of sports development*. Routledge.

Inman, P. (2014, December 4). Osborne's spending cuts will change state 'beyond recognition,' says IFS. *Guardian*. http://www.theguardian.com/politics/2014/dec/04/george-osborne-spending-cuts-change-state-beyond-recognition-ifs

Ives, J. (2016, February 9). Letter from the editor: 'A strategy in which the deeds can't match the words'. *The Leisure Review*. http://www.theleisurereview.co.uk/editorial/editorial81.html

Jackson, D. (2008). Developing sports practice. In K. Hylton & P. Bramham (Eds.), *Sports development: Policy, process and practice* (2nd ed., pp. 25–41). Routledge.

Jeffreys, K. (2012). *Sport and politics in modern Britain: The road to 2012*. Palgrave Macmillan.

John, P. (2014). The great survivor: The persistence and resilience of English local government. *Local Government Studies, 40*(5), 687–704. https://doi.org/10.1080/03003930.2014.891984

Keech, M. (2013). Sport and adult mass participation in England. In B. Houlihan & M. Green (Eds.), *The Routledge handbook of sport development* (pp. 217–230). Routledge.

King, N. (2009). *Sport, policy and governance: Local perspectives*. Butterworth-Heinemann.

King, N. (2012). *Local authority sport & recreation in England: Where next?* Halliwell King.

King, N. (2013). "Sport for all" in a financial crisis: Survival and adaptation in competing organisational models of local authority sport services. *World Leisure Journal, 55*(3), 215–228. https://doi.org/10.1080/04419057.2013.820503

Lentell, B. (1993). Sports development - Goodbye to community recreation? In C. Brackenridge (Ed.), *Body matters: Leisure, images, and lifestyles (No. 47)* (pp. 141–149).Leisure Studies Association.

Lindsey, I. (2014). Prospects for local collaboration into an uncertain future: Learning from practice within Labour's partnership paradigm. *Local Government Studies, 40*(2), 312–330. https://doi.org/10.1080/03003930.2013.805690

Local Government Association. (2021). *A guide to the emergency insourcing of leisure facilities.* LGA.

Lord Justice Scarman. (1981). *The Brixton disorders 10–12 April 1981.* Home Office.

Lowndes, V., & Gardner, A. (2016). Local governance under the conservatives: Super-austerity, devolution and the 'smarter state'. *Local Government Studies, 42*(3), 357–375. https://doi.org/10.1080/03003930.2016.1150837

Lowndes, V., & Pratchett, L. (2012, February). Local governance under the coalition government: Austerity, localism and the 'big society'. *Local Government Studies, 38*(1), 21–40. https://doi.org/10.1080/03003930.2011.642949

Murray, J. (2015). *Policy paper: The role of local government in the modern state.* Centre for Labour and Social Studies.

Painter, C. (2012). The UK Coalition government: Constructing public service reform narratives. *Public Policy and Administration, 28*(1), 3–20. https://doi.org/10.1177/0952076711427758

Pamben, D. (2016, November 14). GLL awarded 25-year Cornwall contract. *Sports Management.* http://www.sportsmanagement.co.uk/Sports-news/latest/HKS-Texas-Rangers-stadium-development/328245

Pamben, D. (2017, January 18). Cash-strapped council signs leisure centres over to GLL. *Leisure Opportunities.* http://www.leisureopportunities.co.uk/detail.cfm?pagetype=detail&subject=news&codeID=329658

Parnell, D., Millward, P., & Spracklen, K. (2015). Sport and austerity in the UK: An insight into Liverpool 2014. *Journal of Policy Research in Tourism, Leisure and Events, 7*(2), 200–203. https://doi.org/10.1080/19407963.2014.968309

Public Health England. (2020). *Engaging NHS system leaders in whole systems approaches to physical activity.* Public Health England.

Sport Council. (1982). *Sport in the community: The next ten years.* Sports Council.

Sport England. (1999). *Delivering best value through sport.* Sport England.

Sport England. (2004). *A framework for sport in England.* Sport England.

Sport England. (2015). *In it for the long run* [Online]. Retrieved June 5, 2015, from http://www.sportengland.org/our-work/local-work/local-government/in-it-for-the-long-run.

Sport England. (2021). *Uniting the movement: A ten-year vision to transform lives and communities through sport and physical activity.* Sport England.

Stewart, J. (2014). An era of continuing change: Reflections on local government in England 1974–2014. *Local Government Studies, 40*(6), 835–850. https://doi.org/10.1080/03003930.2014.959842

Stoker, G. (2004). *Transforming local governance: From Thatcherism to new Labour.* Palgrave Macmillan.

Swim England. (2021). *A decade of decline: The future of swimming pools in England.* Swim England.

UK Parliament. (2021). *A national plan for sport, health and wellbeing.* House of Lords.

Weaver, M. (2022, April 26). Going under: Energy price rises leave UK pools in deep trouble. *Guardian*. https://www.theguardian.com/lifeandstyle/2022/apr/26/swimming-pools-in-uk-will-close-without-energy-bailout-ministers-told

Wilson, D. (2003, August). Unravelling control freakery: Redefining central-local government relations. *British Journal of Politics and International Relations*, 5(3), 317–346. https://doi.org/10.1111/1467-856X.00109

Wilson, D., & Game, C. (2011). *Local government in the United Kingdom* (5th ed.). Palgrave MacMillan.

Chapter 6

Public Health Agencies and Policy Implementation in Sport and Physical Activity

Re-thinking Partnerships and Priorities

Phil Brown and Aaron Beacom

Introduction

This chapter explores how the 'physical activity agenda' has become a central pillar of contemporary government sport policy within England. We consider public health in the context of wider government health spending priorities and national policy priorities of the Department of Health, NHS England and Public Health England, as well as local policy enactment and implementation through commissioned services. Central to the consideration of the impact of public health agencies is the recognition of their powerful advocacy of the health agenda, which then influences both national and local policy priorities in sport, education, transport and community policy, delivered by organisations in sport, local authorities and schools. The *implementation* of the physical activity agenda is therefore enacted through a diverse web of government departments, agencies and organisations who contribute to a wider public health agenda, as well as through some direct delivery by public health agencies.

Specifically, the investigation illustrates through deliberately selective examples, how sport and physical activity (PA) have shifted within the public policy hierarchy, reflecting the salience of sport and PA to wider public policy agendas in health. We illustrate the web of relationships between sport and PA in the context of public health agencies, outlining interdisciplinary and interagency complexity. Through the historical sections below, we briefly outline how political ideology influenced the perception of social and cultural 'problems' and 'solutions,' and readers will be able to identify the policy coalitions and organisational structures in these eras through sport and health policy. The Advocacy Coalition Framework draws attention to the scope of government priorities and that sports policy communities cannot 'insulate themselves from other, more powerful, and politically important, policy communities' (Weed, 2001, p.135). Houlihan invoked Kingdon's conception of policy 'spill-over,' from stronger to weaker policy areas and the 'vulnerability of sport policy to manipulation by diplomatic, health and educational interests' (Houlihan, 2005, p.172). While the chapter identifies primarily with ACF to help articulate the

DOI: 10.4324/9781003162728-6

fundamental shifts in perspective which underpin policy change, we acknowledge the validity of the Multiple Streams Framework (MSF) (Kingdon, 1984; Paredis & Block, 2013) in that the concept of the 'policy window' helps the conceptualisation of the new policy landscape. In this new landscape, there is potential for cross-sectoral working where policy windows emerge and stakeholders engaged in public health, PA and sport respond to systemic health and well-being challenges of sedentary lifestyles, exacerbated further by the Covid-19 pandemic. The framework accommodates interrogation of key actors and individuals fulfilling a strategic role as boundary spanners and policy entrepreneurs[1] (at both national and local levels) seeking to maximise opportunities emerging from public health realities. At the same time, Lipsky's concept of 'Street Level Bureaucrats'[2] provides the basis for understanding the actions of practitioners as they seek to develop and deliver programmes in fluid environments.

When considering the strength of the public health advocacy, readers may attune their focus to the extent to which the health and PA agenda is evident in the analysis of non-health organisations in this book, and the extent to which health and PA have become a policy priority for implementation by these organisations. Whilst other chapters have been able to take a sharper focus on a 'type of organisation' (National Governing Bodies, Local Authorities, Schools, Active Partnerships), what will become apparent is that there is not a single 'type' of organisation that is responsible for the implementation of PA. To be clear, there are no *public health* agencies with a single remit for PA. We will demonstrate the breadth of the public health agenda and show that PA is strongly advocated, but there is limited direct implementation by public health agencies. Direct public health focus and resources (devolved locally) are orientated towards high-impact services and interventions, targeted to people already experiencing ill health, which have more direct impact on health (such as smoking cessation), rather than on population-wide PA interventions as a preventative measure for ill health.

We contend there has been a fundamental shift in the centre of gravity of 'sport' policy to fill the policy space for PA promotion and delivery, aligned to the health and well-being agenda. This is evident in the realignment of national policy objectives by the Department of Culture Media and Sport (DCMS) – policy outcomes concerned with physical and social well-being, alongside individual, community and economic development objectives (DCMS, 2015). The orientation towards the PA agenda by the DCMS and Sport England and their regional partners (including Active Partnerships linked with local Clinical Commissioning Groups (CCGs)) and local Health and Well-being Boards is indicative of the new funding imperatives across the public sector, reflecting the sharing of policy objectives and resources. PA promotion is integrated within a complex web of national, regional and local health agencies, working with local partnerships and consortia that interpret and enact local policy. There is hyper-complexity in diffused implementation approaches for PA that transcends sectoral and organisational boundaries of public, private and voluntary sector organisations.

Funding for Health: The Wider Health Agenda in Context

UK government-financed healthcare expenditure was £166.7 billion in 2018 (pre-Covid-19 pandemic), which represented 10.0% of GDP (ONS, 2021). Real-term per person spending is reported to have almost doubled between 1997 and 2018, rising from £1,672 per person in 1997 to £3,227 in 2018, representing a 4.7% annual increase between 1997 and 2009, falling to a 1.2% increase between 2009 and 2018 (ONS, 2021). Government health spending comes second only to pensions and welfare benefits, which demonstrates the significant political and social prioritisation of the health of UK citizens.

The World Health Organisation (WHO) advocates the Primary Health Care model as optimal for achieving population-wide health outcomes, prioritising primary prevention and health promotion, alongside local delivery of medical services (WHO, 2008). This approach is linked to wider recognition of the social determinants of health. The Socio-Ecological Model (SEM) is aligned to this holistic understanding of health care and considers interventions through four levels: (i) institutional/legislative, (ii) organisational/environmental, (iii) interpersonal and (iv) personal levels. The SEM transforms our understanding of health from an individualised medical model to a broader social model (see Murphy et al., 2009). Aligned to this, there is recognition of a gradient of public health interventions from having the largest to smallest impact: (i) addressing inequality in socio-economic factors (e.g., poverty, housing, education), (ii) changing the context for default choices to be healthy (e.g., banning smoking inside public spaces), (iii) long-lasting protective interventions (e.g., vaccinations), (iv) clinical interventions (e.g., medicating diabetes, weight loss surgery) and (v) counselling and education (e.g., promotion of healthy diet and physical activity, targeted interventions) (see Moreland-Russell et al., 2016).

Following the logic of these perspectives and the international momentum towards an appreciation of the range of determinants influencing health and wellbeing, it is unsurprising to find clear reference in UK government policy documentation, to this socio-ecological narrative (UK Government, 2018). In practice, given the breadth of the Socio-Ecological Model, all government interventions that improve life chances, such as early years education and social welfare policies, contribute to social determinants of health. However, focusing specifically on direct government spending on health care reveals that approximately two-thirds (64%) is spent on curative or rehabilitative care (hospitals/doctors treating immediate medical issues) (ONS, 2020). Only 5% of government healthcare expenditure is directed towards preventative primary care, to avoid diseases and their associated risk factors, and secondary prevention, such as health screening for early disease identification (ONS, 2020). Direct spending on preventative measures through public health prevention is dwarfed by the immediate demands to treat people who are already experiencing ill health. The advocacy of the Primary Health Care model of addressing the root causes of health inequalities is superseded in practice by spending on clinical interventions.

Organisations Concerned with Public Health

Key organisations concerned in some way with public health include the Department of Health and Social Care (DHSC),[3] the NHS, the UK Health Security Agency (UKHSA), the Office for Health Improvement and Disparities (OHID),[4] General Practitioners (GPs), local Clinical Commissioning Groups and local authorities. Public agencies are wholly funded by government, through general taxations, and are part of the state's apparatus for developing and implementing public policy objectives. The Department of Health (2010) defined public health as 'the science and art of promoting and protecting health and wellbeing, preventing ill health and prolonging life through the organised efforts of society' (Department of Health, 2010, p.11). DoH (2011, p.11 cited in Griffiths et al., 2005) laid out three domains of public health:

1. health improvement (e.g., healthy lifestyles and addressing health inequalities and the wider social influences of health);
2. health protection (e.g., infectious diseases, environmental health and emergency plans); and
3. health services (e.g., service planning, audit and evaluation).

The public health agenda saw significant changes since the nineteenth and early twentieth centuries, where the focus was on infectious diseases, but as Covid-19 demonstrated, transmissible diseases can still significantly impact society. Prior to Covid-19, the public health agenda focused upon chronic diseases, coronary heart disease (CHD), cancer, respiratory diseases/stroke (Wanless, 2002; DoH, 2004), and mental health and well-being (PHE, 2019). These conditions affect mortality (death) and morbidity rates (living with disease) and 'healthy life expectancy' (how long self-rated good health will be enjoyed). Lifestyle factors such as smoking, obesity, poor diet, excessive alcohol consumption and physical inactivity are all associated with chronic diseases. These issues are influenced by wider social determinants of health that include early years, income, employment status, education, housing and social isolation (Wanless, 2002; DoH, 2004; DoH, 2011). The antecedents of health inequalities are derived from broader social inequalities. There is a clear social gradient; those at the lower levels have lower life expectancy and lower 'healthy life' expectancy (Wanless, 2002; WHO, 2008; Marmot, 2010). The inverse is true of people who enjoy higher socio-economic positions; these social advantages have a multiplying effect, resulting in them having better health (Marmot, 2010). The Marmot Review identified a difference of 7 years in life expectancy, and 17 years in disability-free life expectancy, between the richest and poorest neighbourhoods; these in-country differences illustrate stark consequences of health inequality (WHO, 2008; Marmot, 2010). Rather than reducing, the social gradient gap has increased to 19 years between the richest and poorest communities (PHE, 2019, Marmot et.al., 2020).

Interventionist Conservatism, 1992–1997

This chronological oversight begins with John Major as prime minister from 1990 to 1997. Against a backdrop of the increasing prominence of ideas associated with New Right ideology (advocating free market economics, personal choice and responsibility, reflected in the rolling back of the welfare state and concerns with the so-called 'nanny state'; Henry, 2001; Houlihan & White, 2002), Major adopted a more interventionist tone – articulated not least in the policy areas of sport and health. During this period, Major introduced *Health of the Nation* (HotN) (DoH, 1992) which was the first attempt by government to have a single strategy for health, which was followed by the first sports strategy, *Sport: Raising the Game* (DNH, 1995).

HotN set out to tackle the risk factors of five major diseases: coronary heart disease/stroke, cancer, mental illness, HIV/AIDS and accidents. The status of PA and exercise was underplayed in comparison to other areas such as diet and smoking. HotN established the role of primary care health education promotion, led by Local Health Education Authority Officers, premised upon the belief that individuals would modify their own behaviours once they had greater understanding of healthy choices. The Physical Activity Task Force was responsible for the emergence of the now very familiar 'five-a-week message' for PA and the overt promotion of PA (Robson & McKenna, 2008). Physical activity and sport were not directly linked. The sports strategy, *Raising the Game* (DNH, 1995), promoted traditional competitive sports, both in schools linked to a new national curriculum and in communities through school–club links (Henry, 2001; Houlihan & White, 2002). There was no direct formal connection between health, PA and sport in policy or practice during this era.

New Labour, 1997–2010: Establishing the Trajectory of Collaborative Approaches with Sport and Health

The 'New' Labour era of Tony Blair saw unprecedented intervention in all areas of public policy. 'New' Labour's political project was underpinned by the cross-cutting, 'social inclusion agenda' that sought to tackle social inequality which required 'joined up solutions to joined up problems' (Newnam, 2001, p. 53) and promoted a modernisation agenda that was reliant upon cross-departmental and cross-sectoral partnerships as the central mechanism to achieve social policy objectives and implement services (McDonald, 2005). The ideology of social inclusion underpinned both *Game Plan* (DCMS/SU, 2002) and Sport England's (2004) *Framework for Sport. Game Plan* outlined a proposal for an unprecedented change in population-wide PA, from the baseline of 30% meeting Chief Medical Officer (CMO) recommendations to 70% over a 20-year period. The CMO established a minimum of 30 minutes moderate PA on at least five days per week for adults, and at least 60 minutes per day for children to prevent ill health from physical inactivity (DoH, 2004). In 2004 the CMO outlined the consequences of physical inactivity upon the health of the nation, physical inactivity increases:

the risk of premature death by about 20-30%. The annual costs of physical inactivity in England are estimated at £8.2 billion – including the rising costs of treating chronic diseases such as coronary heart disease and diabetes. This does not include the contribution of inactivity to obesity – an estimated further £2.5 billion cost to the economy each year.

(DoH 2004, p. iii)

The CMO at the time, Derek Wanless, in *Securing Good Health for the Whole Population* recommended a 'medium-term' *Game Plan* target by 2020 (50% participation rather than the aspirational 70% target) which equated to a 1% per annum increase (DoH, 2004). *Game Plan's* rationale aligned to the wider health and social inclusion agendas that were cognisant of the social determinants of health (Wanless, 2004; WHO, 2008). The health policy *Saving Lives: Our Healthier Nation* (DoH, 2000a), NHS National Service Frameworks for CHD (DoH, 2000b) and the NHS Cancer Plan (DoH, 2000c) recognised the positive contribution of PA to health prevention and rehabilitation.

Under New Labour, Public Health (PH) was under the remit of the Department of Health and the NHS nationally and locally. Regional leadership and oversight came from regional NHS Strategic Health Authorities (SHA), who agreed on joint local priorities, objectives and delivery mechanisms with Primary Care Trusts (PCTs) and Hospital Trusts through Local Delivery Plans (LDPs) to achieve 'top-down' national targets (NHS, 2021). Introduced in April 2000 as statutory NHS bodies, PCTs were responsible for the local delivery of national policy (The NHS Confederation, 2011). As a result of the government's publication of *Creating a Patient-Led NHS* (DH/NHS, 2005), PCTs were reconfigured to align with the number of local authorities in England (152 reduced from 303) in order to increase opportunities for local partnership working. PCTs were responsible for up to 80% of the NHS budget and had both a commissioning of services and service delivery role. PCTs 'locally commissioned' other local NHS services including NHS Hospital Trusts, GPs and dental services. Commissioned services also included district nursing, health visiting, children's services, mental health services and PCTs and had statutory responsibility for Public Health (The NHS Confederation, 2011). PCTs appointed Directors of Public Health (DPH), but resource constraints resulted in small public health teams with an 'insufficient "critical mass" to fulfil responsibilities' (Wanless, 2004, p. 44).

Limited capacity in local Public Health teams necessitated local partnerships working within and beyond health. The collaboration between sport and health was demonstrated through the joint publication from the DCMS & DoH (2005), *Choosing Activity: A Physical Activity Action Plan*. This publication brought together commitments to promote PA from health, sport, schools and transport and environment departments and related government agencies, further demonstrating the diffuse nature of policy implementation of the public health agenda related to PA. Part of the approach was to promote the benefits of PA through social marketing, online tools (*Change for Life* and NHS *Healthy Choices*) alongside Sport

England's *Everyday Sport* campaign which promoted everyday PA (DCMS & DoH, 2005) to provide information for the public to 'choose' healthy behaviours. The core public health workforce is made up of four key roles: health visitors, school nurses, public health practitioners and environmental health professionals (CfWI, 2014). Peripheral partner professions include midwives, occupational health nurses, community pharmacists, GPs, trading standards officers, teachers and sport and leisure workers, who may 'promote public health, but this is not the primary function of their role' (CfWI, 2014, p.3). It was the ability of health professionals to harness the political priorities of health and to make these shared priorities with other sectors (such as sport and the promotion of PA) that enabled public health agencies to shape policy and divert resources and efforts towards the PA agenda.

Preventative Public Health services are often characterised as a 'Cinderella service' in terms of funding and resources, despite the often-repeated importance of tackling both individual lifestyle factors and the wider social determinants of health. Public Health resources are allocated to interventions that have the greatest efficacy for lifestyle risk factors and health improvement (and achieving national targets); therefore, 'smoking cessation' services often have taken priority, over PA, where no specific PH targets existed for public health agencies. Instead of Public Health being accountable for PA targets, these were made the responsibility of the DCMS, as expressed through *Game Plan* (DCMS/SU, 2002), and local authority Public Service Agreement (PSA) targets, with performance measured through Sport England's Active People Survey (Sport England, 2021).

Primary care interventions aimed to take a whole-system approach to PA aligned to a wider focus on tackling obesity. National policy advocated that doctors, nurses, pharmacists and allied health professionals incorporated the promotion of PA into patient interactions, apply behaviour change approaches, and refer patients for 'exercise referral' (DoH, 2005). The National Institute for Health and Care Excellence (NICE) identified four commonly used methods to increase PA in primary care settings: (1) exercise referral, (2) pedometers (step counters), (3) community walking schemes and (4) cycling schemes (NICE, 2006).

Choosing Activity (DCMS & DoH, 2005) demonstrated cross-departmental collaboration in Whitehall and local-level partnerships who ultimately implemented policy. Due to the limited capacity of PCT Public Health, the sports sector took up the mantel for coordinating PA through sports agencies. Community-based sport and PA were led at a strategic level by Sport England and their regional offices working with Regional Sports Boards, County Sports Partnerships, local authorities, National Governing Bodies (NGBs), third-sector organisations and community sport clubs to promote sport and PA to communities. The Local Government Act 2000 gave powers to local authorities in England and Wales to promote economic, social and environmental well-being of communities and citizens within its boundaries (Gov.UK, no date). Local partnership complexity came through Local Strategic Partnerships (LSPs) that aligned to local authority (LA) boundaries, made up of LAs, PCTs, commercial and third-sector organisations, who were tasked to create Sustainable Community Strategies and deliver Local Area Agreements (LAAs). LAAs negotiated local priority outcomes agreed with the central government. In addition, local PSAs were funded targets aligned to national government departments. For example, in health PSA targets were focused on reducing childhood obesity (shared with the DCMS) and increasing life expectancy and health outcomes for people living with long-term conditions (DoH, 2005). There were shared PSA targets through the Department for Education and Skills (DfES) and the DCMS to increase the number of pupils who took part in two hours of high-quality Physical Education (PE) and School Sport (DfCSF, 2008). Also for schools to engage with the PE School Sport and Club Links strategy and to work with School Sports Partnerships to increase participation in sport and the numbers of pupils who achieve 3×30 minutes of sport/PA per week in school (DfCSF, 2008). This shared PA agenda crossed national government departmental boundaries and local delivery partnerships.

The so-called obesity epidemic and physical inactivity in communities were of growing concern in this era. 'New' Labour established Local Exercise Action Pilots (LEAPs) to build an understanding of effective community-based PA interventions, in keeping with their claims of making 'evidence-based policy' (Coalter, 2017). LEAPs were led by PCTs who designed and developed a variety of community PA interventions with priority target groups. LEAP findings were disseminated to policymakers and local health commissioners (DCMS and DoH, 2005) in the hope that these would influence local policy decisions by public health agencies. LEAP also aimed to increase the evidence base to contribute to the development of best practice for Free Swimming interventions, which were popular with local authorities in the early 2000s.

In summary this period saw significant intervention across the public sector. It established shared priorities for health between public health agencies and wider branches of the state. There was an overt coupling of the sport and health agendas in national and local politics. Public sector sport agencies and local delivery partners were expected to make a significant contribution to improving population-wide levels of physical activity. This period established the context and trajectory of contemporary sport and physical activity policy.

2010 Coalition: Consensus Building and Austerity

The period following significant public spending in the 'New' Labour era and the economic downturn following the banking crash of 2008 resulted in a new era of economic austerity from the Conservative and Liberal Democrat coalition government. In contrast to an expanding PA system under 'New' Labour, the public sector was faced with a financial squeeze and a period of significant contraction and realignment. Sport, PA and local government were all subject to real-term budget reduction (Hastings et al., 2015). Core funding for elements of the PA infrastructure established under 'New' Labour, such as the School Sport Partnerships and Specialist Sports Colleges, was cut. The DCMS (2012) strategy *Creating a Sporting Habit for Life: A New Youth Sport Strategy* advocated a specific focus on young people (rather than the whole population) and promoted traditional competitive sports, in contrast to New Labour's pre-Olympic Games focus on social inclusion and population-wide PA. The promotion of competitive sport was prioritised in schools which replaced the holistic approach to increasing sport and PA through the Physical Education, School Sport and Club Links (strategy), and then the PE School Sport and Young People (PESSYP) initiatives (Phillpots, 2013). Primary schools though benefited from £150m ring-fenced funding from the PE and School Sport Premium, which devolved PA and sport funding decisions to head teachers (DoE, 2014). Primary schools were expected to play a dual role in policy implementation, leading the way on young peoples' CMO PA policy objectives and increasing the levels of competitive school sport aligned to DCMS and DfE targets (Lindsey, 2020). Lindsey et al. argue that the health-related objectives 'sat uneasily alongside continued commitments to competitive sport' (Lindsey et al., 2021, p.278) given that competitive sport is problematic in the context of raising levels of PA (Lindsey, 2020).

There was continuity through the *Let's Get Moving* (LGM) PA care pathway (a Primary Care led PA initiative) (DoH, 2012) that was initiated under New Labour in 2009. LGM was an evidence-based approach to PA behaviour change for primary healthcare professionals. The enactment and implementation of LGM was a devolved decision of local commissioners due to the nature of localised commissioning and local funding decisions. LGM promoted PA delivered in NHS primary care settings to commissioners on the basis that it was clinically cost-effective. Through LGM, GPs and Practice Nurses were trained to identify inactive patients, promote PA through behaviour change approaches, set personal PA goals for patients and refer patients to exercise referral programmes. LGM would only run if this service was bought by local commissioners who may target specific communities to address health inequalities or adopt a community-wide approach.

The most significant act of the Coalition government for public health came through the introduction of the Health and Social Care Act (2012). This significant piece of legislation resulted in the abolition of PCTs and the transfer of the statutory responsibility for Public Health from PCTs (Health) to local government (county/unitary authorities) and a responsibility to improve the health of their constituents. The legislation also saw the creation of local CCGs which replaced PCTs (Heath, 2014). In addition, there was the creation of a new national public body, Public Health England, the executive agency of the Department of Health and Social Care, on April 1, 2013 (DoH, 2012).

The transfer of Public Health to local authorities brought with it statutory responsibility, ring-fenced funding and director-level influence at a policy and strategic level. Directors of Public Health work with local politicians and senior leaders in LAs and hold a statutory position on Health and Well-being Boards. Public Health in local authorities enjoys a higher status and profile than it did within the

NHS, and there is closer alignment with the preventative agenda. Local authorities' fundamental purpose is to provide local services to improve the lives and health of their residents through their functions, including public health and social care integration, housing, schools, planning, green spaces and sports and cultural provision. Collectively this offers the potential to improve the quality of lives of residents and tackle wider social determinants of health.

Clinical Commissioning Groups, constituted by GPs, determine local policy and commissioning services to meet the needs of the local population and their patients. CCGs effectively buy services to meet the needs of their local community from organisations including NHS hospitals, social enterprises and commercial or third-sector providers. CCGs are responsible for acute services (emergency and planned hospital services) and mental health and community care (NHS, no date). Policy planning and implementation are locally determined through local Health and Well-being Boards. Local authorities' Public Health remit can combine with CCGs to pool budgets through Section 75 agreements and make joint commissioning decisions based upon the evidence from Local Needs Assessments that align to national health outcome targets.

The advocacy in national guidance for the direct commissioning of PA interventions from CCGs was refined. NICE guidance on PA referral stated that:

> policy makers and commissioners should only fund exercise referral schemes for people who are sedentary or inactive **and** have existing health conditions or other factors […] that put them at increased risk of ill health.
>
> (NICE 2014, emphasis added)

NICE guidelines also promoted walking and cycling with the expectation that this can benefit the entire population and include those in chronic disease pathways. The multiagency cross-sectoral approach to consider walking and cycling in wider planning and transport infrastructure and the cross-cutting benefits of this to communities, with specific guidance for schools and workplaces, further demonstrate the effectiveness of the advocacy of the public health agenda to influence policy direction and diffuse approaches to implementation, rather than direct delivery of public health policy exclusively by public health agencies.

Contemporary Issues: Emerging Policy Configurations, 2015–2022

When considering recent shifts in policy priorities relating to PA and health, it is important to appreciate the wider policy context against which such developments have taken place. Beacom and Ziakas (2022) noted that a deteriorating fiscal environment reflected in the sport sector, unfulfilled expectations relating to London 2012 Olympic and Paralympic Legacy, responses to the plateauing of PA levels, enhanced expectations concerning the capacity of activity-based interventions to deliver social, health and educational benefits (Coalter, 2013), Brexit and the impending decline of supra-national policymaking and concerns regarding the code of sport governance have all played their part in shaping the policy environment within which priorities are determined and decisions are made.

It was against this backdrop that attempts were made to re-calibrate sport policy; re-imagining physical culture more broadly defined, as a route through which to address the health and well-being agenda, focusing on the importance of building cross-sectoral engagement and partnerships outside the traditional sporting community as a means of promoting behavioural change amongst those alienated by the mainstream sporting culture. While there were concerns about aspects of the new policy direction – not least, the potential impact on stakeholders concerned with the development and delivery of orthodox forms of competitive sport (for example, National Governing Bodies of sport lost their 'preferential funding' status during this period) – the essential narrative of re-focusing efforts on those engaging in the most sedentary lifestyles was absorbed across the sector.

Whilst the full impact of the pandemic on the characteristics of PA and sport participation is still not fully understood, the restriction of opportunities to engage with formalised sport and PA has aided the shift towards more informal forms of activity. In this way, it could be argued that the pandemic has promoted wider shifts already underway since the launch of Sporting Future. Informal forms of physical activity have been promoted further by, for example, concerns over the relationship between obesity and mortality rates resulting from Covid-19 – and the need to encourage interventions from a wider range of organisations and agencies (Mitchell, 2020). Such developments have the potential to expand the 'policy window' for Active Partnerships, who have a history of engagement with the obesity agenda and increased synergies between local CCGs to commission services of what could loosely be termed third-sector delivery organisations.[5] Alongside potential for cooperative projects evident in such synergies, readers should bear in mind the limited capacity for the engagement of many third-sector organisations such as grassroots sports clubs whose infrastructure, volunteer base and operational practices are necessarily restricted in a number of contexts. The challenge is evident across societies where there is significant third-sector engagement in the delivery of sport and PA. In response, Marlier et al. (2020), for example, consider strategies for capacity building as a route to addressing this deficit. Such strategies seek to identify conduits to 'intersectoral' working which would help to enhance robustness and efficiency of actors. In part this requires understanding and empathy between organisations with different cultural and institutional backgrounds – promoted, for example, through engaging cross-sectoral teams of practitioners (youth, health and cultural practitioners) in initiation planning and delivery of community sport development programmes. At the same time, however, challenges remain. The capacity of the many grassroot sports clubs is severely restricted beyond their core activities – we argue that the task of facilitators such as public health organisations and Active Partnerships will, in part, be to identify where the greatest potential for further capacity building lies.

From an operational perspective, we would suggest the key issues that have emerged over the past six years, which have shaped the interface between public health and the sport/PA sector:

Public Health Agencies and Policy Implementation 105

1. Recognition at policy and practitioner level – that the greatest health benefits are achieved by moving individuals with sedentary lifestyles to moderately active lifestyles.
2. Recognition of the revised parameters of public health bodies as facilitators and mediators, where PA is part of a wider policy agenda. In the words of one practitioner 'Public health is about getting things lined up; identifying where gaps are and which organisations can fill the gaps.' The sport/PA sector is increasingly filling some of these gaps through national programmes delivered via locally managed cross-sectoral partnerships.
3. Recognition of stagnation of growth (core market saturation) through traditional approaches to sport – diversification of offer and delivery both through more informal approaches to sport/PA and working with non-sporting organisations (see Sport England Uniting the Movement).
4. Adoption of Behaviour change methodologies – such as the Capability, Opportunity, Motivation, Behaviour (COM-B), influencing the practices of sports organisations through PA pilots (see *Tackling Inactivity: What We Know: Key Insights from Our Get Healthy Get Active Pilots* (Sport England, 2016a) and *Applying Behaviour Change Theories: Real World Examples from the Get Healthy Get Active Projects* (Sport England, 2016b)).
5. Core funding budget constraints have led to competition for externally funded projects which are time-limited – which by definition limits continuity and narrows operational scope.

When considering current pre-occupations, practitioners are particularly vocal regarding the impact of Covid on the health and well-being agenda – as well as the potential for PA-based interventions to contribute to addressing the challenges. The significance of the impact was first articulated by Sport England in April 2021 through a report based on the Active People survey (Sport England, 2021). While the report did attempt to retain a positive note concerning numbers who continued to engage with physically active lifestyles, it did acknowledge the unequal spread of the impact of the pandemic – with particular concerns regarding older people and those with disabilities – a factor that would continue to dominate the subsequent narrative of PA during the pandemic.

Conclusion and Future Directions

Organisational responses to policy change and strategic challenge continue to evolve. In relation to the sport and public health interface, particular challenges are noteworthy:

1. The national policy discourse of physical activity has not been matched with significant funding for implementation by public health agencies.
2. There is an inconsistent approach regarding prioritisation of PA since it is a shared objective across multiple government departments and sectors. This

is reflected in fragmented policy objectives and fragmented approaches to implementation. While superficially a diffused approach might appeal intuitively in the sense that 'many hands make light work,' there is limited overall control or oversight and a corresponding lack of focus. The sports/PA sector nationally and locally is filling this void.

3. The national government continues to advocate PA as a cross-cutting issue in guidance to commissioners, schools, LAs, etc., but there is limited central control due to local resource constraints and the breadth of the Public Health agenda.

4. Local budgetary pressures have seen limited direct commissioning for PA beyond that which is targeted to patients on care pathways or obesity programmes. Direct funding for wider PA interventions is not available from local budgets.

5. Policy enactment for PA implementation and *delivery* on the ground is limited through local public health agencies. Much of the delivery of PA interventions is not directly funded by public health agencies. There is some targeted delivery of local services by third-sector organisations, Community Trusts, Social Prescribers, GP referral and walking groups, but this is not widespread.

6. Significant resources are available through external funding sources, but these are often competitive in nature, short-term and focused on communities most in need.

The policy convergence examined in this chapter is indicative of the adoption and integration of PA as a core aspect of the sports policy community. The significant advocacy power from public health agencies has resulted in non-public health agencies contributing, and in the case of Sport England and Active Partnerships, leading on PA policy. We have moved beyond 'policy-spill-over' (Weed, 2001; Houlihan, 2005) of PA from the health policy community to whole-scale adoption of PA by sport, to achieve wider physical and mental health outcomes as identified in *Sporting Future* (DCMS, 2015), superseding traditional sporting outcomes. We contend that this is partially driven by the scale and scope of the wider public health agenda and resource and capacity restrictions of public health agencies to prioritise PA over alternative interventions. In seeking greater legitimacy beyond traditional sports, the sports policy community has become a willing partner and contributor to the PA agenda. It has therefore become part of the policy implementation apparatus of public health agencies. Smith et al. (2016) identify the growing convergence between the fields of sport and health nationally and a decentralised locally determined approach to policy implementation and the delivery of local public services. National policy establishes the parameters for devolved local policy prioritisation and implementation, which requires strong local strategic and operational partnerships for policy implementation. In the context of budgetary constraints, local professionals in public health and sport are required to operate as boundary spanners and policy entrepreneurs to secure political attention and resources for their local communities for PA interventions. Given the limited resources available, and taking account of the social gradients in health inequalities, interventions are increasingly targeted at individuals and communities most in need, consequently limiting population-wide preventative approaches to PA. Allied to this must be recognition of the limitations of many traditional third-sector sports organisations (such as grassroots sports clubs who continue as central providers of sport and PA across the UK) to readily engage with such interventions. A key challenge for policymakers and strategists will be to identify organisations with the most potential for such interventionist work and focus capacity building at these locations.

PRACTITIONER REFLECTION AND INSIGHTS

Dwain Morgan, Head of Business and Impact, Plymouth Argyle Community Trust

Introduction

This response aims to contextualise the role of Community Club Organisations (CCOs) and showcase the significance of their output within the contemporary sport development landscape and the sphere of public health. As levels of physical inactivity continue to be a major public health concern, the growth in the use of professional and community sports clubs for delivering physical activity and health improvement interventions is important because of the large number of potential participants that can be reached through the programmes offered. Further thoughts are shared through the lens of a specific CCO (Argyle Community Trust) outlining their current work within an applied health, well-being and physical activity context.

The Broad Role of CCOs

The creation of CCOs as a concept was a direct response by Professional Football Clubs who were becoming increasingly challenged by National Governing Bodies to utilise their influence within local communities. This has been done mostly by using the Community Trust delivery model, which allows clubs to deliver a broad range of sport development projects, within their hyper-local communities, as a means of fulfilling elements of a professional clubs' corporate social responsibility (CSR).

Each professional football club has a supporting CCO that is governed and operates as a stand-alone sport-for-change charity. The projects are often funded by external organisations or public sector grants that in turn allow CCOs the resource required to work with a wide range of partners. Commonly, CCOs use these funding partnerships to deliver projects to those often most at-risk of disengagement, exclusion or experiencing health inequalities within their specific localities. The growing role and responsibilities of football clubs and more importantly their CCO in supporting social change are evidenced by the increased levels of funding being awarded by NGOs, UK government and Sport England. For example, in 2021 the English Football League Trust (EFLT) provided £59m and the Premier League Charitable Fund (PLCF) invested a further £35m into CCOs to deliver sport development projects.

Introducing Argyle Community Trust (ACT)

ACT is the official charity of Plymouth Argyle Football Club (PAFC) and uses the power of football to inspire, engage and help individuals to achieve their full potential. ACT aims to use their affiliation to PAFC, alongside a variety of sporting initiatives, to engage individuals from all populations, breaking down potential barriers (health, well-being, education, employment, low levels of physical activity, high deprivation and low attainment) and building stronger, more employable communities. ACT receives funds from both local and national funding sources to deliver projects that are deemed to meet the needs of its local community.

Significant Priority/Funding Shifts

Whilst CCOs will have a core offer that rarely changes its focus or priority away from being a self-sustainable provider of grassroots sport development opportunities, many also have skilled capacity and appetite to deliver across multiple, often complex sectors not traditionally associated with football such as public health, community development and alternative education. Whilst CCOs could attain the required capacity and skill sets to work deeper within these complex landscapes, funding cycles are rarely guaranteed long enough to make a sustainable investment into the necessary infrastructure (staffing, resources, training and development, etc.). As a result, CCOs tend to move dynamically (and regularly) between the complex sectors and tend to follow available funding streams, ensuring that they are servicing the needs of local people whilst remaining a financially viable charity. Whilst they no doubt make a positive impact, they often do not operate in a targeted space for a sustained period to truly make long-term community/personal development improvements.

Current Health and Well-Being Output

ACT currently delivers several health and well-being-themed sport development programmes that are funded through a diverse range of local and national partners. Like the aforementioned examples, ACT operating in a public health space is a relatively new concept, yet a space where they have adapted to meet local needs. Unlike the previous examples, ACT made this shift based upon local insight, instead of explicit public health funding being the driver. It is noteworthy the ACT has been influenced by a wider public health policy but is not *directly* funded by public health bodies, nationally or locally. The projects below are examples of ACT delivering health benefits to local people.

Active Through Football (ATF) is a five-year Sport England programme, funded by National Lottery and delivered by local partners on behalf of the Football Foundation. The project aims to engage key target audiences who face some of the greatest inequalities in being physically active. Using a 'place-based approach,' ATF aims to increase activity levels and create sustained behaviour change. Project outcomes aim to be achieved through a suite of recreational and informal small-sided football activities that have been developed through a community engagement process.

Nationally, delivery partners have the autonomy to design and deliver a project based on community needs (i.e., female underrepresentation, lack of disability provision, specific target groups including over-55s and ethnically diverse communities, etc). Within a local context, ACT has opted to deliver their project aligned specifically to the local public health strategy, Thrive Plymouth. Locally, ATF aims are to reduce the link between community deprivation and four key negative lifestyle behaviours: poor diet, lack of exercise, tobacco use and excessive alcohol consumption. These specific behaviours are prominent risk factors for four diseases (coronary heart disease, stroke, cancer and respiratory problems) which collectively account for 54% of all deaths in Plymouth. Aligning the five-year delivery plan to these public health issues reinforces an ACT commitment to the well-being of their local people and further signifies the synergy between the CCO's work and the public health agenda. ATF further highlights a willingness to diversify ACT's output in support of local strategic priorities and through relationships with local Public Health Officers who contribute to the ATF Steering Group.

Further work currently being delivered within a health, well-being and physical activity space includes '*Argyle Fans in Training*' and '*FIT Fans*,' both weight management and behaviour change programmes; '*It's a Goal*,' a mental health and physical activity support project; and '*Greens Social Prescribing*,' an exercise programme using green spaces and informal activity. Whilst each of these aligns explicitly to local and national health strategies, none received direct public health funding. Instead, this work is funded by a range of sources, all of which sit outside of the immediate public health landscape. Whilst it is widely recognised that ACT (and other CCOs) can add value within this field, it is often done through in-kind partnership support as opposed to direct funding, based on a mutual desire to improve community health. However, there remains a risk that should national policy/focus shift significantly, CCOs would be forced to decide about where to deploy available resources, how to meet funder/stakeholder targets and how long they can operate within a public health space without receiving financial support.

Conclusion

CCOs have a distinct ability to adapt their delivery output to remain in line with government policy and national trends. They too have a unique connection with local people that allows them to become significant influencers of community behaviour. As a result of both, CCOs tend to be a strong connector that sit somewhere between national policymakers and local communities. This in turn makes them an ideal facilitator of sport development programmes that focus on a diverse range of outcomes and impacts.

Like many of its counterparts, ACT has built robust links with the local community. Whilst the chapter illustrates the constantly changing nature of policy, CCOs are embedded within their communities and therefore offer relatively novel, practical and workable options for health improvement interventions with local priority population groups. CCOs have become a key focal point for both football and health-related organisations. The impact of football and health improvement continues to grow, yet the funding is fragile, and challenges CCOs face are complex. A greater understanding of the challenges related to the successful implementation of local programmes will be at the heart of the future viability of CCOs work in public health.

Whilst their ability to differentiate their delivery and deploy skilled staff internally to new programmes appears a strength, it could be argued as a weakness. CCOs are built upon strong relationships with local people who are often passionate about their brand, and therefore, there is often a highly emotive connection. Therefore, there is a risk that CCOs move dynamically to service local needs through a commitment to their communities and for the overall well-being at the expense of not being suitably funded for their contribution by relevant bodies. This appears evident within an ACT/public health context whereby project outcomes are being shaped around public health demands with no direct local authority funding being committed. There appears a risk that CCOs may be perceived and/or utilised as a credible 'first-responder' to community complexities, as opposed to receiving direct funds to become a strategic long-term solution. Considering the unique offer CCOs can provide and the credibility many already hold within their local authority, a stronger commitment to funding would only enhance their ability to reduce societal issues.

Acknowledgement

The authors would like to acknowledge the contribution of Paul Johnson whose critical practitioner's insights from the fields of sport development and public health helped to inform this chapter.

Notes

1 Individuals are viewed as policy entrepreneurs in the sense of their potential to maximize leverage at critical junctures in the policy process (Paredis & Block, 2013). Typically, senior practitioners working at strategic level and networked across the sector have the potential to engage in this way.
2 Street-level bureaucrats is a term used to articulate the behaviours of practitioners working at an operational level as they interpret and implement policy in ways which align with organizational capacity, available resources, individual interpretations of professional responsibility and operational limitations (Lipski, 2010; Belabas & Gerrits, 2017).
3 Health-related policy and practice have historically been located under a wide range of government departments. The UK government departments most directly engaged with health policy over the past 50 years have been:
  Department of Health and Social Security (1968–1988), Department of Health (1988–2018), Department of Health and Social Care (2018 to present).
4 UKHSA replaced Public Health England in 2021 as the Executive Agency of the DHSC responsible for public health protection relating to infectious diseases and a range of other threats (having the managerial and budgetary autonomy required to enable it to carry out executive functions of government). DHSC agencies and partner organisations (in England) also include NHS England, Care Quality Commission, National Institute for Health and Care Excellence, Health Education England and Health Research Authority. OHID was launched by government in 2021, to lead in development of strategies to improve health and well-being and to address health disparities. While linked to DHCS, it necessarily works across a number of government departments.
5 Walker and Hayton (2018) comment on the 'vast' and diverse range of third-sector organisations within the UK – typically including charitable trusts, social enterprises, mutual, civic associations, cooperatives, voluntary and community organisations, neighbourhood groups and advocacy networks. Sports organisations located within the myriad structures which sit between the state and the market include voluntary sports trusts (for example, those associated with professional football clubs), youth associations such as the YMCA, voluntary organisations providing for specific needs in communities (such as the Special Olympics) as well as education and development organisations (such as the Scout movement), independent sports trusts linked to businesses and public services, National Governing Bodies of sport and a multiplicity of voluntary grassroots sports clubs which are central to national sport and PA provision. Each grouping has its own particular challenges, limitations and strengths in relation to their capacity to deliver PA-based interventions for the purposes of public health.

References

Beacom, A., & Ziakas, V. (2022). Managing grassroots sport development: The role of UK active partnerships in policy implementation. In V. Ziakas (Ed.), *Trends and advances in sport and leisure management: Expanding the frontiers* (pp. 1–19). Cambridge Scholars.

Belabas, W., & Gerrits, L. (2017). Going the extra mile? How street-level bureaucrats deal with the integration of immigrants. *Social Policy and Administration, 51*(1), 133–150. https://doi.org/10.1111/spol.12184

Coalter, F. (2017). Sport and social inclusion: Evidence-based policy and practice. *Social Inclusion, 5*(2), 141–149. https://doi.org/10.17645/si.v5i2.852

Department for Children, Schools and Families. (2008). *Autumn performance report 2008: Progress against public service agreements.* https://assets.publishing.service.gov.uk/government/uploads/system/uploads/attachment_data/file/341270/autumn_performance_report_2008.pdf

Department for Culture Media and Sport. (2012). *Creating a sporting habit for life.* Department for Culture Media and Sport

Department for Culture Media and Sport. (2015). *Sporting future: A new strategy for an active nation.* Department for Culture Media and Sport

Department for Culture Media and Sport/Strategy Unit. (2002). *Game plan: A strategy for delivering Government's sport and physical activity objectives.* Department for Culture, Media & Sport/Strategy Unit

Department of Education. (2014). *PE and sport premium for primary schools.* https://www.gov.uk/guidance/pe-and-sport-premium-for-primary-schools

Department of Health. (1992). *Health of the nation: A strategy for health in England.* Department of Health.

Department of Health. (2004). *At least 5 a week: Evidence on the impact of physical activity and its relationship to health: A report from the chief medical officer.* https://webarchive.nationalarchives.gov.uk/ukgwa/20130107105354/http:/www.dh.gov.uk/prod_consum_dh/groups/dh_digitalassets/@dh/@en/documents/digitalasset/dh_4080981.pdf

Department of Health. (2005). *Department of health autumn performance report 2005.* https://assets.publishing.service.gov.uk/government/uploads/system/uploads/attachment_data/file/272208/6704.pdf

Department of Health. (2010). *Healthy lives, healthy people: Our strategy for public health in England.* The Stationery Office.

Department of Health. (2011). *Start active, stay active: Report on physical activity in the UK.* https://www.gov.uk/health-and-social-care/exercise-physical-activity

Department of Health. (2012). *Let's get moving; information for partners.* https://assets.publishing.service.gov.uk/government/uploads/system/uploads/attachment_data/file/216263/dh_133102.pdf

Department of Health/National Health Service. (2005). *Creating a patient led NHS–delivering the NHS improvement plan.* https://www.plymouth.ac.uk/uploads/production/document/path/1/1921/dh_4106507.pdf

Department of National Heritage. (1995). *Sport: Raising the game.* Department of National Heritage

Griffiths, P., Harris, R., & Ullman, R. (2005). *Self assessment of health and social care needs by older people: A multi-method systematic review of practices, accuracy, effectiveness and experience.* NCCSDO.

Hastings, A., Bailey, N., Bramley, G., Gannon, M., & Watkins, D. (2015). *The cost of the cuts: The impact on local government and poorer communities.* https://www.jrf.org.uk/sites/default/files/jrf/migrated/files/Summary-Final.pdf

Heath, S. (2014). *Local authorities' public health responsibilities (England).* House of Commons Library, SN06844. https://researchbriefings.files.parliament.uk/documents/SN06844/SN06844.pdf

Henry, I. P. (2001). *The politics of leisure policy* (2nd ed.). Palgrave.

Houlihan, B. (2005). Public sector sport policy: Developing a framework for analysis. *International Review for the Sociology of Sport, 40*(2), 163–185. https://doi.org/10.1177/1012690205057193

Houlihan, B., & White, A. (2002). *The politics of sports development: Development of sport or development through sport?*. Routledge

Kingdon, J. (1984). *Agendas, alternatives and public policies*. Little, Brown.

Lindsey, I. (2020). Analysing policy change and continuity: Physical education and school sport policy in England since 2010. *Sport, Education and Society, 25*(1), 27–42. https://doi.org/10.1080/13573322.2018.1547274

Lindsey, I., Metcalfe, S., Gemar, A., Alderman, J., & Armstrong, J. (2021). Simplistic policy, skewed consequences: Taking stock of English physical education, school sport and physical activity policy since 2013. *European Physical Education Review, 27*(2), 278–296. https://doi.org/10.1177/1356336X20939111

Lipsky, M. (2010). *Street-level bureaucracy: Dilemmas of the individual in public service* (30th Ann. Ed.). Russell Sage.

Marlier, M., Constandt, B., Schyvinck, C., De Bock, T., Winand, M., & Willem, A. (2020). Bridge over troubled water: Linking capacities of sport and non-sport organizations. *Social Inclusion, 8*(3), 139–151. https://doi.org/10.17645/si.v8i3.2465

Marmot, M., Allen, J., & Boyce, T. (2020). *Health equity in England: The Marmot review 10 years on: Health equity in England*. https://www.instituteofhealthequity.org/resources-reports/marmot-review-10-years-on/the-marmot-review-10-years-on-full-report.pdf

Marmot, M., Allen, J., & Goldblatt, P. (2010). *Fair society, healthy lives: The Marmot review executive summary*. https://www.instituteofhealthequity.org/resources-reports/fair-society-healthy-lives-the-marmot-review/fair-society-healthy-lives-exec-summary-pdf.pdf

McDonald, I. (2005). Theorising partnerships: Governance, communicative action and sport policy. *Journal of Social Policy, 34*(4), 579–600. https://doi.org/10.1017/S0047279405009165

Mitchell, G. (2020). Clear link between Covid-19 complications and obesity. *Nursing Times*. https://www.nursingtimes.net/news/research-and-innovation/clear-link-between-covid-19-complications-and-obesity-27-07-2020/

Moreland-Russell, S., Zwald, M., & Gilsinan, J. (2016). Use of policy theory in prevention policymaking. In A. E. Ayler & J. F. Chriqui (Eds.), *Prevention, policy, and public health* (pp. 41–66). https://doi.org/10.1093/med/9780190224653.003.0003

Murphy, R., Dugdill, L., & Crone, D. (2009). Physical activity, health and health promotion. In L. Dugdill, D. Crone, & R. Murphy (Eds.), *Physical activity and health promotion: Evidence-based approaches to practice* (pp. 3–20). Wiley Blackwell

NHS. (2021). *Strategic health authority*. https://www.datadictionary.nhs.uk/nhs_business_definitions/strategic_health_authority.html#ariaid-title2

National Institute for Health and Clinical Excellence (NICE). (2006). *Four commonly used methods to increase physical activity: Brief interventions in primary care, exercise referral schemes, pedometers and community-based exercise programmes for walking and cycling*. NICE.

National Institute for Health and Clinical Excellence (NICE). (2014). *Physical activity: Exercise referral schemes: Public health guideline [PH54]*. https://www.nice.org.uk/guidance/ph54/chapter/1-recommendations

Newman, J. (2001). *Modernising governance: New Labour, policy and society*. Sage.

ONS. (2020). *UK health accounts, healthcare expenditure, UK health accounts: 2018 2022*. https://www.ons.gov.uk/peoplepopulationandcommunity/healthandsocialcare/healthcaresystem/bulletins/ukhealthaccounts/2018

ONS. (2021). Healthcare expenditure, UK Health Accounts provisional estimates. https://www.ons.gov.uk/peoplepopulationandcommunity/healthandsocialcare/healthcaresystem/bulletins/healthcareexpenditureukhealthaccountsprovisionalestimates/2020

Paredis, E., & Block, T. (2013). The art of coupling: Multiple streams and policy entrepreneurship in Flemish transition processes. Research paper 1. Policy Research Centre, Ghent.

Phillpots, L. (2013). An analysis of the policy process for physical education and school sport: The rise and demise of school sport partnerships. *International Journal of Sport Policy and Politics, 5*(2), 193–211. https://doi.org/10.1080/19406940.2012.666558

Public Health England. (2019). *Public health strategy: 2020–2025 – Executive Summary*. Public Health England.

Robson, S., & McKenna, J. (2008). Sport and health. In P. Bramham, K. Hylton, & D. Jackson (Eds.), *Sports development: Policy, process and practice* (pp. 164–185). Routledge.

Smith, A., Jones, J., Houghton, L., & Duffell, T. (2016). A political spectator sport or policy priority? A review of sport, physical activity and public mental health policy. *International Journal of Sport Policy and Politics, 8*(4), 593–607. https://doi.org/10.1080/19406940.2016.1230554

Sport England. (2004). *The framework for sport in England*. Sport England.

Sport England. (2016a). *Tackling inactivity: What we know: Key insights from our get healthy get active pilots*. https://sportengland-production-files.s3.eu-west-2.amazonaws.com/s3fs-public/tackling-inactivity-what-we-know-full-report.pdf

Sport England. (2016b). *Applying behaviour change theories: Real world examples from the get healthy get active projects*. https://sportengland-production-files.s3.eu-west-2.amazonaws.com/s3fs-public/applying-behaviour-change-theories-real-world-examples-from-ghga.pdf

Sport England. (2021). *Active lives survey*. https://www.sportengland.org/know-your-audience/data/active-lives/active-lives-data-tables

The Centre for Workforce Intelligence (CfWI). (2014). *Mapping the core public health workforce: Final report*. The Centre for Workforce Intelligence. https://assets.publishing.service.gov.uk/government/uploads/system/uploads/attachment_data/file/507518/CfWI_Mapping_the_core_public_health_workforce.pdf

UK Government. (2018). *Health profile for England 2018 (Chapter 6, Wider Determinants of Health)*. https://www.gov.uk/government/publications/health-profile-for-england-2018/chapter-6-wider-determinants-of-health

Walker, C. M., & Hayton, J. W. (2018). An analysis of third sector sport organisations in an era of 'super-austerity'. *International Journal of Sport Policy and Politics, 10*(1), 43–61. https://doi.org/10.1080/19406940.2017.1374296

Wanless, D. (2002). *Securing our future health: Taking a long-term view* [Final report]. HM Treasury.

Wanless, D. (2004). *Securing good health for the whole population: Final report*. https://webarchive.nationalarchives.gov.uk/ukgwa/+/www.dh.gov.uk/en/Publicationsandstatistics/Publications/PublicationsPolicyAndGuidance/DH_407442

Weed, M. (2001). Towards a model of cross-sectoral policy development in leisure: The case of sport and tourism. *Leisure Studies*, *20*(2), 125–141. https://doi.org/10.1080/02614360110049931

WHO. (2008). *Commission on social determinants of health (CSDH): The final report of the commission: 'Closing the gap in a generation': Executive summary.* https://www.who.int/publications/i/item/WHO-IER-CSDH-08.1

Chapter 7

Implementation of Equality Policies

From Legislation to Lived Practices

Lauren Kamperman and A. J. Rankin-Wright

Introduction

Policy-driven attempts to tackle inequalities, discrimination and exclusion in sport have been a key feature of UK governance since the 'Sport for All' discourse in the 1970s. Mandatory requirements from equality legislation and wider awareness of inclusion in society have arguably strengthened the narrative of equality progress within UK sport organisations. However, huge disparities and inequalities still exist across the sporting landscape from grassroots participation to board leadership. As such, the actual engagement with and implementation of equality policy legislation into practice by sport organisations and national governing bodies (NGBs) has been a recurrent subject of debate (Shaw & Penny, 2003; Lusted, 2014; Spracklen et al., 2006; Turconi & Shaw, 2021). The narratives of the dominant policy makers and implementers regarding equality and inclusion have received some attention in the literature (see Turconi & Shaw, 2021; Rankin-Wright et al., 2016). However, the perspective of those working in key national equity agencies remains largely unexplored. Such national equity organisations include independent charities, such as Kick It Out, independent bodies and charities partnered with Sport England, such as Sporting Equals, Women in Sport and Activity Alliance, and charities that support equality policy and implementation in society (including sport), such as Disability Rights UK.

This chapter addresses these gaps and focuses on the implementation of national equality policies in UK sport broadly while also highlighting those working within sport institutions concerned with challenging the systemic processes and structures that sustain exclusionary power relations (Burdsey, 2014; Omi & Winant, 2002).

The first section of this chapter provides a brief history of sport equality policy in the UK, including key legislative developments and wider contextual influences that have focused sport equality policy discourses. The second section examines challenges, constraints and successes regarding the implementation of equality policy for UK sport under three themes, namely high performance versus inclusion, outcomes over processes and rhetoric versus real action. The final section offers some concluding thoughts and implications for practitioners.

DOI: 10.4324/9781003162728-7

Equality Policy/Legislation Development

As sport scholars have expounded (Houlihan & White, 2002; Hylton & Totten, 2013), sport became a public policy concern from the late 1960s with focus on encouraging and increasing participation, with a particular agenda to combat social exclusion through sport. The 1970s also represented a key point for the introduction and enactment of major statutes against sex and race discrimination in the UK (Dickens, 2007). Key legislation included: the Race Relations Act (first legislation in 1965, amended in 1976 and 2000), the Equal Pay Act (1970, fully implemented in 1975 and amended in 1983) and the Sex Discrimination Act (1975). Twenty years later, the Disability Discrimination Act (DDA) (1995, updated in 2004 and 2005) was finally enacted. Thus, to oversee these statutes, three equality organisations were established: the Commission for Race Equality (CRE), the Equal Opportunities Commission (EOC), and later, the Disability Rights Commission (DRC). The baton has since been passed in recent years to organisations working directly in sport, including Sporting Equals, Women in Sport and the Activity Alliance.

In the 1980s and 1990s, the equality agenda in sport largely focused on promoting women's representation, rights, and inclusion. The Women's Sport Foundation (now rebranded as Women in Sport) was founded in 1984 as the first charity to campaign for women's rights in sport. Women in Sport, along with the Sports Councils and the International Olympic Committee organised the first International Conference on Women and Sport in 1994. This led to the publication of the *Brighton Declaration on Women and Sport* (International Working Group on Women and Sport, 1994), which placed gender equity as a central agenda for sports organisations (Shaw, 2001) and was subsequently adopted by 200 countries.

During this time, several activist groups and some NGBs began to address racial equality in sport through anti-racism initiatives and campaigns (Long, 2000; Long & Spracklen, 2011). Examples included the Let's Kick Racism Out of Football (now known as Kick It Out) campaign, jointly launched in 1993 by the CRE and the Professional Footballers' Association (PFA), and the Tackle It campaign initiated by the Rugby Football League. Following recommendations from Sport England's Racial Advisory group, in 1998, the CRE in partnership with Sport England established 'Sporting Equals', a sports equity organisation established to promote racial equality in sport. For Sporting Equals, it was a logical move to re-write the CRE's standards for monitoring and evaluating racial equality for the sport context. The CRE standards had been primarily aimed at the public sector but were being applied indirectly to sport through local authorities for grassroots sports development (Hylton & Totten, 2013). With the backing of Sport England, Sporting Equals (2000) launched *Achieving Racial Equality: A Standard for Sport*, specifically for sports organisations and NGBs (Long & Spracklen, 2011). This document provided a tool to plan, develop and achieve racial equality, as well as evaluate progress against set levels of achievement. Crucially, evidence of achievement against the objectives of this standard was later linked by Sport England to continued funding of NGBs (Long & Spracklen, 2011). This led to every NGB funded by Sport England bar one achieving the preliminary level of the racial equality standard by the end of March 2003 (Spracklen, 2003).

From 1997, after a New Labour government was elected, a number of policy documents were published that linked sport to a broader policy rhetoric of social inclusion, equality and diversity (Long & Spracklen, 2011). Key equality policy documents from this time included, but were not limited to: *Making English Sport Inclusive: Equity guidelines for governing bodies* (Sport England, 2000), *A Sporting Future for All* (Department for Culture Media and Sport, 2000), and *The Equality Standard: A Framework for Sport* (Sports Council Equality Group, 2004, re-launched in 2012 and updated in 2014).

A Sporting Future for All (DCMS, 2000) formalised the mainstreaming of disability sport policy, a process started in 1989 (Minister for Sport Review Group, 1989), as there is no separate disability sport policy in the UK. This plan made the development and promotion of equity and inclusion a prerequisite for state funding, a trend that has since prevailed in subsequent strategies and codes for sport governance. However, studies have shown that incorporating disability sport into mainstream sport has not necessarily led to successful inclusive outcomes (Kitchin & Howe, 2014; Thomas & Guett, 2014). In the UK, disabled people are the biggest underrepresented group when it comes to sport participation, with 41% of disabled people not participating in sport compared to 20% of non-disabled people (Sport England, 2019a). Established in 1998, the Activity Alliance (formerly the English Federation of Disability Sport) drives and supports the inclusion of disabled people in sport, alongside Disability Rights UK. Focused on getting more disabled people active, they deliver the Get Out Get Active Campaign as well as many other projects, programmes and trainings around the inclusion of disabled people and tackling ableism in sport and leisure.[1]

With the launch of *The Equality Standard: A Framework for Sport* in 2004, a shift towards an integrated and intersectional approach to equality was signalled (Sports Council Equality Group, 2012). The Standard provided some standardisation for NGBs and sports organisations in providing key definitions of terms, such as equality: 'the state of being equal – treating individuals equally which is not necessarily treating people the same' (Sports Council Equality Group, 2014, p. 6). The purpose of this equality framework was to support NGBs and organisations to develop structures and processes to become more equitable in organisational and service development. Performance was assessed against four levels: foundation, preliminary, intermediate and advanced (Shaw, 2007). As an impetus for NGBs to engage with this standard, key sport funding organisations (Sport England and UK Sport) set measurable targets linked to the achievement of the various levels of *The Equality Standard*.

The establishment of the Equality and Human Rights Commission (EHRC) in 2007 marked a shift from single-issue politics to an overarching approach to equality, as the commission which subsumed the three previous separate equality bodies. This along with a single Equality Act, introduced initially in 2006 and then rewritten in 2010 (see Gedalof, 2013), replaced the numerous discrimination statutes, regulations, and orders (Dickens, 2007) and enforced 'equality' as a public duty by law within publicly funded organisations across sectors.[2] Within several NGBs, *The Equality Standard*, along with the equality statutory legislation documented in the Equality Act (*Equality Act 2006, C.3*; *Equality Act 2010, C.15*), had a major impact in terms of updating policies and documents to ensure that they were compliant within the new legal framework. This standard was re-launched in 2012 and is now the longest-standing effort by the combined UK Sports Councils to address inequality in sport and a range of factors that impact upon inclusion/exclusion (Turconi & Shaw, 2021). *The Equality Standard* identified the following protected characteristics: age, disability, gender reassignment, marriage and civil partnership, pregnancy and maternity, race, religion or belief, sex and sexual orientation, with the addition of political opinion and dependents for Northern Ireland only (Sports Council Equality Group, 2012).

Following a few years of grappling with *The Equality Standard* as well as celebrating accomplishments at the 2012 Olympic Games in London, the UK government's *Sporting Future: A New Strategy for an Active Nation* was published which placed renewed focus on getting more of the population active and addressing lack of diversity, especially in sport leadership (Department for Culture, Media, and Sport, 2015). This led to UK Sport (2016) establishing *A Code for Sports Governance*, which outlined standards of governance for organisations seeking (and those in receipt of) funding from UK government and National Lottery funding from UK Sport and/or Sport England. Since its launch, this code has been applied to more than 4,000 organisations ranging from national charities down to grassroots organisations.

Recent Influences and Current Landscape of British Sport Policy

The year 2020 marked a moment rife with turmoil as the world grappled with the Covid-19 pandemic, which seemed to exacerbate and bring forward ongoing societal issues in the western world (e.g. cost of living crisis, police brutality, racial inequalities and injustices). Perhaps the most prominent and influential movement during this time was Black Lives Matter (BLM). Starting in the United States in 2013, BLM is a social movement focused on affirming the lives of black people and combating systemic racism and acts of violence against the black community. BLM had a resurgence in May of 2020 after the death of George Floyd at the hands of a police officer in Minneapolis. Across the world, individuals as well as many organisations chose to respond to the movement with messages of support and pledges online. Internationally, sporting athletes showed their activism through kneeling before competitions, wearing BLM slogans on their clothing, and showing solidarity on their social media accounts (The Guardian, 2020). Athletes in the UK took note from their US counterparts and began to 'take a knee' on their respective playing fields before competitions (Premier League Football News, 2020). While the BLM movement sparked much-needed conversation around the lived experiences of black people in white-majority nations, activists and advocates quickly critiqued what they claimed to be performative activism instead of the necessary investment and real action into the cause (Jenkins, 2020; Kalina, 2020; Malone Kircher, 2020).

Extending beyond the social sphere, BLM had an influence in UK sport policy and practice. First, the Sports Minister decided to review the Sports Governance Code, previously set in 2016 (Sky Sports, 2020). Following this announcement, the Sport and Recreation Alliance initiated a pledge to commit to tackling inequality, which had over 120 signatures from sport and recreation organisations across the UK. This pledge stated that 'it is time to confront racism and inequality' and that 'systemic change must be made at all levels' (Sport and Recreation Alliance, 2020). Organisations like Sport England made their own individual pledges to commit to increasing diversity (Sport England, 2020). In response to these pledges, Sporting Equals (2022) created the Race Representation Index (RRI) to hold organisations accountable and to monitor progress, as there were critiques that many of these pledges and messages were performative, reactionary, and didn't equate to real commitment to structural change (Evans et al., 2020; Hylton, 2020). The RRI scores the progress made by sports bodies on policy and strategy, workforce, coaching and elite talent profile. The Sport Monitoring Advisory Panel, also launched by Sporting Equals, oversaw the RRI and published the inaugural results in March 2022. Additional responses to BLM and the need to challenge racism in the sport sector include Sporting Equals' Race Equality Charter (2020) and the Tackling Racism and Racial Inequality in Sport Review (Shibli et al., 2021).

Lastly, the Covid-19 pandemic led to England/the UK having to 'lock down' and impose restrictions on access to sport and physical activity for many months during 2020 and 2021. This pause in play led many sport organisations to adopt new strategies and equality, diversity and inclusion (EDI) plans to combat surging inactivity (due to pandemic) as well as the systemic and intersectional inequalities raised during this time and also conversations sparked by BLM. Sport England unveiled their *Uniting the Movement: 10-year strategy for 2021-31*, which initially came with a one-year implementation plan until March 2022, due to the lockdowns. The strategy's key mission involves 'tackling inequalities' and highlights the need to better support disabled people, lower socio-economic groups, women, and people from Asian and Black backgrounds (Sport England, 2021). Following suit, UK Sport (2021) announced their new EDI strategy for 2021-2025, *The power of our differences*, which was drawn from their new strategic plan. At the heart of this EDI action plan are four priority areas: (i) power a more diverse and inclusive team that delivers more diverse champions, (ii) increase the diversity of leadership on national and international sporting bodies, (iii) promote and embed inclusion across UK Sport's programmes and (iv) drive the EDI agenda with accountability (UK Sport, 2021).

The UK sport sector is working towards progress around diversity and inclusion, as shown in recent policies and initiatives. However, it is clear that there is tension between rhetoric and reality of such pledges and plans. The next section outlines some of the key challenges and constraints of such work.

Equality Policy to Equality in Practice: Challenges, Constraints and Successes

In her article 'The language of diversity,' Ahmed (2007, p. 249) makes a valid point in distinguishing between those organisations which value diversity and those which are committed to diversity. Ahmed argues that claiming to value or aspire to diversity, through legislation, for example, acts only as a 'lip-service' model if the claim or aspiration is not followed through with action or by the re-allocation of resources to enable action. The same can be argued of equality legislation; as Long et al. (2005, p. 47) state: 'a measure of a policy's true worth is in how it is put into practice.' The often gestural nature of commitment statements in equality policy documents have been described as 'non-performative' defined as the 'reiterative and citational practice by which discourse *does not produce* the effects that it names' (Ahmed, 2012, p. 117). In sport, Lusted (2014, p. 85) has described this wide-ranging commitment to implementing policy as follows:

> At one end, achieving non-compulsory 'Standards' (such as The UK Equality Standard) can require the submission and external evaluation of extensive portfolios of evidence. At the other end, very general position statements on websites and 'cut-and-paste' codes of conduct in local club documentation provide what Horne (1995) calls a basic 'gestural' commitment.

In understanding policy as both text and discourse, it is also important to highlight that policies are ultimately 'constructed within a particular social, political, and historical context and prevailing lines of power' (Walker, 1997, p. 41). Thus, they bring with them an 'interpretational and representational history' (Ball, 1993, p. 11). Traditionally, the development, representation, implementation and reporting of equality policies have given preference to discourses that exemplify dominant groups' interests, statuses and positions of power. Lusted (2014, p. 87) describes progress towards equality as 'patchy,' and other researchers claim that well-intended equality policies fall short of their desired outcomes due to piecemeal implementation and competing priorities (Shaw & Penney, 2003).

The following sections examine key challenges and constraints to equality policy implementation. These are discussed under three headings: (1) high performance versus inclusion, (2) outcomes over processes and (3) rhetoric versus real action.

1. High Performance versus Inclusion

Rankin-Wright (2015) has previously likened the constant state of flux, inconsistent funding and policy implementation tensions for those attempting to drive equality and diversity work within sport as a constant '*tug of war*' and '*uphill battle*'. Despite being pushed to achieve equality and inclusion targets, funding and organisational priorities for key funders, aligned to high-performance success, have been a significant and often prohibitive challenge for those implementing equality strategies.

When the UK won the bid to host the 2012 Olympics and Paralympics, the priority and funding for winning medals was reinforced. This desire for medal success created a remit within UK sport organisations and Olympic-funded sports for medal achievements, rather than diversity of participants and inclusion agendas. Some organisations took the view that equality work was neither seen as compatible nor relevant for the high-performance discourse (Rankin-Wright, 2015). Green (2007) noted that because of the dependence of NGBs on their external funding grants and government resources, there has been little, if any, resistance to the high-performance drive. The pursuit of the high-performance discourse, and resulting funding cuts for other peripheral objectives, such as equality, highlighted the fragility of directive funding models with changing priorities (Bury, 2015; Shaw & Frisby, 2006).

Additionally, many past equality policies have failed to recognise the harsh reality that sport did not reflect the diversity of British society (Hylton & Totten, 2001). This remains the case today, as Team GB especially is criticised for its lack of diversity (Sutton Trust, 2012; McElwee, 2020; Topping, 2021). Critiques show that elite athletes (representing Team GB) do not reflect the larger national population in regard to education level, race/ethnicity and socio-economic background. Furthermore, historically Team GB's most successful sports are the ones with the most funding and the lowest levels of diversity. If the top of the talent pathway is struggling with diversity and many sports are playing down reports of exclusive cultures and athlete abuse (Roan, 2017a, 2017b; Martin, 2020; Scott, 2020a; Whyte, 2021), what does that say for the grassroots level of sport participation?

While recent policy places the onus on the talent pathway and international medals, equality targets and aspirations are pushed to the side. In particular, the 'no compromise' funding framework has led to this trend of prioritising medals over other agendas. This policy has been detrimental to many organisations as they fear loss of funding on top of pressure to meet other standards set out by UK Sport or Sport England (Bostock et al., 2018). While UK Sport claims to be softening their approach to the 'no compromise' policy by changing their funding strategy leading into Paris 2024 (Scott, 2020b), it remains to be seen if the pressure to win medals continues to make inclusion efforts difficult or if these changes to funding alleviate some of that strain and allow NGBs to spend more time fostering an inclusive culture.

2. Outcomes over Processes

A key shift in the understanding of 'equality' in UK sport policy came with the update to *The Equality Standard* where the former definition of equality as *opportunity* in 2004 changed to defining equality as *outcome* in 2012. Turconi and Shaw (2021) believe that this definition of equality as *outcome* makes the achievement of equality unlikely. Research has critiqued audit-based approaches to policy development and implementation that conceptualise and measure a social justice aim such as equality, as a 'tangible' outcome. As Shaw (2007; Turconi & Shaw, 2021) noted, achievement of the first two levels of *The Equality Standard* requires the development of an equality policy and action plan with no evidence required of any change to the organisation or its service provision. Consequently, many organisations have reached the preliminary levels but have failed to implement any change beyond this basic rhetorical commitment (Lusted, 2014). Research has been critical of this focus on equality *outcomes* rather than *processes*, as it fails to 'encourage organisations to be reflective on their history and culture and to promote organisational involvement in creating equality policies' (Dwight & Biscomb, 2018, p.171). As a result, sport organisations and NGBs may just pay lip service to required objectives without regard for the structures, cultures and processes by which outcomes can be achieved (Shaw, 2007; Spracklen et al., 2006). Shaw (2007, p. 426) has further argued that such an approach 'ignores the complex power and political relations that are inherent in considering the intersectionality of marginalised and under-represented groups.'

Currently, there is top-down pressure for NGBs to meet diversity targets in their sport governance. This outcome-based approach to more equality in leadership seems to be an easy way to increase diversity, but stakeholders and researchers alike recognise the struggles of this process and the difficulties around implementing or driving change from these targets. Focusing on gender in particular, Sport England began setting gender governance targets in 2012, stating that NGBs funded by them needed to have at least 25% female representation on their boards by 2017 (increased to 30% in the 2016 *Code for Sport Governance*). Despite the short-term success of some organisations reaching the target numbers, neither meeting these targets nor other statistics show a complete picture of gender equity (Piggot, 2022). While board numbers may sometimes look equitable in terms of gender, additional senior roles (e.g. CEO, President) at the same organisations do not reflect that gender representation (Piggot & Matthews, 2021), and numbers are bleaker when looking at the severe lack of minority group representation (e.g. Black, Asian, minority ethnic communities, disabled) across both men and women in leadership positions (Sport England & UK Sport, 2019). Furthermore, when NGBs fail to meet these set targets for their boards, no sanctions were applied (Rumbsy, 2020).

Piggot (2022) argues that while top-down targets 'are important steps forward' they 'do not go far enough in transforming deep-rooted gender power relations across all leadership hierarchies within sport governance' (p. 252). While targets or quotas may be a good first step, they do not solve or change exclusionary cultures where people who are different from the norm are tokenised or ignored. Piggot's (2022) recent study of two English NGBs, governing two of the oldest modern sports in England, England Golf and the Lawn Tennis Association, revealed the complexities around the reproduction, resistance and evolution of gendered recruitment and selection processes in English sport governance. Piggot (2022) argues that achieving gender equality within the governance of two organisations that have historically been found to have resistance to change from the dominant men in power is a 'complex process that requires transformational change of long-standing, deep-rooted organizational habitus' (p. 255). Thus, equality or indeed inclusion cannot be attained through mere targets or statistical outcomes, but instead must be approached as an ongoing process of commitment to change.

3. Rhetoric versus Real Action

Policy language is paramount when discussing equality, but current language used by UK sport organisations across all levels is inconsistent and unclear. Equality is often conflated with equity and inclusion, with inclusion now being the most common term used to discuss action plans around equality policy. Most sport organisations use vague and aspirational terminology with no explanations for what they mean by inclusion (see Sport England & UK Sport, 2019; Sport England, 2019b). If inclusion isn't clearly defined, how can it be achieved or assessed?

In sport literature, inclusion is most often interpreted as an equal opportunity to participate (Kiuppis, 2018; Misener & Darcy, 2014; Valet, 2018), despite the shift in sport policy interpreting equality as an outcome (as discussed above). Boiling inclusion down this way assumes that people have a choice to participate or not, as though sport or physical activity is a right and equally accessible to all. But the reality on the ground is that barriers exist for many groups; they cannot simply show up and gain access. This is especially the case for disabled people trying to access sport.

Inclusion is rarely, if ever, defined in policies (Promis et al., 2001) or in the sector at large (Collins, 1997; Spaaij et al., 2018; Thomas, 2004). Christiaens and Brittain (2021) believe that there is an implied assumption that people automatically know what inclusion means when they are confronted with the term. This assumption then allows freedom of interpretation of 'inclusion' which may affect how equality policy, especially the mainstreaming of disability sport provision, is interpreted. Disabled people, in particular, may have varied experiences across the sport sector due to the lack of clarity around what 'inclusion' means (Christiaens & Brittain, 2021). When disability inclusion requires accessibility (Parnell et al., 2017), too often accessibility is reactionary and not the standard.

It has been argued that policy commitment, such as NGBs taking a leading role in delivering sport opportunities for disabled people, is largely rhetorical and based upon vague and poorly developed rationales (Thomas & Guett, 2014). In sport strategy documents, the 'need' for diversity and inclusion is mentioned but specifics around how disabled people will be included are lacking. When Christiaens and Brittain (2021) asked a Sport England representative to explain what inclusion means in relation to disabled people, she said that their inclusion means 'disabled people are going to take part in sport in a mainstream environment, in a non-disabled environment.' Inclusion, in this instance, means that disabled people are incorporated into non-disabled sport structures. While there are other ways that inclusion strategies are implemented (see Christiaens & Brittain, 2021), it is uncommon for disabled people to be given a choice in how they are included. Given that recent reports (Activity Alliance & IFF Research, 2022) reveal that less than three in ten disabled people feel encouraged to return to physical activity after the pandemic, it is vital that sport organisations engage more directly with disabled people around disability provision.

Concluding Thoughts and Practitioner Implications

While the efforts and evolutions of equality sport policy are apparent, the challenges discussed above make it difficult for NGBs to meet equality standards and inclusion goals. There remains a critical need for equality policy to go beyond a compliance approach (i.e. audit or outcome-based) and towards a process-oriented approach where there is a firm commitment to change. Inclusion efforts must expand past setting board member targets and lip service pledges and instead work must involve structural and strategic change. Hopeful and aspirational rhetoric in existing diversity action plans needs to be coupled with real action and clear plans for change (e.g. mandatory targets, restructuring of policies and practices, periodic reviews of progress). Additionally, equality sport policy must involve accountability measures and consequences when organisations do not show progress of such change.

The UK sport sector is diversifying in theory, with the inclusion efforts and diversity action plans discussed above, and thus will increase the talent pool. While the widening talent pathway means there will be more opportunities for medals to feed the high-performance drive, it also means that staff and stakeholders in the system need to be ready to support these new athletes. Best practice trainings around inclusion, cultural competency and unconscious bias would help upskill practitioners and staff to meet the moment and to best support and serve the new wave of talent in UK sport. National equity organisations like Sporting Equals and Activity Alliance have already developed similar trainings and resources, related to their focused communities, that can be readily accessed to help NGBs with this work.

Inclusive leadership is needed from the top of the talent pathway for a complete buy-in of equality and inclusion that echoes throughout all levels of sport and across all sport disciplines. Action is also needed at the grassroots level where athletes begin their sporting journeys. This structural change may involve reconsidering how talent is identified and supported, diversifying all levels of staff, identifying and removing barriers to participation, and outreach to communities that historically have not participated in particular sports. Equality and inclusion can be a collaborative effort, ensuring that the perspectives, experiences and needs of people currently outside the system are heard and met.

PRACTITIONER REFLECTION AND INSIGHTS

Kirsty Clarke, Director for Innovation and Business Development at Activity Alliance

Activity Alliance is the leading voice for disabled people in sport and activity. Formerly known as the English Federation of Disability Sport and founded more than 20 years ago, we are focused on enabling more disabled people to enjoy the benefits of sport and active recreation. Despite targeted interventions over the decades, disabled people remain one of the least active groups in society (Sport England, 2022). Disabled people are almost twice as likely to be inactive as non-disabled people (https://activelives.sporteng-land.org/ showing the respective proportions of inactive people being 42.4% compared to 22.6% in November 2021). Our aim is to close this gap and achieve fairness for disabled people in sport and activity within a generation.

It is this difference between disabled people's and non-disabled people's inactivity levels that we refer to as the 'fairness gap.' We know that by focusing our efforts on embedding inclusive practice into organisations across the sector and beyond and by changing attitudes towards disabled people's sport and activity, we can close this fairness gap within a generation. With one in five of the population considering themselves a disabled person, such a large proportion of our society cannot be ignored or forgotten. Every disabled child and adult deserves the right to be as active as they want to be.

Our approach to achieving fairness is insight-led, as we draw from our own sector-leading research and insight alongside that of others to drive targeted interventions. We share this insight with our sector partners, empowering them to make the best decisions about how to increase and improve the engagement and opportunities for disabled people within their sports and physical activity. In addition, we use this insight to inform the nature of the partnerships that we develop to maximise our reach and influence. Crucially, through our Get Out Get Active (GOGA) programme, we have a platform to continually test this insight and see the role it plays in direct delivery. Having the ability to offer practical application to our insight through GOGA enables us to keep learning but also aggregate our understanding and impact thus informing policy alongside practice.

The application of the social model of disability underpins our work, and as a membership organisation we have a representative voice advocating for fairness in sport and activity across the sector. Our expansive mix of inclusion expertise alongside insight from disabled people's lived experiences drives our work collectively. We champion and base our delivery on a person-centred approach (Activity Alliance, 2020). This means embracing intersectionality to shape better practices to engage the very least active and encourage the use of inclusion principles. With a focus on tackling inequalities, disabled people are part of all other groups with protected characteristics and/or who are underrepresented in sport and activity. It is therefore crucial to ensure an intersectional approach to inclusion is at the heart of any delivery.

When considering the role of Activity Alliance within the sector but also exploring the ways in which policies aimed at tackling inequalities influence delivery, it is important to acknowledge the ways in which the landscapes of sports policy intertwine. As the then English Federation for Disability Sport, we welcomed the 2015 strategic shift in the cross-government strategy of *Sporting Future – A New Strategy for an Active Nation*. The outcome-focused approach had greater alignment to our own objectives, explicitly targeting the less active population along with the broader agenda of activity beyond just sport. The broader focus is especially important as we know that the first steps into activity bring the most significant health benefits. Not every disabled person aspires to be a Paralympian, and a genuine sense of inclusion is required across all elements of the sport and physical activity ecosystem. In acknowledging the important role that being active has to play across the population and securing cross-departmental commitment, the *Sporting Future* strategy set a positive tone.

In many cases, for disabled people to truly engage in sport and activity, there is a greater reliance on other government departments and key policy decisions to support their participation. For example, ensuring that transport links (often public transport) are feasible, appropriate and affordable and making sure that healthcare professionals can advise and actively encourage activity. There needs to be a skilled, competent and confident workforce, so people feel safe when taking part. We also need to ensure all young people have a positive experience of activity from a young age at school.

Importantly, we also need to reduce disabled people's anxiety caused by the fear that being active will be detrimental to their benefits. Our 2018 research, *The Activity Trap* (Activity Alliance, 2018), explored disabled people's fear of being active. Almost half (47%) are fearful of losing their benefits if they are seen to be more active. More than half (55%) said they were likely to be more active if benefits weren't at risk of being taken away. These areas are still creating significant barriers to disabled people's sport and activity levels. It is clear that working across government departments is vital for the successful delivery of any strategy that aims to increase participation levels for the least active.

Unfortunately, in delivering against the strategy, it has often felt that the real-time policy decisions that could positively impact upon the challenges noted above and that would require genuine cross-departmental working haven't necessarily come to fruition. We cannot emphasise enough the need for dynamic, committed and engaging partnership working to create the very best environments and opportunities to enable the least active, particularly disabled people. Our GOGA programme offers examples of these partnerships at a local level and demonstrates the positive outcomes of local delivery, co-production and having the right partners around the table. To shift towards a national policy context which enables the best decisions making, the right bodies must be involved to inform those decisions.

Our research has continued to highlight the importance of working closely with others, for example the health sector. We will continue to strengthen our engagement with the health sector after our Annual Survey showed that 78% of disabled people say their impairment or health condition stops them from being active. While this is linked to a lack of availability or awareness of suitable activities, it also reflects individual worries about safety and risk. This is despite clear evidence on the benefits of activity for disabled people and those with health conditions, and with healthcare professionals being cited as the most trusted individuals (GPs, doctors or nurses 64% and physios, occupational therapists and other medical professionals 53%) when it comes to disabled people making decisions about their participation (Activity Alliance, 2022).

More recently, we have welcomed Sport England's (2021) *Uniting the Movement* strategy, particularly the unequivocal focus on tackling inequalities. In addition, we welcome the acknowledgement of the challenges of the post-Covid environment, especially when considering the disproportionate impact that the pandemic has had on disabled people. However, as we look forward to delivering against this strategy, we continue to highlight what the last 20 years of well-informed delivery has taught us. Truly tackling inequalities and driving inclusion means embracing an intersectional approach. While the application of a mix of bespoke engagement skills, understanding, lived experiences and delivery methods is required, a person-centred approach is key. Ensuring inclusion allows sport and physical activity to reflect on changing stages in an individual's life journey, which influences their own identity, behaviour and, ultimately, how and with whom they wish to be active.

Embedding inclusion principles is unlikely to be attached to quota-based systems or having a single point of legislative action. Instead, it needs strategic engagement, appropriate levels of expert support and crucially an innate willingness from leadership to acknowledge that tackling inequalities is non-negotiable. This is particularly the case for disabled people, who are part of every community. Instead, previous approaches to increasing sport and activity among the least active have focused on specific characteristics and/or demographics. This has led to a mixed picture in outcomes. For example, interventions targeting low socio-economic groups may fail to acknowledge the needs of disabled people within that group. But we know that four million disabled people in the UK live in poverty. They are more than twice as likely to be in poverty than non-disabled adults (Office for National Statistics, 2021). Disabled people from lower socio-economic groups are much more likely to be physically inactive than disabled people from higher socio-economic groups (44.7% vs 29.8% as per https://activelives.sportengland.org/ November 2021). It is important that the current proposition to tackle inequalities does just that with more holistic and inclusive approaches.

It is important to also emphasise the need for strategic partnership working and engagement in order to impact positively. Enhancing the ability of key funders to see the best route to supporting disabled people to become active and make strategic decisions about targeted investment is key. While there is positivity in increasing the range of investments and subsequently funded bodies across the sector, it remains crucial to understand the roles of each of these organisations. Actively encouraging coordinated collective action to support fellow organisations, and the sector more broadly, to navigate how to include disabled people is critical, as opposed to having a multitude of agencies funded to deliver very similar services.

Ultimately, sport and physical activity's power to change lives cannot continue to be a marginalised interest area in government policy. Disabled people's equal access to activity must have broader merit and a central place within the wider discussions concerning civil society and inclusion, across agendas such as those for public health, employment and welfare, health, transport, social justice and education.

Notes

1 Ableism is the discrimination of and social prejudice against people with disabilities based on the belief that typical abilities are superior. Ableism is discrimination in favour of able-bodied people.
2 Government departments and ministers, educational bodies, the NHS, the armed forces, local authorities, the police and the information commissioner.

References

Activity Alliance. (2018) (rep.). *The activity trap*. https://www.activityalliance.org.uk/how-we-help/research/the-activity-trap
Activity Alliance. (2020) (rep.). *Inclusive activity: Taking a person-centred approach.* https://www.activityalliance.org.uk/how-we-help/resources/5856-inclusive-activity-taking-a-personcentred-approach
Activity Alliance & IFF Research. (2022) (rep.). *Annual disability and activity survey 2021–22.* https://www.activityalliance.org.uk/how-we-help/research/7236-activity-alliance-annual-disability-and-activity-survey-june-2022
Ahmed, S. (2007). The language of diversity. *Ethnic and Racial Studies, 30*(2), 235–256. https://doi.org/10.1080/01419870601143927
Ahmed, S. (2012). *On being included: Racism and diversity in institutional life.* Duke University Press.
Ball, S. J. (1993). What is policy? Texts, trajectories, and toolboxes. *Discourse, 13*(2), 10–17. https://doi.org/10.1080/0159630930130203
Bostock, J., Crowther, P., Ridley-Duff, R., & Breese, R. (2018). No plan B: The Achilles heel of high performance sport management. *European Sport Management Quarterly, 18*(1), 25–46. https://doi.org/10.1080/16184742.2017.1364553
Burdsey, D. (2014). One week in October: Luis Suarez, John Terry and the turn to racial neoliberalism in English men's professional football. *Identities, 21*(5), 429–447. https://doi.org/10.1080/1070289X.2014.924415
Bury, J. (2015). Non-performing inclusion: A critique of the English Football Association's Action Plan on homophobia in football. *International Review for the Sociology of Sport, 50*(2), 211–226.

Christiaens, M., & Brittain, I. (2021). The complexities of implementing inclusion policies for disabled people in UK non-disabled voluntary community sports clubs. *European Sport Management Quarterly*. https://doi.org/10.1080/16184742.2021.1955942

Collins, D. (1997). *Conference report: National disability sport conference*. Kings Fund Centre.

Department for Culture Media and Sport. (2000). *A sporting future for all*. DCMS.

Department for Culture Media and Sport. (2015). *Sporting future: A new strategy for an active nation*. Department for Culture Media and Sport.

Dickens, L. (2007). The road is long: Thirty years of equality legislation in Britain. *British Journal of Industrial Relations*, *45*(3), 463–494. https://doi.org/10.1111/j.1467-8543.2007.00624.x

Dwight, A., & Biscomb, K. (2018). Ten years of the UK's Equality Standard for Sport. *European Journal for Sport and Society*, *15*(2), 171–188. https://doi.org/10.1080/16138171.2018.1458181

Equal Pay Act 1970, c. 41. Retrieved from https://www.legislation.gov.uk/ukpga/1970/41/enacted

Evans, A. B., Agergaard, S., Campbell, P. I., Hylton, K., & Lenneis, V. (2020). 'Black lives matter': Sport, race and ethnicity in challenging times. *European Journal for Sport and Society*, *17*(4), 0.289–.300. https://doi.org/10.1080/16138171.2020.1833499

Gedalof, I. (2013). Sameness and difference in government equality talk. *Ethnic and Racial Studies*, *36*(1), 117–135. https://doi.org/10.1080/01419870.2011.644310

Green, M. (2007). Olympic glory or grassroots development?: Sport policy priorities in Australia, Canada and the United Kingdom, 1960–2006. *International Journal of the History of Sport*, *24*(7), 921–953.https://doi.org/10.1080/09523360701311810

Horne, J. (1995). Local authority black and ethnic minority provision in Scotland. In M. Talbot, S. Fleming, & A. Tomlinson (Eds.), *Policy and politics in sport, physical education and leisure* (pp. 159–176). Moray House Institute/Heriot-Watt University, LSA Pub. 95.

Houlihan, B., & White, A. (2002). *The politics of sports development*. Routledge.

Hylton, K. (2020). Black lives matter in sport …? *Equality, Diversity and Inclusion*, *40*(1), 41–48. https://doi.org/10.1108/EDI-07-2020-0185

International Working Group on Women and Sport. (1994). *Brighton declaration on women and sport*. Auckland, New Zealand.

Jenkins, J. (2020). The blurred lines between genuine allyship and performative activism. *Yale News*, Yale Daily News Publishing Co., Inc., November 12. https://yaledailynews.com/blog/2020/11/12/the-blurred-lines-between-genuine-allyship-and-performative-activism/

Kalina, P. (2020). Performative allyship. *Technium Social Sciences Journal*, *11*, 478–481. https://doi.org/10.47577/tssj.v11i1.1518

Kitchin, P., & Howe, D. (2014). The mainstreaming of disability cricket in England and Wales: Integration 'One game' at a time. *Sport Management Review*, *17*(1), 65–77. https://doi.org/10.1016/j.smr.2013.05.003

Long, J. (2000). No racism here? A preliminary examination of sporting innocence. *Managing Leisure*, *5*(3), 121–133. https://doi.org/10.1080/13606710050084829

Long, J., Robinson, P., & Spracklen, K. (2005). Promoting racial equality within sports organizations. *Journal of Sport and Social Issues*, *29*(1), 41–59. https://doi.org/10.1177/0193723504269883

Implementation of Equality Policies   131

Long, J., & Spracklen, K. (2011). Positioning anti-racism in sport. In J. Long & K. Spracklen (Eds.), *Sport and challenges to racism* (pp. 3–18). Palgrave Macmillan.

Lusted, J. (2014). Equality policies in sport: Carrots, sticks and a retreat from the radical. *Journal of Policy Research in Tourism, Leisure and Events, 6*(1), 85–90. https://doi.org/10.1080/19407963.2013.822461

Malone Kircher, M. (2020). Your black square Instagram isn't helping. *Vulture.* https://www.vulture.com/2020/06/dont-use-black-lives-matter-on-blackout-tuesday-instagrams.html

Martin, A. (2020). Yorkshire investigate 'institutional racism' claims made by Azeem Rafiq. *The Guardian,* September 3. https://www.theguardian.com/sport/2020/sep/03/azeem-rafiq-yorkshire-cricket-club-institutionally-racist

Minister for Sport Review Group. (1989). *Building on ability: Sport for people with disabilities.* HMSO.

McElwee, M. (2020). Over half of British Olympic and Paralympic teams at Rio 2016 fielded only white athletes, report shows. *The Telegraph,* July 5. https://www.telegraph.co.uk/olympics/2020/07/05/half-british-olympic-paralympic-teams-rio-2016-fielded-white/

Office for National Statistics. (2021). *Family resources survey: Financial year 2019 to 2020.* Department of Work and Pensions.

Omi, M., & Winant, H. (2002). Racial formation. In P. Essed & D. T. Goldberg (Eds.), *Race critical theories* (pp. 123–145). Blackwell.

Piggott, L., & Matthews, J. (2021). Gender, leadership, and governance in English national governing bodies of sport: Formal structures, rules, and processes. *Journal of Sport Management, 35*(4), 338–351. https://doi.org/10.1123/jsm.2020-0173

Piggott, L. V. (2022). "You only go from what you know": The reproduction, resistance and evolution of gendered recruitment and selection processes in English sport governance. *European Journal for Sport and Society, 19*(3), 250–269. https://doi.org/10.1123/jsm.2020-0173

Rankin-Wright, A. J. (2015). *Racial and gender equality and diversity in sport coaching in the United Kingdom.* Leeds Beckett University Doctor of Philosophy.

Rankin-Wright, A. J., Hylton, K., & Norman, L. (2016). Off-colour landscape: Framing race equality in sport coaching. *Sociology of Sport Journal, 33*(4), 357–368. https://doi.org/10.1123/ssj.2015-0174

Roan, D. (2017a). British Swimming apologises for 'climate of fear' findings. *BBC Sport,* October 11. https://www.bbc.co.uk/sport/disability-sport/41586743

Roan, D. (2017b). Was 2017 the year British sport lost its way? *BBC News,* December 29. https://www.bbc.co.uk/news/uk-42353175

Rumbsy, B. (2020). Exclusive: Quarter of taxpayer-funded sports organisations fail government gender target for board diversity. *The Telegraph.* https://www.telegraph.co.uk/sport/2020/08/11/quarter-taxpayer-funded-sports-organisations-fail-government/

Scott, L. (2020a). *UK sport notified of 19 allegations of emotional abuse or neglect of athletes since 2017, BBC sport.* BBC. https://www.bbc.co.uk/sport/53837137

Scott, L. (2020b). *'Big shift' in UK sport funding for Olympics and paralympics, BBC sport.* BBC. https://www.bbc.co.uk/sport/54562195

Shaw, S. (2001). *The construction of gender relations in sport organisations.* De Montfort University.

Shaw, S. (2007). Touching the intangible? An analysis of the equality standard: A framework for sport. *Equal Opportunities International, 26*(5), 420–434. https://doi.org/10.1108/02610150710756630

Shaw, S., & Penney, D. (2003). Gender equity policies in national governing bodies: An oxymoron or a vehicle for change? *European Sport Management Quarterly*, *3*(2), 78–102. https://doi.org/10.1080/16184740308721942

Shibli, S., Gumber, A., & Ramchandani, G. (2021). *Provision of tackling racism and racial inequality in sport - Data gathering and analysis services*, rep., UK Sport. https://www.uksport.gov.uk/news/2021/06/23/tackling-racism-and-racial-inequality-in-sport-review

Sky Sports. (2020). Government set to review sports governance code. *Sky Sports*. https://www.skysports.com/more-sports/other-sports/news/29877/12005034/government-set-to-review-sports-governance-code

Sport and Recreation Alliance. (2020). Sport and recreation sector commit to tackling inequality. https://www.sportandrecreation.org.uk/news/industry/Sport%20and%20recreation%20sector%20commit%20to%20tackling%20inequality

Sport England. (2019a). *Active lives adult survey 18/19 report*. Sport England.

Sport England. (2019b). *Diversity action plan*. Sport England. https://www.sportengland.org/about-us/equality-diversity/commitment-to-diversity/

Sport England. (2020). Our commitment to increasing diversity in sport and physical activity. Sport England. https://www.sportengland.org/news/our-commitment-increasing-diversity-sport-and-physical-activity

Sport England. (2021). *Uniting the movement: A 10-year vision to transform lives and communities through sport and physical activity*. Sport England.

Sport England, & UK Sport. (2019). *Annual survey 2018/19: Diversity in sport governance*. https://www.uksport.gov.uk/-/media/files/resources/executive-summary--diversity-in-sport-governance-report-final.ashx

Sporting Equals. (2000). *Achieving racial equality: A standard for sport*. Commission for Racial Equality.

Sporting Equals. (2022). *Race representation index, 2021*. Sporting Equals.

Sports Council Equality Group. (2012). *UK equality standard - equality in sport*. The Equality Standard, A Framework for Sport. https://equalityinsport.org/wp-content/uploads/2014/02/Guidance-for-Sports-Organisations.pdf

Sports Council Equality Group. (2014). *UK equality standard resource pack, glossary of terms*. The Equality Standard, A Framework for Sport. https://equalityinsport.org/wp-content/uploads/2014/02/Glossary-of-Terms.pdf

Spracklen, K. (2003). Setting a standard? Measuring progress in tackling racism and promoting social inclusion in English sport. In A. Ibbetson, B. Watson, & M. Ferguson (Eds.), *Sport, leisure and social inclusion* (pp. 41–57). Leisure Studies Association.

Spracklen, K., Hylton, K., & Long, J. (2006). Managing and monitoring equality and diversity in UK sport. *Journal of Sport and Social Issues*, *30*(3), 289–305. https://doi.org/10.1177/0193723506290083

Sutton Trust. (2012, August). *Over a third of British medal winners were private educated*. https://www.suttontrust.com/newsarchive/third-british-olympic-winners-privately-educated/

The Guardian. (2020). Taking a knee: Athletes protest against racism around the world – In pictures. *The Guardian*, August 27. https://www.theguardian.com/sport/gallery/2020/aug/27/nba-strike-athletes-kneeling-black-lives-matter-protest

Thomas, N., & Guett, M. (2014). Fragmented, complex and cumbersome: A study of disability sport policy and provision in Europe. *International Journal of Sport Policy and Politics*, *6*(3), 389–406. https://doi.org/10.1080/19406940.2013.832698

Topping, A. (2021). Team GB still too white and suburban, says Sport England board member. *The Guardian*, August 9. https://www.theguardian.com/sport/2021/aug/09/team-gb-still-too-white-suburban-sport-england-official

Turconi, L., & Shaw, S. (2021). 'Turning the tanker around': Examining the requirements, interpretations and implementation of the equality standard: A framework for sport. *European Sport Management Quarterly*, 1–20. https://doi.org/10.1080/16184742.2021.1879190

UK Sport. (2016). A code for sports governance. https://www.uksport.gov.uk/resources/governance-code

UK Sport. (2021). *The power of our differences: Introducing our equality, diversity and inclusion strategy 2021–2025*. UK Sport.

Walker, M. (1997). Simply not good chaps: Unravelling gender equity in a South African university. In C. Marshall (Ed.), *Feminist critical policy analysis: Perspectives from post-secondary education* (pp. 41–59). Falmer Press.

Chapter 8

Sporting Charities and Non-sporting Community Agencies

Kate Mori

The Evolution of Community Sport Policy as an Enabler of Third-Sector Provision

Community sport has long been central to sport policy. The use of the term 'community' generally invokes a feeling of positivity, a 'feel good factor,' an 'inner glow.' The word 'community' brings with it images of an ideal past, when people had time for each other and placed a value on being part of their local community (Etzioni, 1995). In that respect, placing community at the heart of sport policy can act as a means of associating this positivity with governmental and political aims. As Mackintosh (2021) highlights, community sport is historically, politically and socially situated and can be viewed as a conceptual construct. Conceptually, the legitimisation of government funding for community sport has taken many forms. From community sport as a means of encouraging a fitter and healthier population (Siedentop, 2002; Warburton et al., 2006), to promoting community cohesion and social inclusion (Smith & Waddington, 2004; Tonts, 2005; Morgan & Parker, 2017; Parker et al., 2019), to its contribution to crime reduction (Hartmann & Massoglia, 2007; Nichols, 2007; Parker et al., 2014), the instrumental use of community sport has spanned all political parties and sport policies. Looking at sport policy over time, we can see that interest in community and community development has become increasingly prevalent (The Sports Council, 1982, 1988; Department for Culture, Media and Sport, 2000, 2012; Department of Culture, Media and Sport/Strategy Unit. 2002; HM Government, 2015, Sport England, 2016) and this is made explicit within Sport England's latest sport strategy that cites the overwhelming evidence that community sport and physical activity plays in improving lives (Sport England, 2021). This chapter aims to trace the historical development of governmental interest in the use of sport to develop communities and beyond this we look to examine how this plays out 'on the ground' from a policy-to-practice perspective.

The evolution of the welfare state from the early 1950s strongly influenced community sport development and its role in delivering welfare outcomes (Coalter, 2007). During the 1960s, the preferred mode of improving welfare was a professionalised public service that was deemed to bring subject expertise, neutrality and

DOI: 10.4324/9781003162728-8

Sporting Charities and Non-sporting Community Agencies 135

local knowledge to overcome social problems within locales (Houlihan & White, 2002). During this time, the report of the Wolfenden Committee, the Wolfenden Report (The Central Council of Physical Recreation, 1960), had a lasting impact on sport development. The Committee was given a broad remit:

> To examine the factors affecting the development of games, sport and outdoor activities in the UK and to make recommendations to the CCPR as to any practical measures which should be taken by statutory or voluntary bodies in order that these activities may play their full part in promoting the general welfare of the community.
>
> (The Central Council of Physical Recreation 1960, p. 1)

The underpinning themes of the Wolfenden Report highlighted the welfare of the community and via its recommendation for a Sports Development Council (SDC) set in place an arm's length non-governmental structure for public funding of sport. This process could be viewed as a pivotal moment for community sport as it moved away from being solely within the domain of civil society towards being a central pillar of government social welfare issues (Houlihan & Lindsay, 2013). During the late 1960s to the mid-1970s, sport was emphasised as a means of promoting community wellbeing, and therefore found legitimacy in the delivery of sport and physical activities by sports development officers working within a local authority setting.

The acceptance of sport and leisure as aspects of welfare provision and the role sport played in the quality of life in communities was further emphasised by the Council of Europe's (CoE) European Sport for All Charter in 1975 and publication in the same year of the White Paper on Sport and Recreation. Such policy developments occurred within a political paradigm that until the mid-1970s emphasised a commitment to Keynesian economics and the belief in the positive value of state provision (Henry, 2001; Houlihan & White, 2002).

Whereas the left viewed the state as a key provider of funding and resource to enable community welfare, this started to change with the election of a Conservative government in 1979, which began to move away from Keynesian economics to neoliberal ideals, proposing that welfarism had undermined self-reliance and promoted self-seeking welfare professions whose primary interest was to secure further government expenditure (Minford, 1984; Houlihan & White, 2002). Margaret Thatcher set in place a series of fundamental reforms both within local government and the NHS that not only affected the rest of her tenure but also affected her Labour and Conservative successors that followed. The shift towards neoliberal, free-market economic policies was particularly evident during Thatcher's reign (Houlihan & Lindsey, 2013) as government policies emphasised a reduction in the role of government, alongside support for the private sector within public services delivery. The sporting offer of local authorities, which was previously seen in a social or political context, was increasingly conceptualised within an economic context, and for local authorities this shift highlighted a transition from local government as provider to enabler (Aitchison, 1997).

The Conservative government of 1981 chose to further a 'Sport for All' philosophy by focusing the campaign, originally started by the GB Sports Council in 1972, to specific underrepresented 'target groups' within the community. The campaign, championed by the GB Sports Council, ran throughout the 1980s and targeted the disabled, women, older adults and the unemployed. Target groups have continued to be a key narrative within sport policy, and it could be argued that the Sport for All campaign was influential in this continued focus. For example, the Labour government's sport strategy, Game Plan (Department for Culture, Media and Sport, 2002), emphasised increasing participation in sport and physical activity for those from lower socio-economic groups, young people (up to 24), women (16+) and older people. The rationale for these target groups promoted a need to encourage a more active lifestyle amongst those who had traditionally been less active than the general population (Department for Culture, Media and Sport, 2002).

'New' Labour's rise to power in 1997 sought to combine the social democratic principles of greater equality with the dynamism of market-led approaches and, in doing so, tried to distance themselves from the centralised bureaucratic hierarchy (and perceived outdated socialist ideals) of 'old' Labour and the market emphasis of the previous Conservative government (Giddens,1998). In simple terms, the 'Third Way' rejected the 'old left' and the 'new right' and sought to establish a middle way based on a mix of the perceived strengths of both (Giddens, 1998; Stevens & Green, 2002). In doing so, 'New' Labour was instrumental in emphasising sport for social good (Devine, 2013; Mackintosh & Liddle, 2015) and sport achieved a more clearly articulated and prominent role in social policy (Coalter, 2007; Bloyce & Smith, 2010). The strengthening of focus on the instrumental use of sport to achieve social objectives was bolstered by the creation of the Department for Culture, Media and Sport (DCMS) in July 1997. A result of the renaming of the Department of National Heritage, the DCMS helped to legitimise sport policy at cabinet level. The establishment of Policy Action Teams (PATs) was an influential mechanism designed to cut across policy divisions. PATs were established to inform policy that would underpin social inclusion by focusing on regeneration, lifelong learning and healthier and safer communities. The Policy Action Team for sport and the arts (PAT 10) was one of 18 teams established after the publication of 'Bringing Britain Together: A National Strategy for Neighbourhood Renewal' (Social Exclusion Unit, 1998).

Central to New Labour's 'Third Way' was a firm belief in the value of community and a commitment to equality of opportunity (Giddens,1998), and this belief flowed through to New Labour's sport strategy, 'Game Plan' (DCMS/Strategy Unit, 2002). The strategy evidenced the shift from an ideology of the development of sport to development through sport and articulated the growing relationship between social and economic policy. The social investment state model views spending on passive welfare such as unemployment benefits as 'bad' (Perkins, 2008) and instead seeks to move beyond redistributive social welfare to one that encourages people to actively participate in society through initiatives such as return-to-work schemes (Palme, 2006). Within the Third Way paradigm, the community rather than the individual or the state became the primary focus (Jarvie, 2003). More participative forms of governance were emphasised such as multi-agency partnerships in which communities were strongly represented as stakeholders and local 'experts' encouraged (Powell & Exworthy, 2002). Participative forms of governance placed social inclusion at the heart of government policy and gave increased emphasis to using sport as a 'tool' to engage those at the margins of society. Schemes such as Positive Futures, Street Games, Playing for Success, Splash and a plethora of other local and national schemes were established during the Blairite years. At the heart of such schemes was a continued focus on social inclusion and social/personal development through sport, rather than the development of sporting ability per se (National Foundation for Educational Research, 2003). These schemes emphasised a 'sport for good' rather than 'sport for sport' approach, and an elevated role was given to sport as a contributor to social inclusion and community cohesion.

According to Hoye et al. (2010), third-way policies represented a shift away from direct government service provision to 'whole of government' partnerships with private and third-sector agencies. During this time, New Labour placed an emphasis on the third sector and social enterprises as opposed to for-profit organisations in relation to public sector delivery (Alcock, 2010). The importance of the third sector for New Labour led to them, in 2006, establishing the Office of the Third Sector (OTS) within the Cabinet Office and the appointment of a Minister for the Third Sector. Social enterprise was seen to exemplify the Third Way through promising a combination of social justice and market dynamism with ethical values at the centre of business goals (Teasdale, 2012). During this time, community sport delivery evolved from being a key focus of local government towards partnership working, in which local authorities became enablers of community sport provision rather than playing a delivery role.

The promotion of social enterprise as a means of delivering community sport continued beyond 'New' Labour and this is evidenced within both the 2015–2020 sport strategy (HM Government, 2015) and the current sport strategy (Sport England, 2021), which positively emphasises diversified funding and delivery. The 'New' Labour administration paved the way for the delivery system we see today, which encourages sporting charities and non-sporting community agencies to assume a key role in community sport delivery.

Under the Conservative-led coalition government, elected in 2010, the mantra was 'small state, big society' (Nicholls & Teasdale, 2017). The social justice discourse framed Britain's 'broken-society' as an individual-level problem exacerbated by an overbearing 'nanny state' (Bochel & Powell, 2016) and, to this end, the Conservative-led coalition sought to further reduce the size of the state and cut public expenditure, positioning the politics of austerity at the heart of its approach. David Cameron's Big Society remit highlighted that social enterprises and third-sector organisations should have less state interference and instead be driven purely by market forces (Macmillan, 2013). Neoliberalist ideals were evident through the promotion of support for the creation and expansion of co-operatives, social enterprises and the establishment of a Big Society Bank with the aim of providing new finance for such initiatives. In turn, more emphasis was placed on the role of volunteers in sport as a means to achieve community involvement, but also, importantly, as a means of lessening the financial burden of staffing costs for the public sector and broader sporting organisations (Department for Culture, Media and Sport, 2011).

Charities and non-sporting community agencies continued to flourish during this time and became increasingly recognised within the delivery system with large-scale investments. Organisations aligned with the sport for wider social purposes agenda, often termed as a 'sport for development movement,' saw a growth beyond the 2012 Olympics as local authority spending on sports development services tightened or ceased. This created not only a space for the third sector but opportunity to evidence its methods, including its ability to reach priority groups, being responsive, asset based and sustainable by attracting investment from diverse sources. As of 2019, an estimated 60,000 (Sported, 2019) not-for-profit organisations using sport as a means for wider outcomes were in existence. Whilst the vast majority are run on minimal resources and the goodwill of volunteers, the potential to scale up, reach and impact via charities and non-sporting community agencies is vast. During this period, Sport England sought to appoint national partners from the third sector (such as Street Games, Sported, and Sporting Equals) to grow and sustain participation and non-sporting outcomes with priority groups.

The Sporting Future strategy (HM Government, 2015) emphasised the importance of a diversified funding model for sporting organisations and a clear message that Sport England and UK Sport would reduce the percentage of income that sporting organisations received from a single public sector body, whilst encouraging such organisations to increase the overall level of non-public investment they receive. Whilst focusing on diversified funding models, the strategy also recognised the 'crucial role' that local authorities play in delivering sport and physical activity opportunities (HM Government, 2015), which to many seemed contradictory.

Sport England launched *Uniting the Movement*, a ten-year strategy, in 2021, against the backdrop of the Coronavirus pandemic. Underpinning the strategy is the concept of 'proportionate universalism,' which paves the way for targeted investment into areas deemed most in need or on the margins of society whilst retaining universal funding opportunities. This distinct shift in discourse potentially re-enforces a deficit reduction approach by targeting localities deemed troublesome or under-resourced. The strategy does acknowledge that 'people' and 'leaders' require investment, and trusting relationships are required as a driver for change (Sport England, 2021). Tackling inequalities is positioned at the core of the strategy, which seeks to establish a delivery system couched in broader societal outcomes beyond participation, a mantra that has been at the heart of government sport policy for many years.

It is debatable how positive the move towards multiple delivery agents such as charities and non-sporting community agencies has been for community sport participants. Mori et al. (2021) found that as the focus of sporting agencies involved in community sport delivery shifted from collaboration to competition, they were increasingly less likely to share information about the communities they served,

Sporting Charities and Non-sporting Community Agencies   139

resulting in the duplication of services and an unnavigable and confusing delivery system, all of which can result in poor attendance and sporting initiatives that have deemed to have 'failed.'

Approaches to Delivering Community Sport

Community sport has seldom succeeded in evidencing its impact (Coalter, 2007). This is problematic and has caused much scholarly debate since the 1990s, not least with the emergence of the 'sport for development movement.' Weiss (2016) laments sport's use as a tool for positive youth development as 'old wine, new bottle,' arguing that a legacy of a lack of robust data capture and impact assessment has paved the way for third-sector organisations to market their services and represent models of delivery (previously delivered) as something new and dynamic, when in fact such models of delivery have been in existence for many years. The fragmentation of the delivery system and ongoing promotion of localism through a place-based approach has offered much scope for third-sector organisations (TSOs) to innovate and offer what appears to be freshly developed and branded programming.

National TSOs are prime examples of organisations that have followed wider business approaches, investing in building relationships with key policymakers and influencers, with the goal of unlocking resources for future programming. Many TSOs operating in community sport have established business development teams, and this can shift the focus to bidding and winning contracts, which can prove a challenge for community sport to remain connected to its grassroots missions and objectives, as business principles increasingly prevail. Further it has enabled TSOs to diversify its workforce, by appointing expert fundraisers, insight and data managers, communications and PR specialists and national/regional programme managers. The career pathway for a community sport practitioner, focused on delivery and meeting community needs, can be limited within such an environment both in terms of earning potential and organisational responsibility, as TSOs look towards the business community for leadership. This step towards managerialism brings into question the value of the practitioner who delivers in communities within TSOs. In turn, TSO's operating national programming is modelling the managerialist focus which impacted leisure services during the 1990s. A consequence of this has been a devaluing of the community sport practitioner, with careers being perceived as something 'anyone can do' and exhibiting low pay, minimal opportunity for career progression and a lack of status within larger TSOs.

Two Key Approaches to the Third-Sector Delivery System

Asset-Based Community Development

Often referred to as ABCD (Kretzmann & McKnight,1993), this approach looks at a community in a holistic sense, working 'with the community, for the community' to build on their strengths and make best use of its people, its physical assets and its resources. The lived experience of the community and how they are connected to each other through public spaces, clubs, organisations and services provide a foundation that ABCD approaches build upon. Community sport practitioners are ideally identified from within the community, are representative of the community and offered professional developmental opportunities to enhance their knowledge and skills in delivery. The underlying common facets of delivery include:

Individualism: The approach to ABCD recognises that each participant has strengths that can be built on. For example, a community sport intervention that takes a group of young people works with them and identifies their strengths such as leadership ability and potential. These strengths can then be realised by the individual/s concerned, the TSO and the community working together (Russell, 2021).

Altruism and volunteerism: ABCD is built on the values of supporting the community, their needs and interests. Within communities ABCD focuses on mobilising groups of people around a common cause or need. For example, the community identifies that a weekend multi-sports club for children would be beneficial. An ABCD approach would support the group of parents who have identified this need to develop and run weekend sports clubs within their community (McNight & Block, 2012).

Inclusive: ABCD challenges the hegemonic culture of male dominance, racial inequalities and discriminatory practice that can prevail in some sports clubs. The sporting offer is not predetermined by TSOs, but instead is discovered and developed via conversations with the community, empowering them to make decisions, plan activities and take ownership of them (Kretzmann & McKnight, 1993).

Connection and bonding: ABCD promotes community interaction, building relationships, collaboration and the creation of new positive connections within a community that can build on the assets that already exist and further develop the activities and services offered. Local networks using sport are often mobilised through regular information-sharing exchanges, supported by TSO staff teams to build collaborations and ultimately develop social capital within the community (Russell, 2020).

Contextualised understanding about the environment: ABCD takes the perspective that no community is the same. For example, rural Devon is different to urban Manchester which is different to urban London which is different to rural Yorkshire. ABCD capitalises on this, taking time to understand community dynamics and nuances and situating the development of activities and services within a local context. Sports practitioners are developed from within the community and their knowledge, understanding and ability to connect with others within that community capitalised upon.

Sport intersects with broader community and societal developments: A strength of ABCD is its ability to position sport within wider community priorities and developments. Examples of regeneration strategies that consider sports and

Sporting Charities and Non-sporting Community Agencies 141

community facilities within their plans become integrated, the commissioning of services such as health, libraries and education are considered and embedded within community sports programming, creating multi-agency advocacy and pooled resourcing.

Deficit Reduction

Deficit reduction focuses on fixing a 'social problem' and sport is used as an instrument in doing so (Coalter, 2007). This instrumental use of sport is well evidenced within sport policy across the years (as discussed earlier) and focuses primarily at targeting resources to those deemed most in need, either through place-based interventions (deprived communities where crime is high, for example) or targeted intervention groups (such as relying on referrals from statutory routes such as GPs or probation services).

A deficit reduction model is underpinned by determination of a community's 'needs' and has the potential to drive a focus on 'problems' rather than solutions. Many organisations retain a vested interest in ensuring that this cycle of dependency continues as it ensures their existence and has implications regarding transparent and effective evaluation. An unintended consequence of this cycle of dependency can be a policy directive that supports and exacerbates a focus on problems, due to biased evaluations undertaken by those organisations that have a vested interest in such cycles continuing. Added to this, funding to alleviate social problems is based on problem-oriented data such as the Index of Multiple Deprivation (IMD) and other such quantifiable metrics which help funders determine levels of 'need.' Kretzmann and McKnight (1993) emphasise, making resources available on the determination of need can have negative effects on the nature of local community leadership. If, for example, one measure of effective leadership is the ability to attract resources, then local leaders are, in effect, compelled to conceptualise their community by highlighting its problems and deficiencies and potentially ignoring its capabilities and strengths. The key aspects of a deficit reduction approach to community sport include:

Concern for public welfare and societal problems: Commissioned projects are designed to change behaviour patterns which will benefit society – such as reduced crime by young people or reducing drug and alcohol consumption.

Paternalism: Paternalism as protection of the public. Taking the examples of crime or drug and alcohol consumption, a deficit approach would promote community sports that embed a focus on life skills and activities that reinforce state priorities, such as the consequences of carrying weapons or the impact of excessive drug use.

Targeted: Deficit reduction approaches target either communities (deemed in need of intervention) or individuals (also deemed in need of intervention). This approach defines the parameters of users, such as young people at risk of crime or those who are known to be addicts.

Addressing skills gaps: Common approaches to deficit reduction programmes promote interventions designed to foster engagement via coach education programmes accompanied with training courses and leadership programming, with the wider agenda to 'create more employable people' who may therefore have greater economic prospects and be less dependent on the state.

Creating social value: The deficit reduction approach is concerned with creating social value, an approach which includes social returns on investment (SROI) and quantification of outcomes relating to state priorities. Indicators such as increased confidence can be attributed a market value and calculated to evidence each intervention's wider economic and societal impact, making interventions using this approach more marketable.

Managing community Sport

A challenge for policymakers and investment in community sport has been reaching the end user or the 'targeted' community. National management approaches have often looked at investing in enabling focused charities, that don't deliver the interventions or programming, but instead work at 'arm's length' from the commissioning organisation and serves as the interface between the community, those delivering community sport and the commissioning agencies. National management approaches to delivering community sport have created a space for TSOs to act as managing partners or agencies, essentially a 'broker' between funding and delivery and has been used by national agencies for specific programmes, such as Positive Futures, a Home Office-funded youth development programme designed to prevent and divert young people from drug and alcohol use. The Home Office appointed Catch-22 (previously Crime Concern) as a managing agent for Positive Futures, deploying national teams to oversee the distribution of grants, provide quality assurance and strategic guidance to over 100 funded projects. Kickz (Premier League and Metropolitan Police) followed a similar model and so, more latterly, has Street Games through its Doorstep sports clubs. This delivery model has its merits as it offers an overarching support function to community sport delivery and a degree of expertise and guidance. It also enables localised projects to respond within their context within a common delivery framework. This approach also requires a split function from the lead TSOs who require management and delivery functions. This dual purposed role can have implications regarding communication and planning between funders, the managing agency and those delivering services.

The Localism Act of 2011 (HM Government, 2011) encouraged localised groups to take ownership of facilities and services within their locales. It is questionable how successful this has been within sport as this requires time, coordinated effort and knowledge of the sporting landscape. However, the Act has supported TSOs and local authorities to champion and commission delivery via localised groups, which has predominantly been achieved via:

- Community groups being commissioned to deliver services by either their local authority, a TSO or another 'arm's length' organisation
- Sports groups and clubs working in localities (non-commissioned)
- Non-sports groups based in the locality (non-commissioned)

What Works?

Harris and Houlihan (2016), in their discussions of community sport development, highlight that it would be more helpful to have a primary agent closer to the point of implementation who understands the local community, is able to provide and promote the right mix of formal and informal activities, link with sports-specific structures such as clubs and NGBs where appropriate, and at the same time work with, empower and support the community to take action itself. This approach aligns with an asset-based community development (ABCD) approach discussed earlier, which starts from an assumption that residing within every community, regardless of the community profile, are assets (Kretzmann & McNight, 1993). Assets may take the form of spaces, such as green space, unused derelict land and buildings that may be reinstated. More essentially, however, ABCD is concerned with the assets that reside within people, the local population and what they can offer (Green & Haines, 2016). As discussed, the traditional deficit model approach to sports development seeks to provide for those who 'lack' provision, or target groups at risk of social exclusion or health issues. What the deficit reduction model can overlook is that within communities there may be qualified coaches, skilled sports practitioners and those who would like to get involved with helping run and develop sporting activities. Yet the CSD structure does not easily facilitate such involvement as TSOs and local authorities do not have methods to 'unearth' such talents, but instead opt to 'parachute' in professionals, often from outside the locale and who have limited knowledge of the community.

Community projects are more likely to achieve effective outcomes if they encourage the engagement of the local community before inception (Bolton et al., 2008; Ledwith, 2016; Bates & Hylton, 2021) which contrasts with a 'top-own' paternalistic approach to programme development and likely assumptions about the community in which such programmes are situated – assumptions that may have been made by people who do not live in that community and of which they have limited knowledge or understanding. Those who live in the local community will have a clearer idea of the types of activities that residents may choose to participate in, how best to promote activities to the community, which community groups are well respected and supported and could help recruit participants. Beyond this, local residents will be aware of social media channels, such as area-based Facebook groups, that could be utilised to source sports coaches and also promote sporting activities to potential participants.

Conclusion

Sport policy has always promoted the positive benefits of community sport and continues to do so within the latest sport strategy (Sport England, 2021). However, this often takes an instrumental approach, focusing on problems within society and how to 'fix' them, which, as discussed within this chapter, can be detrimental to communities. In this respect, it could be argued that the delivery system for community sport is confused about how to get the best from communities, and while promoting a bottom-up approach to delivery via TSOs is still essentially a top-down directive driven by funding.

In order to survive, TSOs very often pursue a mixed economy of funding, which can bring with it specified targets be that, for example, working within a geographical area or with a population that have particular characteristics. Having to meet and juggle multiple aims across a range of different initiatives (to justify funding) can mean that TSOs are pulled in various directions, and this can lead to mission drift. Because of this diversity of funding and aims, the awareness, interpretation and implementation of community sport may take on different meanings to different agencies and individuals involved in delivery. Ultimately, this could result in an interpretation of practice which may not serve the community well if this takes an instrumental approach to delivery to justify funding.

Staff working in community sport will need a broad set of skills (beyond sport delivery) to understand the complexity involved in meeting targets, moving far beyond a 'tick box' approach to meeting specified objectives, and instead placing a communities' needs at the heart of delivery and fully reflecting on how funding can help meet those needs. Community sport has traditionally received low levels of investment in its workforce. A workforce that is often transient, low paid or voluntary and lacking in status. While TSOs have brought a level of business acumen to the sector, this has rarely translated to those at the grassroots responsible for the delivery of community sport sessions. We argue for more recognition and investment in those delivering community sport, as ultimately the success of any community sport initiative will be dependent upon them. There is a danger that we lose focus on what matters, and that is the community, the participants and what we are ultimately trying to achieve through community sport. If we take our gaze away from this, then the quality of provision is likely to suffer, attendances fall and engagement weakened. That said, an ability in knowing how best to monitor, evaluate and evidence the impact of community sport is crucial and something that the community sport sector has seldom practised adequately. The responsibility for doing so is a management responsibility and will need further consideration if community sport is to remain within political thought.

PRACTITIONER REFLECTION AND INSIGHTS

Kevin McPherson, Director, Square Impact

Twenty years ago, when I embarked on a career in community sport, I viewed the system, policy and sports' role in society starkly different than I do today. Like all my peers, we have learnt, adapted and built our work on 'what works' approaches rather than prescribed delivery frameworks. At the crux of community sport has been its secondary (or tertiary) role within sports policy, despite featuring since the 1960s. Participation has been the driver and medals have mattered (I am not disputing their worthiness) at each spending review (the government's process for setting expenditure limits to deliver policy priorities). Nevertheless, there has been ongoing acknowledgement that policy is failing to 'reach' and yield participation of 'priority' groups.

In the early 2000s, I worked in a local authority sports development department. I expected my work and programming to be traditional in the sense of building infrastructure by supporting a delivery system. The reality was different; it was all about delivery, running weekly timetabled activities within a youth service, where the core objectives were inclusion and working towards the five outcomes laid out in the then 'New' Labour Government's Every Child Matters framework (HM Government, 2003). Youth work was what we were doing, not building sports infrastructure. My interaction with supporting sports clubs and supporting the coaching workforce was limited to using sport to build skills for young people to enter the employment market (as coaches) or to volunteer (to make a social contribution to society). As I reflect on this period, much practice was as it is today. Project work was locality driven, used safe spaces and workers took an individualised approach and integrated programming to ensure the end user was protected and had greater access to opportunity. Further, this work took place at the height of Labour's social inclusion agenda with 18 Policy Action Teams established in 1998. The PAT 10 report recognised that participation in the arts and sport has a beneficial social impact, and that these benefits should be widely available to all sections of society. The sports development programme mirrored that; it sought to include and support those most in need with skills, confidence and access to opportunity. This, however, was by no means an asset-based approach; it was deficit reduction. Whilst on the face of it our success indicators were on engagement and building capabilities, we were also acutely aware of investment concerned with crime rates, antisocial behaviour and having to promote volunteerism in communities.

There were paradoxes that we, as 'officers,' often encountered. We were given carte blanche to deliver activities and further develop sports which we had personal interests in. The approach didn't sit comfortably with me. Just because I am a failed cricketer, why am I given the authority to put my personal interests above that of the community or those direct participants? It is an area which made me think we let ourselves down and was certainly cultural and endorsed by managers leading me to reflect and start to sharpen my own critique of how far apart sport development and community sport could be in their approaches. It is important to recognise that you, as an officer or person entrusted to deliver, have power, often unknowingly. The example could sit well within an NGB context; surely a passion and interest for a sport you love is an advantage I used to think. Yet, be reminded of my earlier comments – this was a service that worked to a government outcomes framework (Every Child Matters) which required us to consider the individual end user's needs. I remain unconvinced that sports development teams at the time understood this, with the vast majority aligning with Sport England's wider participation priority.

My career progressed rapidly, too rapidly on reflection. After four years in the field, I became a senior grant and strategy manager at a national sports funder. The period exposed me to the system. I swiftly understood the power I suddenly had – the phone didn't stop ringing, I was invited to every social event and working group out there. The potential to be influenced and influence was more than I'd ever appreciated. The culture wasn't what we were funding and supporting; it was so far removed that delivery became abstract.

There is one example I will share which highlights the cultural differences between the field and operating in an ivory tower. I left Bristol Temple Meads at 12.45 on a Friday. It was warm and I'd met a number of community groups that morning to discuss potential funding support. I'd run an outreach clinic with some minority groups (priority groups!). The last group cancelled on me, so I returned on an earlier train. I arrived in London around 2.30 pm and decided to go to the office to catch up on some tasks. I arrived around 3 pm. By 3.13 pm I had left the office. No one spoke to me at that time but my manager who sat opposite me emailed:

> 3.05 pm: Manager: 'Do you have your suit?'
> 3.07 pm: Me: 'No.'
> 3.07 pm: Manager: 'OK. It has been noticed (by the CEO) you are not in office attire …'
> 3.09 pm: Me: 'OK, what shall I do?'
> 3.10 pm: Manager 'If you have nothing to change into, I think its best you just go home.'
> 3.13 pm: I left the building.

That was the culture. Only a few hours earlier, I'd been supporting a small Somali community to access funding and new networks and (rightfully) I was in my sports kit. In communities we would have a chat, not get an email. We wouldn't care about these things. I probably would have been told thanks for coming back in when I could have gone home. This is not community sport I kept telling myself, this is power at work. Only a small handful of people had done any practice. Yes, they wore business attire, but it was deeper than that. It was about showing professionalism, marketing, branding and outputs. This was a cultural shift I was not prepared for, but I wasn't out of my depth with the work. It was clear that 'conversations in the corridor' led to decisions being made. Funding decisions that kept people in post or made them redundant! That shouldn't be your concern as a middle manager setting the parameters of a fund, but when you have come from practice, these things bother you. So do outcomes and impact. It wasn't understood at the time in this organisation; they knew outputs yet had some bold ambitions around community development, which we will never know the impact of.

An area which I have often critiqued is the connectivity and interpretation of policy into practice. Over the last 20 years, I have witnessed growth in TSOs diversifying their funding, prioritising resourcing from corporates, government and grant making trusts. On the face of it, this diversification and growth appears a positive step – more parties investing in community, coupled with improved infrastructures, enabled TSOs to become closer to policy, become recognised as a vital cog in the system and positively influence decision-makers. There have been significant challenges put to TSOs to sustain this approach. I've certainly witnessed organisational mission drift, shifting priorities and interpreting delivery programming to 'fit the system.' Rather than call out specific examples, I am concerned with a rhetoric that promotes sport as a tool to contribute to a specific 'priority.' Sport for employability, Sport to reduce crime, Sport to improve mental health are just three examples where TSOs have latched onto evidence and, dare I say it, often present sport as a panacea to the social challenges presented in the UK and, of course, globally, where the UN's Sustainable Development Goals drive all discussion.

I do remain convinced, however, that TSOs who remain connected to delivery and culturally connected to their 'end user' can improve complex systematic issues. The chapter emphasised a frustration that policy and consequent interventions can fail to 'reach' priority groups. TSOs with practitioner roots and networks can mobilise others, offer peer support, mentor and offer technical support to others is an underdeveloped yet potentially impactful approach. TSOs who have strong and well-developed localised networks of altruistic sports/community groups offer an alternative to not only distribution of resources to the 'unheard and undervalued' but also offer an important and often ignored priority – offering peer support, advice, guidance and mentoring. This is coupled with more formalised 'capacity building' functions (organisational priorities such as governance, workforce, marketing, financial management, strategy) that position TSOs with this armoury as having the potential to use their strengths as both practitioners and incubators of like-minded groups.

This chapter has touched on the role of the 'Third Sector Organisation' as a deliverer of community sport. Having moved into leadership roles over the last decade of my career, it's clearly a trend which is not applicable to only community sport. Youth work, arts and other mediums have experienced a growth in national and local TSOs growing and being recognised as a core delivery system. It is also important to recognise that TSOs operating broadly in community sport do not secure their resourcing purely from sports funding. There is a greater mixed economy from across government, trusts and foundations, donations, corporates and philanthropy who are investing into community sport. This is of benefit of course, but it poses an issue to the wider system of organisations' closeness to 'sport.' A challenge with growth is an organisation's ability to stay true to its cause and not mission drift, keep its connectedness to communities, and retain its focus on delivery rather than management. We assume in TSOs that growth is good. I would challenge this by saying, 'have we finished the job we started in that community?'

TSOs have strong benefits over a state-led system. It is (and should be) widely accepted that TSOs are able to engage with communities extremely effectively; they are largely agile, motivated and crucially trusted. These are examples of conditions which policy ought to consider as beneficial and require further understanding.

There are pitfalls, many of which I have experienced in TSOs. I have joked on many occasions about being a jack of all trades and master of none. I have learnt how to manage an organisation, market services and fundraising, financially plan, monitor impact, develop policies and manage HR. No one prepares you for this or offers you leadership advice and guidance. As the reader, you might think none of this has anything to do with the service offered to communities through community sport. You'd be right, but without this, TSOs won't cope with the demands of the system.

Assessing the trends and policy direction of travel, community sport appears well positioned to have a period of renaissance with a discourse emphasising the 'role of the lived experienced leader' and a localism agenda. Couple that with the (relative) resources required to deliver activities, there is one facet above all we need to remember: people. Community sport can only work where people are its central focus, as leaders, as beneficiaries and as residents. Without action and thought about the people who create the community sport eco-system, we will struggle to succeed. People need support, need training, but ultimately need valuing. For too long we have forgotten this, people change communities, people lead others and people's lives and opportunities are what we are attempting to build on.

If there is one piece of advice – don't wear a suit if you are into community sport!

References

Aitchison, C. (1997). A decade of compulsory competitive tendering in UK sport and leisure services: Some feminist reflections. *Leisure Studies, 16*(2), 85–105. https://doi.org/10.1080/026143697375430

Alcock, P. (2010). A strategic unity: Defining the third sector in the UK. *Voluntary Sector Review, 1*(1), 5–24. https://doi.org/10.1332/204080510X496984

Sporting Charities and Non-sporting Community Agencies 149

Bates, D., & Hylton, K. (2021). Asset-based community sport development: Putting community first. *Managing Sport and Leisure, 26*(1–2), 133–144. https://doi.org/10.1080/23750472.2020.1822754

Bloyce, D., & Smith, A. (2010). *Sport policy and development: An introduction.* Routledge.

Bochel, H., & Powell, M. (2016). Whatever happened to compassionate conservatism under the Coalition Government? *British Politics, 13*(2), 146–170. https://doi.org/10.1057/s41293-016-0028-2

Bolton, N., Fleming, S., & Elias, B. (2008). The experience of community sport development: A case study of Blaenau Gwent. *Managing Leisure, 13*(2), 92–103. https://doi.org/10.1080/13606710801933446

Coalter, F. (2007). *A wider social role for sport: Who's keeping the score?* Routledge.

Department for Culture, Media and Sport. (2000). *A sporting future for all.* Department of Culture, Media and Sport.

Department for Culture, Media and Sport. (2011). *Encouraging involvement in big society: A cultural and sporting perspective.* Department for Culture, Media and Sport.

Department for Culture, Media and Sport. (2012). *Creating a sporting habit for life: A new youth sport strategy.* Department for Culture, Media and Sport.

Department of Culture, Media and Sport/Strategy Unit. (2002). *Game plan: A strategy for delivering government's sport and physical activity objectives.* Department for Culture, Media & Sport/Strategy Unit.

Devine, C. (2013). London 2012 Olympic legacy: A big sporting society? *International Journal of Sport Policy and Politics, 5*(2), 257–279. https://doi.org/10.1080/19406940.2012.656674

Etzioni, A. (1995). *The spirit of community: Rights, responsibilities and the communitarian agenda.* Fontana Press.

Giddens, A. (1998). *The third way: The renewal of social democracy.* Polity Press.

Green, G., & Haines, A. (2016). *Asset building & community development.* Sage.

Harris, S., & Houlihan, B. (2016). Implementing the community sport legacy: The limits of partnerships, contracts and performance management. *European Sport Management Quarterly, 16*(4), 433–458. https://doi.org/10.1080/16184742.2016.1178315

Hartmann, D., & Massoglia, M. (2007). Reassessing the relationship between high school sports participation and deviance: Evidence of enduring, bifurcated effects. *Sociological Quarterly, 48*(3), 485–505. https://doi.org/10.1111/j.1533-8525.2007.00086.x

Henry, I. (2001). *The politics of leisure policy.* Palgrave Macmillan.

HM Government. (2003). *Every child matters.* HM Government.

HM Government. (2011). *The localism act.* Crown. Copyright.

HM Government. (2015). *Sporting future: A new strategy for an active nation.* HM Government/Cabinet Office.

Houlihan, B., & Lindsey, I. (2013). *Sport policy in Britain.* Routledge.

Houlihan, B., & White, A. (2002). *The politics of sports development.* Routledge.

Hoye, R., Nicholson, M., & Houlihan, B. (2010). *Sport and policy: Issues and analysis.* Elsevier.

Jarvie, G. (2003). Communitarianism, sport and social capital: Neighbourly insights into Scottish sport. *International Review for the Sociology of Sport, 38*(2), 139–153. https://doi.org/10.1177/1012690203038002001

Kretzmann, J., & McKnight, J. (1993). *Building communities from the inside out: A path toward finding and mobilizing a community's assets.* The Asset-Based Community Development Institute, Institute for Policy Research.

Ledwith, M. (2016). *Community development in action: Putting Freire into practice*. Policy Press.

Mackintosh, C. (2021). *Foundations of sport development*. Routledge.

Mackintosh, C., & Liddle, J. (2015). Emerging school sport development policy, practice and governance in England: Big society, autonomy and decentralisation. *Education 3-13, 43*(6), 603–620. https://doi.org/10.1080/03004279.2013.845237

Macmillan, R. (2013). Decoupling the state and the third sector? The 'big society' as a spontaneous order. *Voluntary Sector Review, 4*(2), 185–203. https://doi.org/10.1332/204080513X668692

McNight, J., & Block, P. (2012). *The abundant community: Awakening the power of families and neighbourhoods*. Berrett-Koehler Publishers

Minford, P. (1984). State expenditure: A study in waste. *Economic Affairs, 4*(3), i–xix. https://doi.org/10.1111/j.1468-0270.1984.tb01608.x

Morgan, H., & Parker, A. (2017). Generating recognition, acceptance and social inclusion in marginalised youth populations: The potential of sports-based interventions. *Journal of Youth Studies, 20*(8), 1028–1043. https://doi.org/10.1080/13676261.2017.1305100

Mori, K., Morgan, H., Parker, A., & Mackintosh, C. (2021). Examining the impact of austerity on community sport development workers and their professional environment. *Journal of Global Sport Management*. https://doi.org/10.1080/24704067.2021.1871803

National Foundation for Educational Research. (2003). *Playing for success: An evaluation of the fourth year*. Department for Education and Skills.

Nicholls, A., & Teasdale, S. (2017). Neoliberalism by stealth? Exploring continuity and change within the UK social enterprise policy paradigm. *Policy and Politics, 45*(3), 323–341. https://doi.org/10.1332/030557316X14775864546490

Nichols, G. (2007). *Sport and crime reduction: The role of sports in tackling youth crime*. Routledge.

Palme, J. (2006). Welfare states and inequality: Institutional designs and distributive outcome. *Research in Social Stratification and Mobility, 24*(4), 387–403. https://doi.org/10.1016/j.rssm.2006.10.004

Parker, A., Meek, R., & Lewis, G. (2014). Sport in a youth prison: Male young offenders' experiences of a sporting intervention. *Journal of Youth Studies, 17*(3), 381–396. https://doi.org/10.1080/13676261.2013.830699

Perkins, D. (2008). Improving employment participation for welfare recipients facing personal barriers. *Social Policy and Society: A Journal of the Social Policy Association, 7*(1), 13–26. https://doi.org/10.1017/S1474746407003971

Powell, M., & Exworthy, M. (2002). Partnerships, quasi-networks and social policy. In C. Glendinning, M. Powell, & K. Rummery (Eds.), *Partnerships, new labour and the governance of welfare* (pp. 15–32). Policy Press.

Russell, C. (2020). *Asset based community development: Looking back to look forward*. Independently Published.

Russell, C. (2021). *Asset based community development: An incomplete guide*. Independently Published.

Siedentop, D. (2002). Sport education: A retrospective. *Journal of Teaching in Physical Education, 21*(4), 409–418. https://doi.org/10.1123/jtpe.21.4.409

Smith, A., & Waddington, I. (2004). Using 'sport in the community schemes' to tackle crime and drug use among young people: Some policy issues and problems. *European Physical Education Review, 10*(3), 279–298. https://doi.org/10.1177/1356336X04047127

Social Exclusion Unit. (1998). *Bringing Britain together: A national strategy for neighbourhood renewal*. HMSO.

Sport England. (2016). *Towards an active nation*. Sport England.

Sport England. (2021). *Uniting the movement: A ten-year vision to transform lives and communities through sport*. Sport England.

Stevens, D., & Green, P. (2002). Explaining continuity and change in the transition from compulsory competitive tendering to best value for sport and recreation management. *Managing Leisure, 7*(2), 124–138. https://doi.org/10.1080/13606710210140684

Teasdale, S. (2012). What's in a name? Making sense of social enterprise discourses. *Public Policy and Administration, 27*(2), 99–119. https://doi.org/10.1177/0952076711401466

The Central Council of Physical Recreation. (1960). *Sport and the community: The report of the Wolfenden Committee on sport*. The Central Council of Physical Recreation.

The Sports Council. (1982). *Sport in the community: The next ten years*. The Sports Council.

The Sports Council. (1988). *Sport in the community: Into the 90s: A strategy for sport 1988–1993*. The Sports Council.

Tonts, M. (2005). Competitive sport and social capital in rural Australia. *Journal of Rural Studies, 21*(2), 137–149. https://doi.org/10.1016/j.jrurstud.2005.03.001

Warburton, D. E. R., Nicol, C. W., & Bredin, S. S. D. (2006). Health benefits of physical activity: The evidence. *Canadian Medical Association Journal (CMAJ), 174*(6), 801–809. https://doi.org/10.1503/cmaj.051351

Weiss, M. R. (2016). Old wine in a new bottle: Historical reflections on sport as a context for youth development. In N. Holt (Ed.), *Positive youth development through sport* (2nd ed., pp. 7–20). Routledge.

Chapter 9

Schools

Helen Ives

Introduction

Over the last 30 years or so, there has been a 'dramatic change in the political salience of school sport and PE' (Houlihan & Green, 2006, p. 74) with an increasing attention on the use of schools to deliver physical activity initiatives and sport-focused policies in the UK and internationally (Mackintosh, 2014). From the late 1990s, physical activity and sport gathered momentum as a central policy theme in the UK (Houlihan & Green, 2006, p. 78), attracting a significant investment of public funds. In England, some £2.4bn was invested in school-based activity via two significant strategies: PE, School Sport and Club Links (PESSCL) between 2003 and 2008 and the PE and Sport Strategy for Young People (PESSYP) between 2008 and 2010. Since 2013, government funding has been through a direct payment to schools called 'The PE and Sport Premium for Schools' (Department for Education, 2013, 2015, 2017, 2018, 2020, 2021) for the purpose of improving the quality and quantity of PE and School Sport (PESS). However, with the impetus of the London 2012 Summer Olympic and Paralympic Games now a distant memory, the focus on PESS is now only receiving 'intermittent' importance from senior ministers (Lindsey, 2020). To fully understand the impact of a curriculum subject attracting unprecedented levels of funding accompanied by a now waning interest, it is first imperative to provide some historical context of the 'rise' in physical education and the use of schools as centres of (national) policy implementation for wider policies associated with innovation and curriculum reform.

Educational Policy: Implementation, Innovation and Curriculum Reform

Schools have been sites of interest for successive governments seeking to implement policy; from innovation[1] in educational policy reaching 'epidemic proportions' (Levin, 1998), accompanied by policy hysteria (Stronach & Morris, 1994) as governments increasingly seek to utilise education for other agendas (Priestly & Rabiee, 2002). More recently, the idea of the curriculum in schools not only includes subjects but, as Zhu et al. (2011, p. 84) propose, 'planned educational

DOI: 10.4324/9781003162728-9

experiences for both students and teachers offered by a school which can take place within and beyond schools.' Thus, we begin to see an extension of the role of the school beyond the delivery of a national curriculum, to beyond the school gates. This diversification of the role of the school brought with it the opportunities to create partnerships and in return become central to programmes, strategies and initiatives. Cuban (1988, p. 86) identifies that 'innovation after innovation has been introduced into school after school.' It is interesting to note that with schools being subject to so much innovation and initiatives an 'overwhelming number of them [initiatives] disappear without a fingerprint' (Cuban, 1988, p. 86) and that there is innovation without change (Sparkes, 1989).

Policy implementation through the guise of curriculum reform happens through one of three approaches: top-down, bottom-up and partnerships (Fullan, 1994), which adds to the complexity of innovation. The top-down approach is still favoured in relation to the PESS reform, a process where the reform is introduced by policymakers external to the school system, minimising teacher influence as the innovation comes packaged with educational objectives, curriculum content and assessment instruments (Macdonald, 2003). Top-down reform is often accompanied by the financial and political support required for success (Curtner-Smith, 1999). Often the enticement of quality marks, performance tables and accompanying badges that schools have access to if they are successful at achieving government targets are motivators of compliance within the top-down approach of policy innovation and implementation. This is evident within PESS programmes and interventions; badges, kitemarks, quality marks are used by schools to market their achievements not merely their policy compliance. Thus, the money required to provide the initiative, the materials and/or human resources to succeed as well as an assessment (monitoring and reporting) process has accompanied the national implementation of PESS policy, strategy and suite of programmes.

It should be noted that, unlike the top-down approach, bottom-up approaches are limited but do recognise teachers as specialist (Gillborn, 1994). This approach relies heavily on teachers, often with little or no supporting funds, to provide the capacity to innovate (Skilbeck, 1982). The bottom-up approach often does not have the financial investment and enticements that support compliance in the top-down approach and thus remain localised and more likely to fail. Since the 1990s, the partnership approach has become a favoured model, mirroring the political system favouring a 'joined up' approach. Within the partnership approach there is a note of caution; there is a need to be aware of the fluctuations within partnership working of who, at any given time, has the power to influence and inform the production of the official texts – be it policy, strategy and/or implementation (Ives, 2014).

The policy space in relation to PESS is a crowded one (Houlihan, 2000) occupied by organisations with health, sport and education agendas. The power relations between those involved in education reform need to be considered (Ball, 1994; Anderson & Holloway, 2020). At the turn of the century, the discourse of PESS was gaining momentum, with politicians understanding and supporting sport in schools but also with an organisation, the Youth Sport Trust, headed at the time by Sue

Campbell[2] working across government departments, extolling the virtues and impact of PESS to deliver government targets. Campbell has been recognised as a 'policy entrepreneur' (Houlihan & Lindsey, 2013; Grix, 2015); appointed as an advisor to government in part due to her background in teaching, coaching and sport, she was able to be central to the development of government policy on PESS. Campbell was able to access ministers and policymakers, forming and accessing opportunities. These opportunities positioned the Youth Sport Trust at the heart of the implementation, administration and management of PESS policies, opportunities not afforded to other organisations such as the Association for Physical Education.

Regardless of the approach of policy in schools, in all cases, it requires the school and teacher to be responsible for translating the policy and realising the content in terms of practice. Policy becomes recontextualised for use in schools and transformed into pedagogy and pedagogical discourse (Bernstein, 2000), notwithstanding the internal environment (teacher knowledge, school budgetary commitment, time and expertise) as well as the external environment and community priorities and 'buy in.' These factors again are influenced by the approach taken for implementation and why, in the case of PESS, the partnership approach to the national implementation of policy has been favoured.

The Historical and Political Context of PE and School Sport

In 1995, *Sport: Raising the Game* was published, the first central government sport policy for 20 years that provided a clear statement of intent, a 'sea change in the prospects of British Sport – from the very first steps in primary school right through to breaking the tape in an Olympic final' (Department of National Heritage, 1995, p.1). The then Prime Minister, John Major, expressed his personal ambition and thoughts on the role of sport within schools:

> My ambition is simply stated. It is to put sport back at the heart of weekly life in every school. To re-establish sport as one of the great pillars of education alongside the academic, the vocational and the moral. It should never have been relegated to be just one part of one subject in the curriculum.
>
> (Department of National Heritage, 1995, p. 2)

Chapter 1 of *Sport: Raising the Game* considers the role of sport in schools, with the focus 'deliberately on sport rather than physical education' (Department of National Heritage, 1995, p. 7). However, Major outlined his expectation for physical education in schools in that the survival of 'sport' is only secure if there is a place for it on the curriculum (PE) and that it was the responsibility of schools to 'offer two hours a week of PE and sport in formal lessons' (Department of National Heritage, 1995, p. 7). For this policy to be taken up by schools and realised, and in keeping with the 'top-down' approach to policy implementation at a national level, accompanying public funds were allocated together with other enticements.

As an enticement for complicity in the uptake of this policy, two kitemarks were developed and which schools could apply for: 'Sportsmark' and 'Sportsmark Gold.' These kitemarks were awarded to schools that were able to demonstrate standards, including a very high level of provision in physical education and sport. Schools submitted their application, which included an audit of their provision for PESS within and beyond the curriculum, as well as plans to show how they would continue to develop the subject. Submission to Sport England was independently assessed against criteria that included offering a minimum of two hours per week of physical education on the curriculum, complimented by an extracurricular programme. The awarding of Sportsmark Gold was accompanied with potential funding for schools able to match fund a similar sum via private/corporate sponsorship being awarded £50,000 post-evaluation by Sport England, giving rise to schools receiving 'Specialist Sports College' status.[3] This form of national implementation of policy by 'reward' was considered successful. In 1999, 1,100 schools from 1,400 applications sought Sportsmark or Sportsmark Gold award status to Sport England (Select Committee on Culture, Media and Sport, 1999).

In 1997, those working within PESS, perhaps wrongly, perceived a threat to the status quo. The result of the UK general election led to the replacement of John Major by Tony Blair as prime minister. In most circumstances new parties with new ideologies come in with new ways of working. The Blair government, expected to do the same, did so with many aspects of governance but the work Major had started in PESS was supported and developed under Labour. Rather than being under threat, the '2 hour offer' of PESS, Specialist Sports College Status and Sportsmark Awards were continued and became the focus of a new policy for sport.

The publication of 'Game Plan' (DCMS / Strategy Unit, 2002) by the Labour government prioritised PESS with the inclusion of a schools-focused strategy, the PE, School Sport and Club Links strategy, and a move to a partnership approach to (national) policy implementation. The network of Specialist Sports Colleges (SSCs) increased and continued to provide, first, a site of advocacy in PESS policy and, second, became central to the School Sport Partnership[4] (SSP) programme transforming not only education but also the 'sporting infrastructure in England' (DCMS, 2000; Penney & Houlihan, 2001; Penney, 2004; Youth Sport Trust, 2005). Through the SSC and SSP infrastructure there was, by 2005, an established network for the national implementation of policy through which government aims and key objectives for PESS were disseminated, delivered and audited.

In 2008, Blair resigned from the position of prime minister and his Chancellor of the Exchequer – Gordon Brown – took up the role. Whilst in post Brown continued the PESS policy focus with the publication of the PESSYP. PESSYP, as a strategy, continued the partnership approach of national policy implementation, accompanied by significant levels of funding and no change to the infrastructure of SSPs and SSCs. With such similarities to PESSCL, there were limited sites of objection with the primary difference being represented in the elevation of the two-hour offer to a 'five-hour offer,' increasing the focus on community sport and recognising the need for coaches to contribute to the achievement of this new policy target.

Policy Implementation: A Partnership Approach with Top-Down Support

With the election of a Labour government there was a shift away from 'top-down' approaches to policy implementation to a partnership approach. The national network of SSPs and SSCs became the organisational infrastructure for the dissemination of the plethora of programmes and initiatives created within PESSCL and PESSYP. Each SSP was led by a Partnership Development Manager (PDM), an experienced professional and the main policy actor tasked with narrating the policy (Ball et al., 2011). PDMs had access to significant funding, working with schools to identify needs, whilst still working within the confines of ensuring the attainment of government targets. To consider how this structure worked, the emphasis on localised 'autonomy' and prioritisation of local need enabled the operational framework to offer some flexibility to addressing local need in each SSP.

The PESSCL strategy consisted of eight identified areas, or 'strands' for development, two of which were Specialist Sports Colleges and the SSP themselves. These two strands together provided a significant infrastructure for national policy implementation, managed and administered by the Youth Sport Trust. SSPs would typically include between four and eight secondary schools which would in turn each work with four to six primary schools. Managed by the PDM, funding released a member of PE staff in each secondary school for two days a week to undertake the role of the School Sport Co-ordinator (SSCo), with a Primary Link Teacher (PLT) released for 12 days each year in each partnership primary school (Ives, 2017). This allowed schools to use their own teachers to identify areas of development in their respective schools to ensure performance against government targets and show improvement in the annual audit process. This form of policy enactment ensured the SSP structure was integral to the management of the PESS strategies from 2003 onwards (Flintoff et al., 2011).

It was not only schools involved in this partnership arrangement for the realisation and national implementation of policy. Other partners included the Department for Education (DfE), Department for Culture, Media and Sport (DCMS)[5], Sport England and the Youth Sport Trust (YST). The operational management of the SSPs was assigned to the YST, an 'independent charity concerned with physical education and youth sport' (Youth Sport Trust, 2016), whilst government also continued to recognise schools and SSPs 'as central hubs for their policy directives' (Phillpotts, 2013, p.196). This positioned the YST at the interface between government (DCMS and DfE) and schools contributing to a blurring of boundaries between physical education, school and community sport, which had been a continued trend over many years (Flintoff, 2003; Bloyce & Smith, 2009; Tannehill et al., 2013). Undertaking this required an increase in the knowledge and skills within the SSP infrastructure. This ultimately resulted in a recruitment change with the Partnership Development Manager role moving away from the essential need to be a qualified teacher post, to one that was now open to recruiting from the sport development sector, recognising a need to be able to operate at the interface between sport and education (Ives, 2014).

As policy actors, the PDMs together with teachers selected, transmitted, translated and realised policy at the local level, influenced by the overarching need to achieve government targets to ensure the continuance of funding. In the case of PESSCL, the government had a specific Public Sector Agreement target, PSA22:

> To enhance the take-up of sporting opportunities by 5 to 16-year-olds so that the percentage of school children in England who spend a minimum of two hours each week on high quality PE and school sport within and beyond the curriculum increases from 25% in 2002 to 75% by 2006 and to 85% by 2008, and to at least 75% in each School Sport Partnership by 2008.
> (Department for Education and Skills, 2006, p. 6)

Regardless of what was developed locally in each school, the annual reporting survey that all schools were required to complete focused on the specific 85% target despite the survey including a wider variety of questions. When the target was reached a year early the success of SSPs, and ultimately the implementation of government policy, was widely reported in the media (Metrowebukmetro, 2007). This success also underpinned continued government funding with the PESSYP policy, from 2008, setting a revised government target colloquially referred to as the '5 hour offer':

> Indicator 5: percentage of 5–16 years old participating in at least two hours per week of high-quality PE and sport at school, and the percentage of 5–19 year olds participating in at least three further hours per week of sporting activities.
> (HM Treasury, 2007, p. 6)

This target not only continued to identify SSPs and schools as the infrastructure for the implementation of PESS policy but also placed a modicum of responsibility on National Governing Bodies of Sport (NGBs) and local authorities to review their associated delivery frameworks. NGBs were required to revise their own submissions for funding to include youth sport and school programmes. With NGBs relying significantly on funding, this potentially influenced how NGBs prioritised national policy implementation above the requirements of their sport. Again, whilst there was an air of autonomy in 'how' the funding was used within organisations, it was within a tightly controlled performance (against policy) culture. Arguably, there was a top-down approach presented in the guise of partnership working, giving organisations a perception that they have the freedom to allocate funding but only in furtherance of wider policy targets and performance measures.

The End of an Era

Whilst the story thus far may be considered as positive, PESS was not able to escape a falling out of favour. In 2010, after 13 years of a Labour government, the UK went to the polls again, and a Coalition Government led by the Conservative

158 Helen Ives

Party and including Liberal Democrats took control. One impact of new government was that the secure conditions for PESS became weakened, and on October 14, 2010, completely decimated. It was on this day that the then Secretary of State for Education, Michael Gove, stood up in the House of Commons and announced the immediate cessation of funding to PESSYP and the network of SSPs. The network that had been so successful as a finely tuned government machine was put out of service. In addition, the YST lost the management of the programme with immediate consequences for their organisational structure and staffing levels. National governing bodies were stripped of funding to support youth sport, and their work in schools and other government initiatives managed by the DCMS and the Department of Health were also affected; the impact of the decision of the DfE had a wider reach internally and externally for government.

Within this chapter, the national implementation of policy during the PESSCL and PESSYP years had been considered a partnership approach with elements identified within a top-down approach (funding, instructional materials, performance targets). The overnight dissolution of PESSYP is indicative of the ideological relationship that schools have within the policy process and the lack of power they have in the relationship. Schools are often obligated to implement policy, often aligned to funding and conditions. A 'top-down' approach is common within schools and education policy and in this case, policy related to physical education and school sport. What is interesting in the case of the SSPs and PESSCL/PESSYP was that whilst the 'policy' and the PSA target was bestowed upon the programme in a 'top-down' approach, the implementation was through a partnership approach with the principles of government 'control' enacted in a watered down, less prescriptive way. A way of disguising government control through a form of local autonomy through SSPs and schools. What hadn't been considered in the removal of the funding for the programme was the nationwide response as well as that within government itself.

Phoenix Rising: The Resurrection of PESS

When it seemed as if the focus on PE and School Sport was no longer important, with SSPs disintegrating over time, a lifeline emerged. A partial U-turn of the decision to cut the funding occurred possibly to quieten the public protestation (Lindsey, 2020) but too late to save the national infrastructure of SSPs[6] and not enough funding to sustain delivery in schools. Whilst £65m was provided to enable one day a week of support via the release of a secondary school PE teacher, the investment in training, administration and the SSP infrastructure was lost (Mackintosh, 2014). Its replacement was a 'new School Games tournament inspired by the 2012 Olympics and Paralympics' (Hunt, 2011) with PDMs transferred into the role of 'School Games Organiser' (Lindsey, 2020) but the focus on improving the quality and quantity of PE and School Sport was over. The focus now was on all children having the opportunity to participate in competitive school sport. The YST also sought to capitalise on this partial lifeline, bidding for and being awarded the programme management, coordination and administration of the School Games. In a case of history repeating, the national implementation of the School Games initiative was once again reliant upon 'School Games kitemarks.' Schools were enticed to achieve bronze, silver or gold status (later extended to include Platinum) based upon their ability to implement, provide and participate in competitive school sport. Had the YST learnt a lesson or two about the national implementation of policy and strategies within schools to ensure targets were met? It certainly could be seen to be a method to ensure the lesser-funded School Games at least provided a weak pulse for PESS to remain, albeit in a critical state, alive in schools.

2013: The Primary PE and Sport Premium

The revival of PESS continued, and in 2013 the government announced a new £152m investment into primary schools via the Primary PE and Sport Premium; a joint initiative between the DfE, Department of Health and the DCMS. Those who had worked within the system for the last decade, who had experienced the loss of funding and the dismantling the SSP network, welcomed the return of funding (Lindsay, 402020). The cynic may argue that this new £152m, primary school-focused PESS initiative was only £10m less than the successful, 'world class system for PE and sport' (APPGFHC, 2019, p. 2) that had been dismantled in 2010. The PE and Sport Premium (the Premium), unlike PESSCL and PESSYP, is structured, firstly, only to benefit primary schools and, secondly, without the infrastructure network of SSPs and is part of a government plan to improve the quality of physical education and sport once again for primary school aged pupils. The objectives were threefold:

> Teachers' professional development; increase the level of competitive sport for children; and educate teachers and children to recognise the value and benefit of high-quality PE and how it can be used for whole school improvement.
> (Department for Education, 2013, p. 198)

The Premium was also accompanied not by performance targets but by five key performance indicators (Department for Education, 2014):

1) The engagement of all pupils in regular physical activity – the Chief Medical Officer guidelines recommend that all children and young people aged 5–18 engage in at least 60 minutes of physical activity a day, or which 30 minutes should be in school.
2) The profile of PE and sport is raised across the school as a tool for whole school improvement.
3) Increased confidence, knowledge and skills of all staff in teaching PE and sport.
4) Broader experience of a range of sports and activities offered to pupils.
5) Increased participation in competitive sport.

Unlike PESSCL and PESSYP, Premium funding is ring fenced and paid directly to schools, alongside their Direct Schools Grant (DSG), and can only be used for the provision of primary school PE and sport in school (Department for Education, 2014). The headteacher becomes responsible for these budgets, and how the funding is used is left to their discretion. In 2016, the government's overall budget included an announcement of a 'Soft Drinks Industry Levy' or more commonly referred to as the 'Sugar Tax,' income from which was allocated to 'double the amount of funding we dedicate to sport in every primary school' (Hansard HC Deb, Vol 607, c964). As such, the total value of the Premium increased to £320m a year, with schools receiving between £15,000 and £30,000 per annum – an unprecedented level of funding within a single subject (Griggs, 2015; Ives, 2017; APPGFHC, 2019; Department for Education, 2019; Foster & Roberts, 2019). With such significant amounts of public funding, it could be expected that the flexibility in accounting for the funding be reviewed, as there was and arguably still is very little accountability for schools as to how the money is 'spent.'

The Absence of Accountability

The removal of the central control and reporting of performance represented a significant change in PESS policy under the Coalition and subsequent Conservative governments. In the early days of the Premium, the government did not want to be seen to be prescribing how the funding should be used beyond schools achieving the KPIs and adhering to the funding guidelines. It was PESS advocate Jeremy Hunt MP who sought to retain 'some accountability for that money' (Lindsey, 2020, p.36). As a result, a condition of funding required schools to publish details of the use and breakdown of expenditure of their Premium allocation on their website (Department for Education, 2013). Compliance was still a concern, and in 2015 official auditing of the Premium was introduced as part of the Ofsted inspection process. The caution here is that Ofsted only inspect schools once every 3–5 years so there is plenty of time to deviate from the guidance.

Transmitting Policy: The Headteacher

At the heart of the Premium implementation is the headteacher, who is responsible for how the ringfenced funding should be used to comply with the terms of the funding and associated KPIs. Headteachers were now positioned at the front line of policy decision-making, translating the focus of the government and transmitting it across the whole school agenda and staff. This form of policy implementation assumes that all headteachers are competent and confident, but what is not accounted for is the individual beliefs and experiences of the headteacher and how this influences policy implementation (Forde & Torrence, 2017). It is not just the interpretation of the headteacher however, as the cycle starts again with the generalist classroom teacher translating the headteachers interpretation – resulting in interpretations of interpretations (Rizvi & Kemmis, 1987). This allows for slippage in policy. For example, while government guidelines strictly forbid the use of Premium funding to cover PE classes in order to release the teacher for 'planning, preparation and assessment' (PPA) time, evidence presented in the APPGFHC (2019) report cites practitioner Kathryn Sexton, who acknowledges that this occurs in practice:

> More than one head teacher has told me that they ... use the money to cover shortfalls in their staffing budgets by buying in 'one stop shop' coaching companies to deliver the entire PE curriculum and giving their teachers the time for PPA (which should be covered by the normal school budget). My understanding of the Premium funding is that this is not only unethical but actually potentially fraudulent.
>
> (APPGFHC, 2019, pp. 33–34)

Whilst the PE and Sport Premium may, on paper, provide schools the freedom to decide how to contribute to the funded KPIs, implementation is reliant on headteachers retaining fidelity to the guidance provided. The use of coaches and the headteachers' interpretation of how PESS is outsourced in their school require more attention particularly as a policy that forbids the practice but seemingly does very little to prevent it.

The Outsourcing of Physical Education and School Sport

The use of coaches and external providers in schools is not a new phenomenon; PESSYP strengthened the business case for using sports coaches in schools to support competition, although not to replace teachers in physical education lessons. Outsourcing of PE through employment of coaches links to a public narrative that primary school teachers lack confidence and competence to teach physical education (Morgan & Bourke, 2008; O'Donovan et al., 2016). The use of coaches and third-party physical activity and sport businesses is increasing 'virtually "ceding" the subject in its entirety to non-qualified individuals, specifically, sports coaches/instructors with limited qualifications' (APPGFHC, 2019, p.18). In the first two years of the Premium, the use of external sports coaches rose from 38% to 78% of schools and a decline in the use of class teachers from 84% to 73% (Department for Education, 2015). There remains a call that physical education should remain 'designed and delivered by well qualified teachers' (APPGFHC, 2019, p.18) and that 'the role of external providers is best placed in extending and supplementing, rather than replacing or substituting, internal provision' (Ofsted, 2019).

But, for a moment, consider yourself in the position of a headteacher. Tasked with implementing change in PE and sport in your school, this sits alongside responsibility for the daily management of the school, staffing and financial decision-making, the academic performance of pupils, SATS tests, health checks and curriculum reform across all subjects. PE is in a crowded policy space, with competing demands on the plate of the headteacher and school leaders. For some, the

162 Helen Ives

solution is to outsource, offering breathing space in a pressure cooker of decision-making. It is now easier to possibly understand headteacher rationales for outsourcing and the use of the Premium in such a way as the KPIs are still delivered on paper and fidelity to the Premium guidance is maintained.

The Future of Physical Education and School Sport

This chapter began with a discussion regarding the salience of PESS against the backdrop of the 2012 Summer Olympic and Paralympic Games in London, unprecedented levels of government funding and involvement, PESS strategies, targets then, a break in the cycle where the future of PESS become uncertain, only to rise out of the ashes via the PE and Sport Premium. Yet another decade of funding and again we are at the point where, in what could be a case of history repeating, PESS faces an uncertain future. At the time of writing, Premium funding for the 2022/2023 academic year has been confirmed, with only weeks before the schools break up for summer, highlighting the disconnect between policy/decision makers and the operational management of schools. It is questionable how future policies in sport will focus, or not, on PESS. With the domains of sport, health and education becoming blurred with multiple government agencies involved in a spectrum of interventions, programmes and performance targets. The alliance of 'PE' 'Sport' 'Physical Activity' 'Health' is becoming more evident (Evans, 2003; McKenzie et al., 2016; Pill et al., 2020) and in doing so, policy needs to consider the relationship within the sporting ecosystem (Sport England, 2021), within government as well as across society.

As with *Game Plan* (2002), it may well be the time to review PESS considering the impact, not just as a legitimised curriculum subject (Ives & Kirk, 2013; Williams, 1985) but also in respect of wider policy outcomes in health and sport. This does not however resolve the decision-making pressure on the headteacher, how the transmission, transformation and realisation of policy can be influenced by an individual's experience or level of understanding. Should it be that the infrastructure of SSPs should be resurrected? Undoubtedly a successful method of national policy enactment that maintained a level of fidelity to government outcomes, exceeded performance targets and had accountability for the use of public funds. The future of funding for PESS in schools is uncertain, but the use of schools as sites of national policy implementation is sure to remain whether top-down, bottom-up or partnership approaches are favoured.

PRACTITIONER REFLECTION AND INSIGHTS

Alan Watkinson, Founder of Sport Impact, Co-founder of the Schools Active Movement

I met Helen Ives, the chapter author, in 2007, after her appointment as Partnership Development Manager at Feltham Community Sports College. I had recently been appointed to the same role at Isleworth and Syon School. My background was educational whilst Helen had huge experience of sport development. We readily agreed to collaborate closely for the benefit of the whole borough. Helen opened up the possibilities for partnerships beyond the school gates. I learnt an enormous amount in terms of developing innovative projects, working with targeted groups and the importance of advocacy and a strategic approach. I offered insight with the management of relationships with schools and was able to provide understanding of the world of education. In short, policy which advocated partnerships changed the way I worked. Having been fully immersed in this world for the last 16 years, I found this paper a fascinating insight into the roles of successive governments in shaping, and in one notable case dismantling, the development of this essential area of policy. One could quite easily conclude that our system leaves so much to chance in terms of effective strategy and continuity.

What should be noted is that John Major's pragmatic expectation of a minimum two hours of PE on the curriculum that was then taken on by the Blair government was highly effective. This, aligned to a clearly defined Public Sector Agreement target with defined lines of accountability, was all that was needed to ignite a transformative effect on PE and School Sport over the following decades. This was top-down but certainly caught the imagination of large numbers of schools and provided space for innovation, creativity and opportunity to have a positive effect on bespoke local issues.

The key components to this success can, in my opinion, be clearly identified:

- First, there was a clear focus on what needed to be achieved. A strategy and an infrastructure were created to ensure that the target could be reached and schools were rewarded for raising their game to meet the targets.
- Second, the infrastructure created accountability at a national and a local level and a dedicated, invested and highly motivated workforce of fiercely competitive people was created.
- Third, as a result, targets were reached and surpassed in double quick time. There was clearly an appetite and a need for such a political and financial intervention.

It could, though, be argued that reaching the target so quickly was completed at the expense of nurturing school leadership teams and the need to embed the changes into a school's culture was a job that was incomplete. Schools were swept away with the agenda, altering their timetables to achieve coveted kite marks and meeting targets within the PESSCL survey. It was suggested that some were target obsessed and were not as focused on quality of delivery. An example of this was the creation of 'virtual competition' to reach competition targets, involving students uploading their results (time/distance or total) to a centrally held database from which the results were announced, reducing the need for schools to go off site, attending fixtures or events. There is nothing wrong with virtual competition when the intent, impact and outcomes of the competition are clear. However, there were many examples of these being created to merely reach and surpass set targets. There was a sense amongst some that we were moving a little fast, that the workforce, whilst passionate and motivated, needed a skill set that they did not necessarily possess. Effective training of PDMs was established to address this and the infrastructure continued to mature. It was a buoyant time and the future of PESS looked incredibly bright.

The 2008 target of the five-hour offer was based on an increasingly mature, locally driven infrastructure. Local Authorities and (what are now called) Active Partnerships attached themselves to the movement and burgeoning, effective partnerships were being developed across the country. Even better, a national mechanism to share and develop outstanding practice was being developed across the country. The system was viewed as 'World Class.' Delegations of international visitors would attend the Youth Sport Trust conferences to learn from this amazing system and the feel-good factor was more than a little evident. What could possibly go wrong?

In 2010, a general election loomed but the sector was not worried. Perhaps naively, the general consensus was this successful movement and force for good was untouchable. This sense of security was shattered in the Comprehensive Spending Review of 2011. The fact that the Youth Sport Trust were a charity and that the PESSYP strategy was proving to be highly effective in creating healthier outcomes for children did not appear to matter and cessation of funding to SSPs was announced. The sector was shocked and Helen clearly explains the grassroots campaign that took the argument to government. The creation of the School Games network was a lifeline but the change in title for the fundamental role from Partnership Development Manager, clearly a very strategic role, to School Games Organiser, implying a delivery-focused role, demonstrated a lack of ambition as did the significantly decreased amount of funding attached to the programme.

Our two local SSPs were bloodied but not bowed. We set about creating a bespoke offer for local schools who were appalled that the support that they had received was under threat. Schools particularly valued the development of teachers' ability to teach PE. The confidence pupils gained through our interventions was noticed by the schools and they valued our input highly. Further, the development of the competition structure was a huge motivation to them to support our continuation. Many other colleagues across the country were not so successful. By 2013, the national infrastructure had been seriously damaged, and whilst it could be argued that focus on local issues rather than national targets could be more effective, the lack of a national network made sustainable change on a local basis more difficult. This bottom-up model may have allowed for greater freedom and creativity to operate, but making things stick and sharing outstanding practice and learning was far more difficult. Additionally, it opened the sector to an unregulated workforce and accountability measures which were not as robust as they might have been.

Since 2016, funding, particularly for the Premium, has been significantly increased despite the unsettling times of the Covid-19 pandemic. Accountability has remained an issue and a trained infrastructure that can advise schools wisely is not available in all areas. Sadly, the commitment of head teachers to the PESS agenda and associated funding is mixed. Where there is an enlightened committed head teacher collaborating with a high-quality local provider, phenomenal progress is being made. However, there are still schools that contract out PESS provision utilising the Premium, and in the worst-case scenarios their management of the quality is non-existent. Can we learn lessons to create high-functioning use of funding with a clear target and an informed measurable, accountable strategy?

Ofsted (2022) provided an extraordinarily thorough review of the subject area. The School Games and Premium funding has been extended until at least September 2023. Ofsted noticeably has identified that 'High-quality PE is a physical and cultural entitlement,' and I have selected three quotes from this document:

> The national curriculum identifies the aims of the subject and, broadly, the subject content to be taught at each key stage. The flexibility that this broad outline enables in PE can be counterproductive if the subject expertise to meet these broad and ambitious goals is absent.
>
> Despite the national curriculum aims, the purpose of PE is still highly contested: it means different things to different people. In the past, PE has been described as a chameleon 'that changes its colours' based on the differing priorities of different stakeholders.
>
> However, extra-curricular activities cannot replace the careful selection and sequencing of content that is required to physically educate all pupils so that they know more and can do more.

This would suggest that the subject is again receiving the serious attention it deserves and that the improvement of delivery is viewed as a priority for Ofsted. PE remains the only subject to receive ring-fenced funding and the only one outside of the core to be compulsory from the Early Years Foundation Stage to the end of Key Stage 4. The School Sport and Physical Activity Plan is being overhauled by government in the autumn of 2022. As an experienced professional, I have often been told how important it is to

166 Helen Ives

learn the lessons of history when planning for the future. Having lived and worked through the period, this chapter offers policy advisors and government ministers considerable food for thought. It interrogates how different political philosophies and approaches have fared in terms of managing effective change and tangible outcomes through physical education, school sport and physical activity. It is enlightening in highlighting what has worked well, what approaches have proved to be less effective. For me, a clear vision, goal and strategy backed up by a well-trained motivated workforce and infrastructure will provide the best opportunities and outcomes for young people.

Notes

1 Innovation is defined by Nisbet (1974, p.2) as 'any new policy, syllabus, method or organizational change which is intended to improve teaching and learning.'
2 Now Baroness Campbell of Loughborough having been appointed to the House of Lords in 2008 as a cross-bencher in recognition for her work within Sport: Chair of the Youth Sport Trust, Chair of UK Sport, Advisor to the DCMS and DfE. Campbell is currently Head of Women's Football as the Football Association (England).
3 The Specialist Schools Programme was introduced by the Conservative government but was continued and expanded by Labour post their election victory in 1997. Schools, selecting sport as their specialism, would have to support their application with confirmation of £50,000 of partnership funding that would then be match funded should their application be successful.
4 A School Sport Partnership was a network of secondary, primary and special schools working together to increase the quality and quantity of PE and sports opportunities for young people lead by a Partnership Development Manager.
5 In 2019, this Department underwent a name change to the Department for Digital, Culture, Media and Sport but is still recognised by the acronym DCMS.
6 In 2022, there is still a patchwork of provision of School Sport Partnerships which, through some changes in relationships with schools and increased commercial enterprise, still operate across more limited geographical areas providing support for schools and teachers as well as delivering the School Games programme. Many of these SSPs charge a membership to the schools payable from the current PE and Sport Premium. Centralised administration of SSPs does not exist resulting in the actual number of SSPs which have survived being unconfirmed.

References

All Party Parliamentary Group on a Fit and Healthy Childhood (APPGFHC). (2019). *The primary PE and sport premium*. Retrieved August 18, 2022, from https://fhcappg.org.uk /wp-content/uploads/2019/07/the-primary-pe-and-sport-premium-report-180219-2.pdf
Anderson, K. T., & Holloway, J. (2020). Discourse analysis as theory, method, and epistemology in studies of education policy. *Journal of Education Policy, 35*(2), 188–221. https://doi.org/10.1080/02680939.2018.1552992
Ball, S. J. (1994). Some reflections on policy theory: A brief response to Hatcher and Troyna. *Journal of Education Policy, 9*(2), 171–182. https://doi.org/10.1080/0268093940090205
Ball, S. J., Maguire, M., & Braun, A. (2011). *How schools do policy: Policy enactments in secondary schools*. Routledge.

Bernstein, B. (2000). *Pedagogy, symbolic control, and identity: Theory, research, critique* (Vol. 5). Rowman & Littlefield.

Bloyce, D., & Smith, A. (2009). *Sport policy and development: An introduction*. Routledge.

Cuban, L. (1988). Constancy and change in schools (1880s to the present). In P. W. Jackson (Ed.), *Contributing to educational change: Perspectives on research and practice* (pp. 85–105). McCutchan.

Curtner-Smith, M. D. (1999). The more things change the more they stay the same: Factors influencing teachers' interpretations and delivery of national curriculum physical education. *Sport, Education and Society, 4*(1), 75–97. https://doi.org/10.1080/1357332990040106

Department for Culture, Media and Sport. (2000). *A sporting future for all*. DCMS.

Department for Culture, Media and Sport/Strategy Unit. (2002). *Game plan: A strategy for delivering government's sport and physical activity objectives*. Department for Culture, Media and Sport/Strategy Unit.

Department for Education. (2013). *PE and sport premium for primary schools*. Retrieved May 6, 2021, from https://assets.publishing.service.gov.uk/government/uploads/system/uploads/attachment_data/file/510865/pe-and-sport-premium_conditions-of-grant-for-local-authorities-2013-to2014.pdf

Department for Education. (2014). *PE and sport premium for primary schools*. Retrieved May 6, 2021, from https://www.gov.uk/guidance/pe-and-sport-premium-for-primary-schools#about-the-pe-and-sport-premium

Department for Education. (2015). *PE and sport premium for primary schools*. Retrieved April 15, 2021, from https://www.gov.uk/government/publications/pe-and-sport-premium-conditions-of-grant-for-2015-to-2016/pe-and-sport-premium-conditions-of-grant-for-the-academic-year-2015-to-2016-for-local-authorities-and-maintained-schools

Department for Education. (2017). *PE and sport premium for primary schools*. Retrieved January 10, 2021, from https://www.gov.uk/government/publications/pe-and-sport-premium-funding-allocations-for-2017-to-2018/pe-and-sport-premium-conditions-of-grant-2017-to-2018-local-authorities-and-maintained-schools

Department for Education. (2018). *PE and sport premium for primary schools*. Retrieved January 12, 2021, from https://www.gov.uk/government/publications/pe-and-sport-premium-conditions-of-grant-2018-to-2019

Department for Education. (2019). *Primary PE and Sport Premium Survey Research Report. July 2019*. Retrieved February 12, 2021, from https://assets.publishing.service.gov.uk/government/uploads/system/uploads/attachment_data/file/816676/Primary_PE_and_Sport_Premium_Survey_research_report.pdf

Department for Education. (2020). *PE and sport premium for primary schools*. Retrieved May 10, 2021, from https://www.gov.uk/government/publications/pe-and-sport-premium-conditions-of-grant-2020-to-2021

Department for Education. (2021). *PE and sport premium for primary schools*. Retrieved May 10, 2022, from https://www.gov.uk/guidance/pe-and-sport-premium-for-primary-schools

Department for Education and Skills. (2006). *2005/06 school sport survey*. TNS.

Department of National Heritage. (1995). *Sport: Raising the game*. DNH.

Evans, J. (2003). Physical Education and health: A polemic or let them eat cake! *European Physical Education Review, 9*(1), 87–101. https://doi.org/10.1177/1356336X03009001182

168 Helen Ives

Flintoff, A. (2003). The school sport co-ordinator programme: Changing the role of the physical education teacher? *Sport, Education and Society*, *8*(2), 231–250. https://doi.org/10.1080/13573320309252

Flintoff, A., Foster, R., & Wystawnoha, S. (2011). Promoting and sustaining high quality physical education and school sport through school sport partnerships. *European Physical Education Review*, *17*(3), 341–351. https://doi.org/10.1177/1356336X11416731

Forde, C., & Torrance, D. (2017). Social justice leaders: Critical moments in headteachers'/ principals' development. *Research in Educational Administration and Leadership*, *2*(1), 29–52. https://doi.org/10.30828/real/2017.1.3

Foster, D., & Roberts, N. (2019). *Physical education, physical activity and sport in schools.* House of Commons Library.

Fullan, M. (1994). Coordinating top-down and bottom-up strategies for educational reform. In R. J. Anson (Ed.), *Systemic reform: Perspectives on personalizing education.* (pp. 7–24). OERI, USDE September 1994.

Gillborn, D. (1994). The micro-politics of macro reform. *British Journal of Sociology of Education*, *15*(2), 147–164. https://doi.org/10.1080/0142569940150201

Griggs, G. (2015). *Understanding primary physical education*. Routledge.

Grix, J. (2015). *Sport politics: An introduction.* Bloomsbury Publishing.

Hansard HC Deb vol 607 col 964 (16 March 2016).

HM Treasury. (2007). *Deliver a successful Olympic games and paralympic games with a sustainable legacy and get more children and young people taking part in high quality PE and sport.* The Stationary Office.

Houlihan, B. (2000). Sporting excellence, schools and sports development: The politics of crowded policy spaces. *European Physical Education Review*, *6*(2), 171–193. https://doi.org/10.1177/1356336X000062005

Houlihan, B., & Green, M. (2006). The changing status of school sport and physical education: Explaining policy change. *Sport, Education and Society*, *11*(1), 73–92. https://doi.org/10.1080/13573320500453495

Houlihan, B., & Lindsey, I. (2013). *Sport policy in Britain.* Routledge.

Hunt, J. (2011). *School games.* Telford Sport College Conference. Telford. Retrieved April 15, 2021, from https://www.gov.uk/government/speeches/school-games

Ives, H. M. (2014). *Physical education and school sport: Transmission, translation and realization* [Unpublished doctoral thesis]. University of Bedfordshire.

Ives, H. M. (2017). Primary physical education in England. In G. Griggs & K. Petrie (Eds.), *Routledge handbook of primary physical education* (pp. 183–193). Routledge.

Ives, H. M., & Kirk, D. (2013). What are the public perceptions of physical education? In S. Capel & M. Whitehead (Eds.), *Debates in physical education* (pp. 188–201). Routledge.

Levin, B. (1998). An epidemic of education policy: (What) can we learn from each other? *Comparative Education*, *34*(2), 131–141. https://doi.org/10.1080/03050069828234

Lindsey, I. (2020). Analysing policy change and continuity: Physical education and school sport policy in England since 2010. *Sport, Education and Society*, *25*(1), 27–42. https://doi.org/10.1080/13573322.2018.1547274

Macdonald, D. (2003). Curriculum change and the post-modern world: Is the school curriculum-reform movement an anachronism? *Journal of Curriculum Studies*, *35*(2), 139–149. https://doi.org/10.1080/00220270210157605

Mackintosh, C. (2014). Dismantling the school sport partnership infrastructure: Findings from a survey of physical education and school sport practitioners. *Education 3-13*, *42*(4), 432–449. https://doi.org/10.1080/03004279.2012.714793

McKenzie, T. L., Sallis, J. F., Rosengard, P., & Ballard, K. (2016). The SPARK programs: A public health model of physical education research and dissemination. *Journal of Teaching in Physical Education, 35*(4), 381–389. https://doi.org/10.1123/jtpe.2016-0100

Metrowebukmetro. (2007). Government hits school sport target. The metro newspaper. Retrieved April 15, 2021, from https://metro.co.uk/2007/10/15/government-hits-school -sport-target-301083/

Morgan, P., & Bourke, S. (2008). Non-specialist teachers' confidence to teach PE: The nature and influence of personal school experiences in PE. *Physical Education and Sport Pedagogy, 13*(1), 1–29. https://doi.org/10.1080/17408980701345550

O'Donovan, T., Ives, H. M., Bowler, M., & Sammon, P. (2016). *Active inspiration playmakers final Report*. University of Bedfordshire. Institute of Sport & Physical Activity Research.

Office for Standards in Education. (2019). *Research review series: PE*. Retrieved April 10, 2022, from https://www.gov.uk/government/publications/research-review-series-pe/ research-review-series-pe

Ofsted. (2022). *Research review series: PE*. Retrieved July 20, 2022, from https://www .gov.uk/government/publications/research-review-series-pe/research-review-series-pe #introduction

Penney, D. (2004). Policy tensions being played out in practice: The specialist schools initiative in England. *Journal for Critical Education Policy Studies, 2*(1), 227–246.

Penney, D., & Houlihan, B. (2001, December). Re-shaping the borders for policy research: The development of specialist sports colleges in England. In *Conference of the Australian association for research in education* (Vol. 14, p. 2010). Retrieved July 10, 2022.

Pill, S., Hyndman, B., & Cruickshank, V. (2020). Physical education during self-isolation: Maintaining the 'E' in PE. *EducationHQ*. Retrieved July 20, 2022, from https:// educationhq.com/news/physical-education-during-self-isolation-maintaining-the-e-in -pe-75994/

Priestley, M., & Rabiee, P. (2002). Hopes and fears: Stakeholder views on the transfer of special school resources towards inclusion. *International Journal of Inclusive Education, 6*(4), 371–390. https://doi.org/10.1080/13603110210143680

Rizvi, F., & Kemmis, S. (1987). *Dilemmas of reform: An overview of issues and achievements of the participation and equity program in Victorian schools 1984–1986*. Deakin Institute for Studies in Education, Deakin University.

Select Committee on Culture, Media and Sport (1999). *Appendices to the minutes of evidence*. Retrieved May 10, 2022, from https://publications.parliament.uk/pa/cm199900/cmselect /cmcumeds/99/99ap26.htm

Skilbeck, M. (1982). Three educational ideologies. In T. Horton & P. Raggatt (Eds.), *Challenge and change in the curriculum* (pp. 7–18). Open University Press.

Sparkes, A. C. (1989). Paradigmatic confusions and the evasion of critical issues in naturalistic research. *Journal of Teaching in Physical Education, 8*(2), 131–151. https:// doi.org/10.1123/jtpe.8.2.131

Sport England. (2021). *Uniting the movement*. Sport England.

Stronach, I., & Morris, B. (1994). Polemical notes on educational evaluation in the age of 'policy hysteria'. *Evaluation and Research in Education, 8*(1–2), 5–19. https://doi.org /10.1080/09500799409533351

Tannehill, D., Van der Mars, H., & MacPhail, A. (2013). *Building effective physical education programs*. Jones & Bartlett Publishers.

Williams, E. A. (1985). Understanding constraints on innovation in physical education. *Journal of Curriculum Studies, 17*(4), 407–413. https://doi.org/10.1080/0022027850170406

Youth Sport Trust. (2005). *Welcome pack for school sport coordinators.* Youth Sport Trust.

Youth Sport Trust. (2016). *Sport changes lives strategic plan – 2013–18.* January 2016. Retrieved May 10, 2022, from https://www.sportsthinktank.com/uploads/yst-strategic-plan-2016-v2.pdf

Zhu, X., Ennis, C. D., & Chen, A. (2011). Implementation challenges for a constructivist physical education curriculum. *Physical Education and Sport Pedagogy, 16*(1), 83–99. https://doi.org/10.1080/17408981003712802

Chapter 10

Voluntary Sports Clubs

Andrew Adams

Introduction

This chapter focuses on voluntary sport clubs as implementers of sport policy and seeks to disentangle process from practice in making sense of how and why voluntary sport clubs are critical to community delivery of any sport strategy. The political/governmental institutional structures of nation states are relatively fixed and enduring. As sport has become a more salient feature of government policy and practice across nation states so has it become part of a political institutional structure that has sought to develop policy that incorporates a full range of delivery mechanisms to ensure reach and compliance. This has meant the inclusion of leisure Trusts, volunteers, local authorities, sport clubs, schools and the Scout Association as willing and/or unsuspecting associates in the delivery of government strategic objectives. To this end, voluntary sport clubs (VSCs) have become an enduring fixture for implementing what might be referred to as community sport policy (Harris & Houlihan, 2014; Adams, 2011).

Because VSCs emerge out of and are a fundamental part of what can be termed the third sector and/or civil society (Rochester, 2013) they can also be considered as private or perhaps 'exclusive' enterprises organised around the enthusiasms of individuals (Bishop & Hoggett, 1986). VSCs are by dint of this arrangement also social entrepreneurial organisations that primarily operate to further their own objectives (Harris et al., 2009), whilst usually operating under the auspices of a particular governing body. In this regard, VSCs are organisationally strong (many have a strong participant and voluntary base) but are structurally weak collectives (limited decision-making capacity/agency beyond the organisation itself) that have become prey to sport policy objectives that have sought to use their potential social outputs as part of a broader policy framework (Parker et al., 2020). This last point suggests that VSCs are victims and are perhaps unwilling to be part of a macro-level policy framework. This is not the case. Nor would it be correct to say that they are willing collaborators. Indeed, necessity and realism are key facets of VSC organisation and the search for survival is at the top of the list for most VSC committees. Of course, we should be aware of not lumping all VSCs in together. VSCs are not a homogenous set of organisations and will vary against many sets

DOI: 10.4324/9781003162728-10

172 Andrew Adams

of indices (Harris et al., 2009), such as size, purpose of the club, NGB structure and organisation and, at a more micro level, the make-up and location of each VSC (Stenling & Fahlen, 2016).

This chapter uses two ideas to organise and structure the discussion. First, the concept of political opportunity structure is used as a descriptive and sensitising device to explain and explore how the institution of the VSC has become a central conduit through which much sport and non-sport policy has been directed. Second, the chapter will outline the idea of street-level bureaucracy as a structuring framework to consider how policy implementation can be considered at the VSC level. The use of these two concepts provides a set of thinking tools that can be used to explore various drivers for implementation that have occurred as the tidal movements of policy and politics have (a) driven sports salience to government (Houlihan & Green, 2009), (b) caused a recognition of sports utilitarian value (Hardman, 2019) and (c) ensured sports subjugation to dominant neoliberal values (Hartmann & Kwauk, 2011). The key paradox as far as VSCs go (and in respect of the sector they represent) is that many of them are increasingly beholden to NGBs, who themselves are beholden to National Sport Organisations (NSOs). This top-down relationship tends to be predicated on financial and operational conditions that stem from the institutionalisation of structural and institutional modernisation, whilst remaining fiercely independent and, in the main, answerable to their members. This idea itself may be slightly whimsical given that (and this is perhaps at the heart of the paradox) accountability has increasingly moved upwards (reflecting top-down implementation strategies) at the expense of downward accountability (bottom-up drivers) (Houlihan & Green, 2009). The dual conceptual framework that this chapter sets out may well enable us to understand and clarify not only who the main players in the world of the VSC are but also to shine a light on the relationship between principals (definers) and agents (doers) as bureaucrats who operate at 'street level' to implement policy in particular local contexts.

The Political Institutionalism of VSCs

There were approximately 62,398 VSCs affiliated to NGBs in England in 2015 (Nichols & James, 2017). VSCs are prime examples of civil society organisations that facilitate the liberty of individuals to associate for a common purpose that does not involve the state directly (Cole, 1945). However, many VSCs in England are now supported by Sport England, which is perhaps at odds with a traditional view of VSCs' 'arm's length' approach (Oakley & Green, 2001). VSCs, with a guiding principle of mutual aid, reflect and enhance the established independent philosophical and consensual tradition of civil society organisations. Critically the fundamentals of VSCs have ensured, that until relatively recently, policymakers have been loath to interfere with these guiding principles, because of the potential knock-on effects for civil society and volunteerism (Bishop & Hoggett, 1986).

The key challenge for VSCs in relation to policy contexts and implementation has arguably come from the simple realisation that sport can play a legitimate role in the construction of government policy. Of course, this has necessitated a particular dominant version of sport that is over-generalised, popular and idealistic (Coalter, 2013). A dominant version that 'teaches valuable lessons' and 'is a central part of Britain's national heritage' (Department of National Heritage, 1995) and which 'teaches us about life. We learn self-discipline and teamwork ... to win with grace and lose with dignity. It gets us fit. It keeps us healthy' but which can 'help Government to achieve a number of ambitious goals' (DCMS/Strategy Unit, 2002, pp. 5–6). By 2015, '*Sporting Future*', the UK government strategy had consolidated VSCs as key partners in local responsibilities to 'unblock participation and improve the local sport delivery system (HM Government, 2015, p. 13). The focus of UK government's sport policy has now moved to increasing movement and tackling inactivity. VSCs in this context are identified as 'trusted' and part of 'community hubs, where people of different ages, cultures and backgrounds, who may otherwise never meet, come together through a shared passion' (Sport England, 2021, p. 13). This very brief recounting of the VSC sport policy context reinforces the point made by the editors of this book in their introductory chapter through citing Houlihan and Lindsey's (2013, p. 188) recognition of 'steady, though uneven, expansion in the role of the state in sport.' It does not suggest that VSCs have developed beyond mutual aid to become 'multi-functional' organisations. This ensures that VSCs are separate to civil society organisations such as Scope, Mencap, Marie Curie Cancer Care and Amnesty International, which typically have several major functions such as service providing, mutual aid, policy advocacy and campaigning, individual advocacy and resource and coordination functions (Kendall & Knapp, 1995).

Political Opportunity Structure

To help make sense of the institutional framework of the VSC, it is useful to consider Andrew's (1989) historical concern, who, from her study of charity in London between 1680 and 1820, identifies that particular forms of voluntary action reflect and are shaped by the specific political context in which they operate. As identified previously (in this chapter and elsewhere – e.g. Kendall & Knapp, 1995), VSCs are increasingly tied into the fabric of social policymaking in the UK and the Political Opportunity Structure (POS) provides a framework for establishing a more contextual analysis of the development and implementation of policy and practice in and through VSCs (Kriesi, 1995; Maloney et al., 2000).

POS is a way of making sense of the political processes that provide a structure for social action to occur (Meyer, 2004). Eisinger focused on whether the political environment was 'open' or 'closed' which he describes as 'the openings, weak spots, barriers and resources of the political system itself' (Eisinger, 1973, pp.11–12). In short, the argument is that political context can be translated into a POS which allows 'For the systematic analysis of the political context that mediates structural conflicts' (Kriesi, 1995, p. 167). The usefulness of the POS concept resides in how it can help us to acknowledge context for the promotion and potential success of particular social movements (Eisinger, 1973). Coming from movement theory, the argument relates to how political structure manufactures and restructures existing power relations with a concomitant impact for social impact (Skocpol, 1979).

The usefulness of the POS concept as a thinking tool for considering VSCs is in the set of clues that can be discerned that may lead to sustained interaction with authorities. In this respect, the POS is not a fixed coordinate and therefore can be interpreted in a more organic rather than mechanistic fashion. The clues arise from the ability of individuals and groups to mobilise particular networks in search of these 'clues,' which include access to power, shifting alignments, the availability of influential allies, and cleavages within and among elites (Maloney et al., 2000). This means that at any one time, VSCs must take the POS in which they are operating as a 'given.' The POS of VSCs thus must consider (a) the formal institutional structure, (b) the informal procedures and prevailing strategies of that structure and (c) an assessment of the configuration of power.

(a) The Formal Institutional Structure

This refers to formal access to state institutions and/or political decision-making processes. Arguably, VSCs are institutionally quite distinct from most voluntary associations. The importance of the mutual aid ethos, the desire for independence and autonomy, and a distinctive managerial framework for sport (Smith & Stewart, 2010) constitute a form of institutional capital that reinforces a differentness to most other civil society organisations. Essentially formal access to the state (the political decision-making processes) is increased in line with how decentralised a state may be. Moves to more decentralised governance in the UK, where there are more opportunities for clubs to interact with state-funded organisations, would indicate a greater potential for formal access for VSCs (Stoker, 1998).

(b) Informal Procedures and Prevailing Strategies

This refers to the extent to which VSCs can informally be mobilised to create potential resources that may become more profitable and more expedient than more formal opportunities for access. This can be a constraining aspect of the POS as it relies on the potential that a VSC may have to engage with 'upper tier' authorities and operate in an 'exclusive or integrative' manner (Kriesi, 1995). Upper-tier authorities such as NGBs, Active Partnerships, Sport England and local authorities may develop different approaches to VSCs. These may be exclusive and/or integrative and are implemented through the processes and practices adopted by upper-tier organisations. For example, an active partnership or local authority may be confrontative, facilitative or assimilative in the strategy it applies to working with VSCs. The outcome for VSCs is strategically related to the issue of informality as not all of the authorities that VSCs have to deal with will treat all VSCs in the same manner. Issues surrounding the nature of particular sports and the specific sub-culture of specific clubs, particularly the socio-cultural make-up of a VSC, its geographical location as well as a concern with its provenance, may all impact on approaches taken towards different VSCs.

(c) The Configuration of Power

As much as it is a truism that power structures and conditions how actors engage in any activity, it is perhaps more important to acknowledge that it is the strategies of authorities and those in a system that are specified by any 'relevant configuration of power' (Kriesi, 1995, p. 168). In this regard, the extent to which the 'success' of a VSC is attainable is largely determined by the constellation of particular central political interests, and then how a VSC or the VSC movement responds to those political interests.

In relation to the VSC environment, the important issue in appreciating the formal institutional structure and the informal procedures and dominant strategies is the extent of the pull and push forces, which can signify how a political environment may be appealing and supportive of volunteerism in general and of VSCs in particular. On the other hand, VSCs themselves (or those who represent them) have signalled a willingness to be supported, be included and be proactive within a government-sponsored policy agenda (Harris & Houlihan, 2016). The receptivity and sympathy of the political context to VSCs can be determined at macro, meso and micro levels (Dorey, 2014). The macro-level concerns central government direction, largely through steerage given by the relevant national sport organisation such as Sport England; the meso level addresses the concerns of regional sports organisations such as Active Partnerships; whilst the micro level focuses on opportunities for VSCs in a particular locality that are likely to be bound up in the nature of the local partnership mix as much as with particular contexts of particular VSCs. It is in this type of scenario where it is possible to consider logics of action for VSCs, where the configuration of power plus the particular alignments of organisations, strategies and relevant political context shapes both formal and informal dimensions of the POS (Maloney et al., 2000).

Towards a POS for VSCs in England

Whilst the discussion thus far has been rather abstract and conceptual, the following section serves as a brief case study of the POS for VSCs in England. Government interest in the voluntary sector is not new. The first Conservative administration under Margaret Thatcher in 1979 saw the emergence of a positively inclined POS towards the voluntary sector (Kendall & Knapp, 1996). An antipathy towards state provision of goods and services, the necessity of a small welfare state and a free rein for the unfettered market to be the dominant provider for people's needs provided an ideological core. The promotion of voluntary associationalism was, between 1980 and 1995, dominated by two factors. First, defensively to protect individuals from the ravages of inequality driven mainly by Conservative economic policies.

Second, it was driven by a service role to supply specific services based upon contractual agreements (Dorey, 2014). The upshot for VSCs at this time was commensurate. VSCs remained steadfastly voluntary in outlook and scope; they were focused on members and tended to be exclusionary, inward looking and were the promoters of sport policy, which was often seen in individual, voluntaristic and even philanthropic terms (Houlihan & White, 2002).

The election of Labour in 1997 changed the ecology for VSCs which was to be located within an overwhelmingly positive POS, with government proactively encouraging volunteering and voluntary associations as agents of the state (Home Office, 1998). It is at this juncture that Stoker's (1998) argument concerning the potential role of governance arrangements informing on configurations of power in developing a more in-depth analysis of the political context has purchase. This can be seen as an invocation for modernisation and how voluntary organisations would be able to modernise effectively. Modernisation can be understood as shorthand for a managerialist framework that is both functional and utilitarian and, as Finlayson (2003) notes, has three components. First, a rhetorical function; an 'up' word that persuades and motivates; it is pragmatic, positive and forward looking (Lister, 2000). Second, a concrete reference; the modernisation discourse enabled the rhetoric and reality of certain policies to be enacted under a more prosaic and pragmatic 'what works' approach, bringing onside politically dissonant elements. Finally, modernisation as a strategy of governance acts as a problematising device ensuring that it 'serves as a mechanism for "diagnosing" errors in the organisation and management of public services and for establishing their cure' (Finlayson, 2003, p. 68). Modernisation is thus a signifier of positive development, a pragmatic and realist-orientated structural framework to manage capitalism, and a strategy of governance where service delivery is problematised with necessary service reform (Adams, 2011). In the UK, this framework was further buttressed by publication of *The Compact* (Cabinet Office, 2010), which 12 years after the publication of the first compact (1998) once again set out how government would systematically work with civil society organisations, including VSCs. Interestingly, at this time, there was a minister for the third sector, and this edition of the compact was supporting the then Prime Minister Cameron's idea of 'Big Society' which was fundamentally about getting citizens more engaged, involved and responsible for the communities around them.

The Coalition government (2010–2015) was arguably re-engineering the 'community' guiding metaphor when following on from 'New' Labour (Levitas, 2000). For VSCs this signified a movement for more enterprising activities underlining a 'mixed economic' role in contributing to the generation of stronger communities, economic development and democratic participation. For VSCs the POS was also reliant on the governance issue of mutual aid, the continual elevation of sport up the political agenda, and the adoption of a super-positive view of sport. The result was that government wanted to incorporate VSCs into wider policy objectives, beyond the idea of partnerships. The apparent importance attached to VSCs by Labour, the Coalition and then successive Conservative governments, particularly as agents

Voluntary Sports Clubs

for promoting sport policy, is reflected by the close alignment of the Department of Culture, Media and Sport, Sport England and NGBs perceptible in successive sport policy documents since 1998. Moving swiftly through the English political landscape from successive Labour governments, through a Coalition government and onto successive Conservative administrations from 2015 onwards (Houlihan & Lindsey, 2013), it is possible to argue that the POS for VSCs has largely remained untouched. Sport policies and strategies published under the auspices of these administrations have pursued a relationship with VSCs to enact elements of policy and meet particular outcomes. VSCs are looked on by upper-tier authorities as part of a solution whilst simultaneously they have come to accept their role in broader policy contexts. In establishing a coherent and direct relationship between governmental objectives – both wider social and the specifically sport related, and the potential for funding – VSCs have had to adopt a more congruent attitude to the key issues of the 'upper tier' authorities.

Street-Level Bureaucracy

In contrast to the structural concept of the POS that has been briefly outlined above as a thinking tool for considering the context within which VSCs operate, the notion of street-level bureaucracy is focused at the individual organisational actor level and associated opportunities for agency. There is a clear resonance here with the editors' outlining of principal-agent theory in the levels of discretion afforded to actors (individuals and organisations) who are likely to find themselves implementing policies in conditions of resource dependency, where power relations and attendant networks are not necessarily clear or transparent. The idea of street-level bureaucracy has a clear practical implementation dimension for VSCs where actors are generally thought to be able to exercise agency and where accountability has traditionally tended to be downwards. Street-level bureaucracy also enables outsiders to make sense of how individuals operating at a grassroots level make common sense decisions on behalf of their club. It is important to separate street-level bureaucrats (SLBts) from bureaucracy (SLBy). SLBts are individuals who can translate and act with discretion in exercising agency. In grassroots sport contexts, this can mean generic or individual sport development officers. It can mean volunteers such as volunteer sports coaches who become responsible for deciding what activities will be undertaken, at what intensity and for how long. It can also mean sport administrators (paid and unpaid) who stand between upper-tier authorities such as NGBs, NSOs and local authorities and the club they represent. Lipsky characterises SLBts as individuals who exercise discretion even though they 'lacked the time, information, or other resources' to perform various functions within their role 'according to the highest standards of decision-making' in their field (1980 [2010], p. xi).

Street-level bureaucracies (SLBys) are organisational structures that can collectively, or within their organisational remit, act with discretion to make their own decisions for and on behalf of an organisation. For VSCs this amounts to how the organisation of each club enables individuals within each club to exercise discretion and make the best decisions for the club members on behalf of the club. Here, in effect, is the mutual aid driver clearly distilled. Importantly, as we shall examine below, some VSCs are more in tune with externally facing demands (Borgers et al., 2018). At this juncture, it is worth reminding ourselves that Lipsky's use of the term SLBy was originally intended to help make sense of the implementation of public policy by bringing together issues of public administration and political science. The extension of the term SLBy to voluntary organisations and associations is largely driven by changes to the framing of public administration, the dominance of neoliberal thought and subsequent developments of governance. It is this latter factor that has promoted outsourcing, hollowing out and a focus on governance rather than government (Stoker, 1998). In this regard, any expectation that VSCs will act as mere implementers is to misread the history and development of the voluntary sector movement and VSCs. It is perhaps useful to consider VSCs as a particular type of social entrepreneurial organisation that is traditionally accountable to their constituent members. The question concerns the extent to which discretion can be exerted by VSCs to ensure they align to a democratic will and the rule of law (Ellis, 2011), which is informal and loosely constituted and subject to a range of social, political, economic and cultural forces. To extend thinking about VSCs, it is noteworthy first, to remind ourselves that a particular POS for VSCs has become institutionalised to the extent that the three dimensions of a POS (the formal institutional arrangements, the informal and dominant processes and how power is configured) have provided the seedbed for how VSCs make sense of their place and purpose. Second, it is necessary to consider how complex dynamics of change may be detected in the institutional logics that may be discernible between types of VSCs.

Borgers et al. (2018) usefully identify two frameworks for considering VSCs. First, they categorise a VSC that offers more individualised treatment of members and membership-generated structures based on bottom-up and spontaneous interaction as 'sport light' organisations. In this definition, bottom-up processes refer to the individual action undertaken by the participants to shape and organise sporting practice. Second, and as a contrast, Borgers and colleagues situate traditional VSCs as 'heavy organisations (2018), which are highly institutionalised, powerful, centrally positioned and are regulated actors in the sports landscape where formal membership 'comes with involvement expectations to interpersonal conduct and organisational practices' (Lorentzen & Hustinx, 2007, p. 105). This distinction is useful to illustrate evolving and developing idioms of VSC structure and participation and institutionalisation of VSCs, but also is indicative of how the bureaucracy of VSCs can mitigate or promote the activities of SLBts. Light and heavy types of VSC usefully denote some of the differences in how VSCs have responded to modernisation processes under the guise of partnership working (Harris & Houlihan, 2016). In employing this typology, it is possible to argue that some institutional realignment has resulted in a contentious landscape where governance, democratic accountability and the ability for individuals to act with discretion are linked to the structure and function of VSCs and their propensity for change (Stenling & Fahlen, 2016). Moreover, in distinguishing between light and heavy organisations it is possible to suggest how the discretionary action of SLBts might differ accordingly and perhaps more importantly who the individuals might be who are able to operate in this capacity. Thus, whilst there are options for SLBts to affect situations differently, depending on organisational status, it is important to be reminded that discretion in itself is neither 'good' nor 'bad' (Evans & Harris, 2004). Rather, in 'heavy' VSCs, the exercising of SLBy may be considered as a professional function or attribute where an individual is expected to link to dominant policy organisations and their agendas. Conversely, in 'light' VSCs, SLBts may exercise discretion aligned to members and the community they serve akin to the development of social capital within a group. In either case, the dominant neoliberal context promotes the marketisation and commodification of VSCs to the extent that policy implementation is individualised for consumption and may represent a type of 'public service gap' (Hupe & Buffat, 2014) that represents how the POS shapes conditions for the translation of policy to action.

As a major contextual factor, neoliberalism can be understood as a set of economic policies that have been widely accepted and include a deferring to the rule of the market, cutting back on public expenditure, deregulation, privatisation and replacing the idea of the 'public good' with individual responsibility (Hall et al., 2013). As part of the neoliberal condition, there is a constant institutional reorganisation to improve competitive position in the global market. VSCs have been subject to these processes and consequently their role as implementers for sport policy has been affected. The greater exposure of VSCs to the need to modernise and take onboard a drive for capital and be party to controlling mechanisms has tapped into VSCs' entrepreneurial roots of mutual aid, reciprocity and self-help. The origins of VSCs, let us not forget, are in an amateurism and volunteerism that has been characterised as a form of sports proselytism (Houlihan & White, 2002; Coalter, 2013), but which has been transformed to enable VSCs to be more inclusive and responsive to social, economic and cultural changes.

As part of cultural changes that have impacted how VSCs can act in a street-level bureaucratic capacity has been the development of governance concerns that have impacted on VSCs. The emergence of partnerships and networks as an organising and structuring structure can be understood as part of a 'governance narrative' (Grix & Phillpots, 2011, p. 6) that Bevir and Rhodes (2006, 2008) call a 'new governance'. Within a proactive POS, VSCs became partner organisations in service delivery where they had to operate in a networked mode with other public and private agents to deliver on policy agendas (Grix & Phillpots, 2011). Other governance structures that have shaped how VSCs can act are New Public Management and New Management. Both concepts describe the commercialisation of public services, the dominance of free market thinking and private enterprise in running often-welfaristic services and a sort of regulatory governance to monitor, evaluate and measure the extent to which services were delivered. This is played out in comments (identified by Grix & Phillpots, 2011, p. 12) made by a senior Sport England figure when discussing partnerships:

> Whether partnership is the right word [for County Sport Partnership] or not I suppose you could argue is up for debate, because within County Sport Partnerships there are commissioning arrangements, contracting arrangements, service level agreements, partnering, partnerships and that is part of the evolution of the new strategy and the new structure.

The emergence of *Game Plan* (Department for Culture, Media and Sport, 2002) under 'New' Labour was a response to, and indicative of, a concern to implement and embed New Management and New Public Management within sport policy. Commensurate processes of implementation involving broader cross-cutting agendas featuring a wide array of partners and deliverers have gradually become the norm (Adams, 2011). Subsequent changes to governance and operationalisation have had a knock-on effect of driving VSCs from being 'light' to 'heavy' organisations that are weighed down within this structural framework.

In considering VSCs as street-level bureaucracies, it is noteworthy that continuity has been at the heart of sport policy for mass participation. This has been characterised by the rhetoric of 'sport for all' that does not have a clearly definable policy goal that is shared by all actors in this sector (Houlihan & Lindsey, 2013). The assumption that the voluntarism at the heart of VSCs can be tapped for political and policy purposes ignores the 'asymmetric network governance' that behoves a set of lopsided power relations which, at best, may limit a VSC's ability to apply discretion in implementing policy and, at worst, render it non-existent. The dependence of government on the delivery network of VSCs should clearly ensure that these clubs have some leverage, but as Houlihan and Lindsey argue, 'it is generally outweighed in significance by the extent of financial resource dependence of NGBs and clubs on public subsidy' (2013, p. 186). However, it should not be assumed that the compliance of VSCs to accept steerage from NGBs, NSOs, local authorities and the like in return for financial or other resources reflects a willingness to trade in their ability to exert agency. Indeed, it would be dangerous in the messy world of mass- or community-level sport policy to assume that policy goals were clear, knowable and operationalisable, with policy decided by politicians and simply implemented by tame policy administrators at club level.

It is important not to homogenise VSCs in the UK or in any country. Individual sports and individual clubs, which are often run by volunteers, are likely to have different cultures and ideologies. The individual context of each and every VSC is likely to create a different framework for how volunteers and clubs reciprocally impact each other in terms of relative autonomy, decision-making and value. Certainly, because VSCs are mutual aid-driven entities that consume the products of their reciprocal structure and functioning, the issue of accountability – towards members rather than to upper-tier authorities

(Adams, 2011) – represents a point of interaction and action where VSCs can demonstrably exert their SLBy status. It is here that the tension between loosely defined policy objectives, modernisation and mutual aid plays out in producing conflict. Prior to the modernisation of sport, its institutions and the public's perception of what sport is and what it can do and the salience of sport to governments were negligible. Sport policy for mass participation sport in the UK from *Raising the Game* (1995), through *Game Plan* (Department for Culture, Media and Sport, 2002) and *Playing to Win: A New Era for Sport* (Department for Culture, Media and Sport, 2008) to *A Sporting Future* (HM Government, 2015) has come to rest on a dominant version of sport (Hartmann & Kwauk, 2011) that is primarily delivered by the country's network of VSCs. It is in this context that Grix and Phillpot's notion of asymmetric governance has resonance as VSCs, notwithstanding the interpretation and discretion that they are able to show or exert, are perhaps prone to currents of power that they are unable to resist. In *Playing to Win: A New Era for Sport* (2008), the drive to develop a world-leading community sport system was to include 'high quality [community] clubs' (p.13) with the presumption that VSCs would willingly comply with a policy context that once again took them for granted.

Conclusion

This chapter has illustrated the complex ways in which VSCs can be thought of in their role as implementers of policy. The increased importance accorded to VSCs has ultimately come as a result of wider political and policy developments. Moreover, these developments and the influence of hierarchical power relations have consistently and substantially shaped the value, role and interpretation of how VSCs can operate in practice.

Two complementary frameworks have been presented to illustrate the complex ways in which the social construction of institutional actors is enmeshed in the particular opportunity structure of the time. As a structural framework, the POS forces an evaluation of configurations of resources, relevant institutional alignment patterns and the historical precedents and political and power relations that can constrain or promote action. The sketch of the POS concept is quite brief and far from foolproof, but it does attest to the value of examining policy implementation within appropriate structural contexts. Intriguingly, it should be possible to compare different POSs of VSCs along, say, temporal and geographical lines to explain differences in how VSCs may adopt a choice of particular strategies or how VSCs may affect the environment in which they find themselves. Whilst we have some understanding of VSCs and the structural forces that both affect them and are affected by them, too often they are not considered on their own terms. This has perhaps begun to be addressed in the second part of my discussion, where the use of the street-level bureaucracy can have purchase. Street-level bureaucracy sits between top-down and bottom-up policy models and focuses attention on the agency of individuals and actors in exercising discretion as implementers of policy.

The apparent objectification of VSCs as policy instruments within a delivery system that is focused on measurable outputs and outcomes and circumscribed by financial conditionality is clearly discernible from the current POS of VSCs. Changes in resource dependency relative to policy and power configurations are likely to determine the array of relationships and influence available to the VSC sector. Individual VSCs are likely to determine particular implementation strategies and impacts relative to their own ability to exercise discretion and agency. Thus, in considering the direction, and formulation of sport policy and non-sport policy, it is necessary to investigate, interpret and understand the context of those policies. The necessity of this approach is that it can shine a light on the structural manufacturing processes at play that may enable and/or constrain the activities of street-level bureaucracies to engage with upper-tier authorities in negotiating their role as policy implementers. As argued above, VSCs can only act as policy implementers within the structure that they find themselves in. Use of the POS and street-level bureaucracy concepts facilitates a nuanced understanding of how and why this occurs.

In closing, it is pertinent to emphasise that whilst VSCs may be constrained by politics and power, they can, by the relatively virtuous position they hold in society, have a level of influence as well. VSCs have expertise, influence, mutuality and volunteerism, a heady mix that creates a dialectic propensity manifest in how VSCs as street-level bureaucracies may operate to resist or acquiesce in relation to their potential for incorporation into state implementation structures (Adams, 2011; Harris et al., 2009). Perhaps we should decide beforehand whether we see VSCs as a means to implement policy or as member-based organisations that are/ should be responsible to their members. A rugby club, after all, is a club for people to come together who enjoy rugby. It is not necessarily designed for other purposes. Yes, a rugby club will want to get new members, encourage young people to play the game, may look to be part of its 'community' and may work with its NGB to develop these aspects, improve governance, coaching and the overall sustainability of the club. But, as argued by Seippel and Belbo in the case of Norwegian sport clubs, it is often quite simply the case that for many VSCs 'the most important strategy will often be to work towards clubs' local constituencies, not other clubs or policy actors' (2021, p. 493).

PRACTITIONER REFLECTION AND INSIGHTS

Daniel Edson, Head Coach for a Voluntary Rugby Club

At the time of writing, I wear many different hats. My primary role within the club is Director of Rugby. I also undertake multiple other positions including Fixture Secretary and Safeguarding Officer. Having been involved as a volunteer in community sports for 15 years, I have held positions across a wide range of environments in various roles, including coaching, workforce and club development.

Being involved in voluntary sports clubs is hugely rewarding but also provides great challenges, not least the increasing pressures placed on volunteers within these organisations and the growing time commitment needed to develop and deliver sporting opportunities to our communities. The red tape from regional (county bodies) and national bodies (The Rugby Football Union) is providing challenges to VSCs like never before, including increased workforce requirements and club operating standards.

In this chapter, Adams has provided theoretical context to the challenges we as the volunteers and administrators of community sport face day to day. Through this commentary, I explore and engage with this theoretical context in relation to some examples from first-hand experiences and drawing upon the notion of street-level bureaucracy.

Our role as a VSC is to provide physical activity and sporting opportunities to the communities we serve. However, as Adams has alluded to, policymakers from government through to localised branches (county bodies) of the National Governing Bodies, who oversee the delivery of national objectives locally, often forget to appreciate that we (the clubs) structure our output to best suit the needs of the members, as it is the members to whom we are answerable and who significantly fund our activities as a club. Therefore, we seek to further our local objectives first – such as ensuring delivery output is achieved (people and teams playing) and financial sustainability – ahead of the objectives of the wider local and national policymakers, with their focus being on broader engagement, workforce and club development projects which often don't reach or impact large swathes of VSCs.

However, individually our ability as clubs to impact change on the policy and decision-makers is weak as stand-alone organisations. Often, as club committees or those delivering sport on the ground, we are dictated to about decisions and policies that impact how we function as a VSC – such as changing season structures, player registration processes and administration systems. It is only when clubs come together creating collective strength that they can influence channels of power and affect real change that will support the operations of VSCs.

An example of the collective strength of community VSCs is the collective action regarding the season and competition structure at a local level. From experience, this collective action is often driven by either frustration on the ground with decisions which have wide-ranging impacts or stem from decision-making without full and proper consultation. A recent example of this is when the county body who organised adult competitions had concluded from a small sample survey that rugby players within the region wanted less travel for fixtures and, as such, imposed change on the competition structure to reduce travel distances for clubs. However, what they had failed to do was present proposals and consult widely with both players and clubs before implementation.

The changes to structure did achieve the aim of marginally less travel for clubs. To create less travel, league sizes were reduced, and this led to large gaps between fixtures which greatly impacted clubs' ability to maintain the engagement of players due to fewer playing opportunities. This, in practice, has much wider implications. National policy aims were to increase engagement and participation, with regional policy aiming to increase available opportunities for people to engage. What we saw, however, was that due to such decisions being made, these policy aims suffered due to a lack of opportunities for people to engage. This then had a knock-on effect for other facets of the running of VSCs, such as club finances.

Several clubs opened dialogue individually with those who administered the competitions (county and regional governing bodies) to outline their concerns and the real-time impact these changes were having on their clubs, but with little to no success. Many clubs were prepared to compromise with changes to the competition format and slightly increased travel distances if it meant increased playing opportunities. What then transpired was that most clubs became involved in a collective action group, which opened opportunities to share ideas, individual issues and best practices, enabling us to collectively represent and reject the changes made and provide the clubs (about 20–25) with a stronger voice to successfully lobby those in positions of power for change. This led to the clubs being invited to provide ideas, thoughts and feedback on necessary changes which directly shaped the implemented competition structure to better suit our local objectives as clubs.

What is clear and has been rightly outlined by Adams is that no two VSCs are alike, and each will vary due to a multitude of different factors ranging from club demographics to operating structures. However, what decision- and policymakers, particularly NGBs, are doing more frequently is making broad-brush assumptions to support policy decisions or relying too heavily on data to decide on where support and investment should be distributed. On a local level, on numerous occasions, certain data and metrics have been used to decide on which clubs and communities to engage with or even which get support without ever engaging with the clubs themselves. What this reliance on data does not account for is the uniqueness of each club's circumstances: for example, because a club sits within a postcode does that mean they shouldn't benefit from being involved in a particular project or programme? Lack of engagement with the VSCs, and more widely with the volunteers when making policy decisions, especially where the funding for programme development and support is involved, can lead to minimised impact and reach due to not always necessarily reaching those VSCs who would benefit most.

Given the further professionalisation of community sport, the operating structures of VSCs have begun to change, and as outlined by Adams, this has coincided with both governmental and societal shifts in policy on what good governance practices look like in VSCs. In practice, this has seen many clubs embarking on reviews of club structures and to the implementation of more professionally aligned management and operating structures, whilst trying to retain their identity and ethos as a voluntary organisation. For example, some clubs have shifted towards a two-tiered approach where people with knowledge and skills are given key areas to lead (e.g. Mini & Junior Rugby, Club Development, Education and Marketing & Growth). These volunteers then establish working groups to enhance, develop and deliver those particular aspects of the VSCs. These leads then feed up the chain to a smaller and more strategic-focused management committee, supporting greater autonomy of and a more streamlined and focused approach to the day-to-day running of a VSC.

However, this shift has been a double-edged sword for many VSCs. Although the outcome within the organisations themselves has been overwhelmingly positive and seen many clubs begin to futureproof their organisations through succession planning for key volunteer roles, conducting regular skills audits to identify new and potential volunteers, implementing appropriate recognition to retain volunteers and engaging beyond those who are currently part of the organisation for support, there has been a downside, too. Whilst this shift has been a necessary exercise for many clubs, it has coincided with a significant reduction in support from professional staff to support the development of VSCs. The gaps left are now having to be filled by the VSCs. For example, the number of full-time staff supporting clubs on the ground in rugby has reduced significantly over the last decade. Our local governing body supports over 60 clubs, which were supported by over a dozen staff a decade ago. However, restructures and changes in national priorities now leave less than a handful of staff on the ground and where they still operate, they are tasked with covering a larger geographical area, limiting the level of support available.

This decrease in professional staffing support has increased the workload placed on volunteers within VSCs and, in VSCs like mine, has led to changes in operating structures to ensure we can continue our levels of delivery and development. Recently, we have seen this first-hand after being invited to be involved with a pilot project to diversify community engagement within rugby. Whilst the clubs are working hard to achieve engagement objectives and deliver key performance indicators (KPIs), the level of impact that we can have is severely impacted due to a decrease in professional staff support. Unlike previously where the professional staff would have taken the lead on the delivery and development of similar projects linked to wider national policy – with clubs supporting this delivery – the workload is now falling to us as volunteers. Ultimately, with this increasing reliance of NGBs on clubs and their volunteer structures to deliver their objectives, it won't be long before VSCs start to see a burnout effect due to the increased pressures on the workforce.

What this is leading to is an increase in VSCs being forced to put themselves at the forefront of their decision-making, ensuring that decisions have the greatest benefit to their clubs and members on a local level. Adams has described this as street-level bureaucracy, which encourages VSCs to reflect upon the wider impact of both national and regional policy decisions on their clubs, and how they subsequently approach implementation with discretion. Previously, the level of this discretion was limited due to the power balance between VSCs and sporting bodies. However, given some of the more recent changes in levels of support and club structures, this balance is beginning to tip in the direction of the clubs – increasing their ability to exercise discretion.

A final example of this would be the shift in recent years towards managing rugby through a central online administration system known as GMS (Game Management System). This shift was widely supported by clubs at first due to the claims it would help volunteers be more efficient and speed up outdated administration processes within clubs. However, what was initially delivered was a system that was often unpredictable and was not fit for purpose. This eventually led to many clubs doing only what was absolutely necessary through the system to either access funding, international tickets or make course bookings, but then outside of this, many used their discretion and reverted to using previous processes to enable them to operate efficiently without breaching their obligations as member clubs.

Adams's contribution to this chapter has provided a theoretical underpinning of what it is like for volunteers who run community sports clubs across the UK. Whilst we are often constrained by policy and the powers that govern our sports, it does encourage the types of street-level bureaucracy as outlined throughout this commentary to ensure we as VSCs protect our organisations and members from changes that may impact or detract from the opportunities and services that they experience. Our organisations contain huge amounts of expertise and influence, and as clubs our focus will remain solely on delivering physical activity and sports opportunities to our communities.

References

Adams, A. (2011). Between modernization and mutual aid: The changing perceptions of voluntary sports clubs in England. *International Journal of Sport Policy and Politics*, 3(1), 23–43. https://doi.org/10.1080/19406940.2010.544663

Andrew, D. (1989). *Philanthropy and police: London charity in the eighteenth century*. Princeton University Press.

Bevir, M., & Rhodes, R. A. W. (2006). *Governance stories*. Routledge.

Bevir, M., & Rhodes, R. A. W. (2008). The differentiated polity as narrative. *British Journal of Politics and International Relations, 10*(4), 729–734. https://doi.org/10.1111/j.1467 -856x.2008.00325.x

Bishop, J., & Hoggett, P. (1986). *Organising around enthusiasms: Mutual aid in leisure.* Comedia.

Borgers, J., Pilgaard, M., Vanreusel, B., & Scheerder, J. (2018). Can we consider changes in sports participation as institutional change? A conceptual framework. *International Review for the Sociology of Sport, 53*(1), 84–100. https://doi.org/10.1177 /1012690216639598

Cabinet Office. (2010). *The compact: The Coalition government and civil society organisations working effectively in partnership for the benefit of communities and citizens in England.* Cabinet Office.

Coalter, F. (2013). *Sport for development: What game are we playing.* Routledge.

Cole, G. D. H. (1945). Mutual aid movements in their relation to voluntary social service. In A. F. C. Bourdillon (Ed.), *Voluntary social services: Their place in the modern state.* Methuen.

Department for Culture, Media and Sport. (2002). *Game plan: A strategy for delivering government's sport and physical activity objectives.* Department for Culture, Media and Sport.

Department for Culture, Media and Sport. (2008). *Playing to win a new era for sport.* Department for Culture, Media and Sport.

Department of National Heritage. (1995). *Sport: Raising the game.* DNH.

Dorey, P. (2014). *Policy making in Britain: An introduction* (2nd ed.). Sage.

Eisinger, P. K. (1973). The conditions of protest behavior in American cities. *American Political Science Review, 67*(1), 11–28.

Ellis, K. (2011). 'Street-level bureaucracy' revisited: The changing face of frontline discretion in adult social care in England. *Social Policy and Administration, 45*(3), 221– 244. https://doi.org/10.1111/j.1467-9515.2011.00766.x

Evans, T., & Harris, J. (2004). Street-level bureaucracy, social work and the (exaggerated) death of discretion. *British Journal of Social Work, 34*(6), 871–895. https://doi.org/10 .1093/bjsw/bch106

Finlayson, A. (2003). *Making sense of new labour.* Lawrence & Wishart.

Grix, J., & Phillpots, L. (2011). Revisiting the 'governance narrative': 'asymmetrical network governance' and the deviant case of the sports policy sector. *Public Policy and Administration, 26*(1), 3–19. https://doi.org/10.1177/0952076710365423

Hall, S., Massey, D., & Rustin, M. (2013). After neoliberalism: Analysing the present. In S. Hall, D. Massey & M. Rustin (Eds.). *After neoliberalism? The Kilburn manifesto* (pp. 210–234). Soundings.

Hardman, A. (2019). Ownership of sport: Philosophical perspectives in A. In Adams & L. Robinson (Eds.), *Who owns sport* (pp. 7–19). Routledge.

Harris, S., & Houlihan, B. (2014). Delivery networks and community sport in England. International Journal of Public Sector Management, 27(2), 113–127. https://doi.org/10 .1108/IJPSM-07-2013-0095

Harris, S., & Houlihan, B. (2016). Implementing the community sport legacy: The limits of partnerships, contracts and performance management. *European Sport Management Quarterly, 16*(4), 433–458. https://doi.org/10.1080/16184742.2016.1178315

Harris, S., Mori, K., & Collins, M. (2009). Great expectations: Voluntary sports clubs and their role in delivering national policy for English sport. *Voluntas: International Journal of Voluntary and Nonprofit Organizations*, *20*(4), 405–423. https://doi.org/10.1007/s11266-009-9095-y

Hartmann, D., & Kwauk, C. (2011). Sport and development: An overview, critique, and reconstruction. *Journal of Sport and Social Issues*, *35*(3), 284–305. https://doi.org/10.1177/0193723511416986

HM Government. (2015). *Sporting future: A new strategy for an active nation*. Cabinet Office.

Home Office. (1998). *Compact: Getting it right together*. The Stationery Office.

Houlihan, B., & Green, M. (2009). Modernization and sport: The reform of sport England and UK sport. *Public Administration*, *87*(3), 678–698. https://doi.org/10.1111/j.1467-9299.2008.01733.x

Houlihan, B., & Lindsey, I. (2013). *Continuity and change in British sport policy in sport policy in Britain*. Routledge.

Houlihan, B., & White, A. (2002). *The politics of sport development: Development of sport or development through sport*. Routledge.

Hupe, P., & Buffat, A. (2014). A public service gap: Capturing contexts in a comparative approach of street-level bureaucracy. *Public Management Review*, *16*(4), 548–569. https://doi.org/10.1080/14719037.2013.854401

Kendall, J., & Knapp, M. (1995). A loose and baggy monster. In J. Davis-Smith, C. Rochester, & R. Headley (Eds.), *An introduction to the voluntary sector* (pp. 65–94). Routledge.

Kendall, J., & Knapp, M. (1996). *The voluntary sector in the UK*. Manchester University Press.

Kriesi, H. (1995). The political opportunity structure of new social movements: Its impact on their mobilization. In J. C. Jenkins & B. Klandermans (Eds.), *The politics of social protest* (pp. 167–198). University of Minnesota Press.

Levitas, R. (2000). Community, utopia and new Labour. *Local Economy*, *15*(3), 188–197. https://doi.org/10.1080/02690940050174193

Lipsky, M. (1980 [2010]). *Street level bureaucracy: The dilemmas of individuals in public service*. Russell Sage Foundation.

Lister, R. (2000). To Rio via the third way: New labour's 'welfare' reform agenda. *Renewal: A Journal of Labour Politics*, *8*(4), 1–14.

Lorentzen, H., & Hustinx, L. (2007). Civic involvement and modernization. *Journal of Civil Society*, *3*(2), 101–118. https://doi.org/10.1080/17448680701554282

Maloney, W., Smith, G., & Stoker, G. (2000). Social capital and urban governance: Adding a more contextualized 'top-down' perspective. *Political Studies*, *48*(4), 802–820. https://doi.org/10.1111/1467-9248.00284

Meyer, D. S. (2004). Protest and political opportunities. *Annual Review of Sociology*, *30*(1), 125–145. https://doi.org/10.1146/annurev.soc.30.012703.110545

Nichols, G. S., & James, M. (2017). *Social inclusion and volunteering in sports clubs in Europe: Findings for policy makers and practitioners in England and Wales*. Report, University of Sheffield.

Oakley, B., & Green, M. (2001). Still playing the game at arm's length? The selective re-investment in British sport, 1995–2000. *Managing Leisure*, *6*(2), 74–94. https://doi.org/10.1080/13606710110039534

Parker, G., Dobson, M., Lynn, T., & Salter, K. (2020). Entangling voluntarism, leisure time and political work: The governmentalities of neighbourhood planning in England. *Leisure Studies*, *39*(5), 644–658. https://doi.org/10.1080/02614367.2020.1763440

Rochester, C. (2013). *Rediscovering voluntary action*. Palgrave Macmillan.

Seippel, Ø., & Belbo, J. S. (2021). Sport clubs, policy networks, and local politics. *International Journal of Sport Policy and Politics, 13*(3), 479–499. https://doi.org/10.1080/19406940.2021.1898441

Skocpol, T. (1979). *States and social revolution*. Cambridge University Press.

Smith, A., & Stewart, B. (2010). The special features of sport: A critical revisit. *Sport Management Review, 10*(1), 1–11. https://doi.org/10.1016/j.smr.2009.07.002

Sport England. (2021). *Uniting the movement: A 10-year vision to transform lives and communities through sport and physical activity*. Sport England.

Stenling, C., & Fahlen, J. (2016). Same, but different? Exploring organizational identities of Swedish voluntary sports: Possible implications of sports clubs' self-identification for their role as implementers of policy objectives. *International Review for the Sociology of Sport, 51*(7), 867–883. https://doi.org/10.1177/1012690214557103

Stoker, G. (1998). Governance as theory: Five propositions. *International Social Science Journal, 50*(155), 17–28.

Chapter 11

Professional Football Clubs and Policy Implementation and Enactment

Jimmy O'Gorman

Introduction

Professional sports clubs are primarily located in the commercial sector. However, they typically operate across multiple social spheres where different institutional logics prevail, engage with a plurality of agendas, and with a variety of people and organisations. As a result, professional sports clubs are institutions that are pluralist in nature, making them extremely difficult to manage, are notorious for high turnover in staff, and face frequent economic problems (Gammelsæter, 2010). Professional sports clubs must be strategically positioned to maximise performance both on and off the pitch whilst simultaneously satisfying a range of stakeholders. This 'on-field/off field' dichotomy presents a range of dilemmas (Wilson & Anagnostopoulos, 2017). Given there has been much examination of professional sports clubs from business, management and organisational perspectives, it is notable that to date, other than some work on the implementation of corporate social responsibility (CSR; Cobourn & Frawley, 2017; François et al., 2019), the literature has rarely explicitly focused on implementation and/or enactment processes.

Taking this into account, this chapter aims to explore and problematise how policy is implemented and enacted by professional sports clubs in the UK. In particular, the chapter will primarily focus on professional football clubs. First, professional sports clubs are positioned as operating within what may be considered the field of elite-level sport. Here, the extent to which such clubs are positioned to implement and enact wider government social policy goals (for example, health) through elite sport is debated. Continuing the focus on social policy, the chapter then explores the extent to which professional football clubs' community arms are positioned to meet an array of government social policy goals. From a multitude of programmes and schemes that exist, the chapter covers some specific examples which illustrate the lack of attention thus far paid to implementation and enactment processes. Third, the chapter then considers the specific role of professional football clubs in implementing and enacting policies centred on achieving their own elite sport objectives. Here, the chapter narrows the focus to youth football where there have been relatively recent policy developments. The chapter is also complemented by practitioner reflection and insights focused on one professional football

DOI: 10.4324/9781003162728-11

club, Tranmere Rovers, in which practitioners have experienced the implementation and enactment of policies detailed in the chapter.

Professional Sports Clubs and UK Government

The extent to which professional sports clubs are involved in or expected to implement government-led sport policy in the UK is an issue rarely investigated or focused on in academic research or practice. At times, the relationships between government and professional sports clubs have been characterised by elusiveness, uneasiness, mutual convenience and, in some instances, opportunism by both entities. Professional sports clubs in the UK are primarily commercially oriented businesses that operate on a for-profit basis in the pursuit of sporting excellence and success. Over the past 50 years or so of increasingly centralised government intervention, policymaking and implementation in sport (Houlihan & Lindsey, 2012), professional sports clubs have largely remained on the periphery of government sport policy goals. This, in part, is due to the modus operandi of professional clubs sitting outside the sphere of government influence. For example, professional clubs have greater control over the recruitment and development of players and other staff in attempting to achieve success in their respective competitions than their governing bodies, which has in part insulated them from interference and influence from government-led implementation of elite sport development systems evident in sports reliant on public funding (Van Hoecke et al., 2013). Alongside this, has been the reluctance of government to directly intervene in professional sport. For example, in *Game Plan* (DCMS, 2002, p. 79), UK government stated that using public money for '"professional" sports, usually those with a consistently high media profile, may simply increase the salaries of highly paid players rather than increase the amount available at the grassroots level.' Nonetheless, professional clubs have, to varying degrees over time, been aligned by government, or aligned themselves directly and/or indirectly, to the implementation of government sport policy goals.

Most recent attempts by government to align policy goals with professional sports clubs can be found in *Sporting Future, Towards an Active Nation* (DCMS, 2015). For example, a key desired output of 'maximising international and domestic sporting success and the impact of major events' was proposed, the achievement of which was aligned with wider strategic outcomes of well-being, social and economic benefits to the nation (p.17). Redolent with the virtuous cycle of high-performance sport policy (see, for example, Grix & Carmichael, 2012), it was cited that sporting success creates a feel-good factor, whereby international and domestic success can inspire people to consider other forms of engagement in sport. Whilst professional sport clubs are recognised as potentially contributing to such goals, examples of modest successes and notable failures or underperformance by international representative teams of commercially funded professional sports clubs in the UK were cited in juxtaposition to the notable Olympic, Paralympic and world championship successes of sports in the high-performance system implemented through UK Sport and funded by the public purse.

The government noted no direct support to commercial sector sports organisations in the same way that has been provided to Olympic and Paralympic sports. Indeed, it was acknowledged that 'the responsibility for success will always rest with the relevant NGB, and we would not seek any involvement in the running of professional clubs or their development programmes' (DCMS, 2015, p. 46). Despite this, it was claimed that the government will do 'all that it can' to support success in pinnacle international competitions where commercially oriented sports demonstrate delivery on the same outcomes as Olympic and Paralympic sports. This rather nebulous statement was to be supported and achieved by 'actions that meet the needs of the professional and elite sports system' (DCMS, 2015, p.18), primarily through interventions made by government at the beginning of the talent pathway (DCMS, 2015, p. 47), such as (i) existing investment in school sport, coaching or facilities for example, through the Football Association's (FA) Parklife scheme and (ii) by sharing world-class expertise from the high-performance sport system implemented by UK Sport in areas like science and medicine, technology and competition to support non-Olympic and non-Paralympic sports in understanding how they can make changes to improve performance (DCMS, 2015, p. 47). The extent to which such initiatives have been implemented either by professional clubs themselves or through professional clubs by government is unclear.

Implementation of Social Policy Goals through Football in the Community

Whilst this modus operandi predominates, the business activities of professional sports clubs have, nonetheless, to varying degrees over time been aligned by government, or aligned themselves directly and/or indirectly, to the implementation of government sport policy goals. This has most prominently been through the programmes and project work of community departments of professional football clubs which have also received most academic attention and critique.

Professional football clubs in England have engaged with their local communities in a variety of guises since their very formation in the 19th century. However, it was not until the 1980s when the local community work and engagement of professional football clubs began to gain political traction and central government concern as conduits through which a contribution to implementing social policy goals could be achieved. Indeed, professional football clubs instigated what came to be known as Football in the Community (FiTC) schemes primarily on the back of socially undesirable high-profile crises related to hooliganism and poor player behaviour (Morgan, 2013). Since then, professional football clubs have been recognised by successive governments as key deliverers for social policy objectives (Mellor, 2008), as FiTC schemes have evolved from a remedial function towards social development priorities. These activities have been embedded within professional football clubs' institutionalised forms of corporate social responsibility activity to varying degrees (Anagnostopolous & Shilbury, 2013). Critical of monotheoretical and mainly macro level content analyses of CSR implementation, Anagnostopolous, Byers and Shilbury (2014) demonstrated from an organisational perspective, the micro-social processes that shaped the decision-making of the managers of charitable foundations. Here too, scholars have examined the complexities of implementation at the micro level, noting managerial challenges associated with the implementation of different and overlapping modes of CSR (Zeimers et al., 2018). FiTC programmes are now enmeshed in increasingly interdependent relationships with a variety of societal, governmental actors and organisations, and public, private and third-sector funding bodies to fund an increasing variety and range of programmes. These complexities will inevitably shape the formulation, implementation and enactment of such programmes and CSR activity, which require further examination if we are to more adequately understand their relative successes and failures in contributing to wider government social policy goals.

The longevity of these schemes is explained, in part, by the perception of successive governments and wider societal actors that football clubs have capacity and ability to deliver on broader social policy objectives, as they are a hook to engage communities in the locations in which they reside (Hindley & Williamson, 2013). Once embedded within the organisational and operational structure of the football club, it is becoming increasingly common for FiTC departments or schemes to have financial, structural and strategic independence, but to maintain association through branding, naming and exposure. There appears to be an increasing variety of schemes under the banner of FiTC, which vary depending on how FiTC is attached to the broader structure of individual clubs. Those with charitable status operate as trusts and are responsible for implementing schemes funded by English Premier League (EPL) and English Football League (EFL).

FitC schemes in the early 21st century were thus often characterised by tackling youth crime and anti-social behaviour (such as through the Positive Futures programme), health improvement programmes including drug awareness education, study support (such as through the Playing for Success programme) and social and employability skills (the latter often linked to youth unemployment and adult learning). Much academic work on FiTC schemes' programme/project work has tended to focus on the impact they have had on particular target groups aligned with government social policy goals. For example, among others, studies have primarily focused on (i) adult general health improvement (Pringle et al., 2011, 2013; Curran et al., 2016), including mental health (Pringle, 2009), weight loss/obesity (Rutherford et al., 2014; Hunt et al., 2020) and (ii) child/youth physical and mental health (Parnell et al., 2013; Haycock et al., 2020). Sanders et al. (2021) have illustrated that the CEOs of professional football clubs' community organisations identify that security and sustainability of delivery and funding, the importance of growth and diversification, engagement with multiple agendas and agencies, 'professionalisation' of the workforce, and brand values and awareness are all challenges that they face. For CEOs, the success of schemes is measured both in terms of financial security of programmes and social impact within the community.

It has become increasingly common for professional football clubs to engage with and contribute to a wide range of government-formulated national social policies and agendas. Much of this work is in the form of programmes or projects delivered in local communities at or outwith club stadia and facilities. One such example is the 'Football Fans In Training' (FFIT) programme. The FFIT programme aims to use the popularity of professional football clubs' facilities as a 'hook' to attract adults to a 12-week group-based, weight management and healthy living programme for those aged 35–65 years who are overweight. Coaches representing professional clubs are employed to support participants in losing weight and to maintain their weight loss long-term through cumulative, sustainable behaviour changes in their physical activity, diet (food and alcohol intake, and eating patterns). Originally developed and delivered in Scotland, the Scottish Professional Football League subsequently supported the scaling up of FFIT via a single licence franchise model. A growing number of professional clubs in England have since become licensed deliverers of the FFIT, receiving funding from the EFL Trust (Hunt et al., 2020). The licensing model presents a support structure for club coaches that was informed by a multi-phase evaluation of the FFIT programme's development (Hunt et al., 2020). This research reported that the goals of these programmes were successfully achieved in conjunction with the development of coaching manuals detailing key delivery points for weekly session topics, alongside coaches being trained to adopt an interactive, non-didactic style of coaching, which encouraged the use of 'positive banter' with and between participants to encourage strong group interactions, mutual support and vicarious learning amongst participants, and between the participants and the club coaches.

Whilst academic work focused on projects delivered by FiTC departments referred to in this chapter and elsewhere (see, for example, Richardson and Fletcher (2020) on Premier League Kicks) illustrate the various efficaciousness and effectiveness for end users, an understanding of how and in what ways such projects are implemented and enacted by various actors is underdeveloped. This is important, as FiTC departments of professional football clubs are reliant on a range of actors whose ability to enact duties is often mediated by a disconnection between qualifications, knowledge and experience required to effectively achieve the goals of the projects for the end users. In addition, many of the actors are involved in the delivery of simultaneous programmes which cover an increasingly complex and multiple set of social and health agendas for which they are often ill prepared (Parnell et al., 2017). Further independent research is needed to understand how and in what ways policy actors seek to enact their duties in contributing to the implementation of community-based programmes in order to ascertain the extent to which the needs of the intended target populations are met in line with government policy priorities. Given the prominence within the communities in which they reside, the charitable status of community arms of professional football clubs appears to be increasingly compatible in contributing to government health and social policy priorities.

Implementation and Enacting Youth Development Policy in Professional Football Clubs

It is perhaps the core business of professional sports clubs where there has historically been a lack of policymaking and cohesion. Individual interests and competition perhaps perpetuated a necessitation for clubs to operate in silos in developing their own strategies aimed at success on the field of play. However, it is in the area of male youth football development aimed at recruiting, nurturing and developing young footballers, particularly in England, where significant policy development and implementation has occurred relatively recently.

The development of young male players by professional football clubs has a long history. Yet, having come under increasing scrutiny and pressure in the context of perceived consistent failures of senior and youth male England national teams at international tournaments, as well as corresponding views that coaches and coaching in English youth football academies had not adequately equipped home-grown players with the necessary attributes to succeed at the highest levels of competitive football (Green, 2009; Mills et al., 2012), the FA took the lead in beginning to develop strategy and policy aimed at maximising engagement within the talent pool available for English football.

Following the *Charter for Quality* (The FA, 1997) which identified the need for a more structured and standardised approach to the development of elite youth footballers, three further initiatives since the turn of the century: *The Football Development Strategy* (The FA, 2001), the *National Game Strategy* (The FA, 2011) and the *FA Chairman's England Commission Report* (The FA, 2014) were developed with the aim to improve youth development and achieve international success. To promote further support for English football players within professional football clubs, the EPL with support from The FA and the EFL launched the Elite Player Performance Plan (EPPP) in 2011 (The Premier League, 2011). In seeking to instigate change from the top (i.e., EPL / EFL), the EPPP encourages increasing isomorphism in the structure and management of English football academies whilst facilitating bottom-up variations as individual clubs develop their own unique and bespoke philosophies for player recruitment and development within the parameters of the regulations (Webb et al., 2020). The EPPP champions a long-term player development model, which focuses on the interface between the technical/ tactical, psychological, physical, and social elements of the players' environment (Nesti & Sulley, 2014; The Premier League, 2011). Couched in terms of 'enhanced efficiency,' 'value for money' and long-term 'financial viability' of the academy system, the EPPP intends 'to foster a working environment that promotes excellence, nurtures talented young players and systematically converts talent into more and better professional home-grown players' (The Premier League, 2011, p.12).

The EPPP was also developed in response to pressures on national governing bodies to modernise the talent identification and development structures of professional sports clubs and to professionalise their workforces alongside the implementation of effective performance measurement and quality assurance processes.

Here, there are parallels with the application of similar policy implementation tools in the UK public sector under successive Labour governments and subsequently Conservative-led administrations into the 2010s, as detailed in the introduction to this book. For example, the setting and monitoring of key performance indicators measured through audits and strategies have been utilised to incentivise clubs with labels and/or categorisations of distinction alongside sources of funding. In England, attention has begun to focus on the implementation of such measures in the youth academy systems of professional football clubs (Van Hoecke et al., 2013; O'Gorman et al., 2021). Classified as optimum development models, Category 1 academies receive most funding, provide up to 8,500 coaching hours for players, a wider range of sport science support and are licensed to recruit and develop players from 5 to 21 years of age. In contrast, Category 4 academies are classified as late development models, receive least funding, provide fewer coaching hours and are restricted to recruiting and developing players in the 16–21 years' age range (Webb et al., 2020).

Whilst no academic work has sought to judge the effectiveness of the EPPP, some research has illustrated how those working in football academies have sought to enact their duties in its implementation. For example, O'Gorman et al. (2021) found that coaches' work had intensified, largely as a result of additional administrative duties in documenting every coaching session plan and subsequent evaluations of player performances stored on an online software package. Coaches expressed concern that no time was allocated for them to complete these additional duties which negatively impacted their focus on actual coaching activity. Coaches engaged in strategic fabrications to enact these duties such as copy and pasting sessions from colleagues or coaches from other clubs on the online software package and depositing coaching session plans and reviews in messy and inconsistent ways that did not accurately reflect their coaching work. Exemplifying an 'implementation gap,' individual and collective fabrications became incorporated into academy documentation to satisfy auditors, rather than to affect the required pedagogical or organisational change of the EPPP (The Premier League, 2011). Coaches were willing to engage in these activities to present an account of themselves and their academy in favourable and policy-compliant ways in line with what were perceived to be the demands of the auditors that scrutinised their work. Policy actors' attempts to fulfil their obligations in these particular ways are redolent with a type of enactment which Ball (2003, p. 222) describes as a 'spectacle' or an 'enacted fantasy' that is provided simply to be seen and judged by others. As such, this research indicates that the enactment of policy is shaped by the actions of policy actors who are variously motivated to act in strategic ways within the constraints of the conditions in which they work. As demonstrated here, this means policy (in this instance, the Premier League's EPPP) may not be implemented in ways desired by policymakers despite appearances to the contrary. However, whilst these local conditions may be outside of the control of the policy makers, it appears the implementation of the EPPP has not been significantly undermined by the discretion, skill and coping practices of implementing agents.

The implementation of the EPPP also aimed to not just produce technically proficient athletes but also good role models who understand the significance of professional football in contemporary culture (Roe & Parker, 2016), alongside safeguarding their welfare. The role of chaplains, attached to professional football clubs but devoid of any involvement in footballing practice or issues, have been found to perform a key role in the non-performance aspects of youth player development which may ultimately benefit team success. In this role, chaplains offer practical, spiritual and pastoral support, as well as providing assistance with wider lifestyle issues (Gamble et al., 2013; Nesti & Sulley, 2014; Oliver & Parker, 2019). Chaplains have also been found to effectively undertake safeguarding policy. Noting safeguarding issues routinely arise from the pressures specific to the highly competitive environment in which elite youth footballers engage, sports chaplains are ideally placed to provide safeguarding and wider welfare support to young players as a consequence of their independence from team management structures and their prioritisation of holistic care above performance-related issues (Oliver & Parker, 2019). This raises questions as to the efficacy and effectiveness of specific player welfare and safeguarding officer and (more recently) player care roles and approaches to implementation of policies within academy structures as required by the EPPP. Related to player welfare criteria of EPPP implementation, Tears et al. (2018) found that the increasingly routinised and increased amount of contact (training and competition) time resulted in a reduction in injuries in the younger age groups U12-U15, but an increase in the severity of the injuries sustained in the older age groups U16-U18. Although restricted to only one club, the findings resonate with established issues that elite youth athletes are likely to experience, such as overtraining, performance-related stress and excessive mental and emotional pressure (Mountjoy et al., 2015). In the context of increasing concerns and efforts to safeguard the welfare of young athletes participating in sports development systems, the effectiveness and efficacy of the EPPP in achieving policy goals in this area are unclear. Specifically, it remains unknown how and in what ways policy actors enact welfare duties.

Some professional football clubs have claimed that the rules and regulations of the EPPP favour 'bigger' clubs at the expense of 'smaller' clubs in developing youth players which has led to some clubs reducing their commitment to the EPPP or electing to withdraw altogether to implement alternative recruitment and development programmes. For example, citing EPPP rules that created a more favourable environment for a number of big clubs with Category 1 status to recruit the best local players in their locality, the board of Huddersfield Town FC decided to downgrade from Category 2 to Category 4 status. As such, Huddersfield Town were drawing funding down for U17 to U21 provision for youth development pathways, after withdrawing provision for U9s through to U16s. The elite-focused player recruitment and development strategy was to recruit players from the age of 16 upwards to the U18s and U23 squads, who had been nurtured within other Category 1 and 2 academy systems. Similar to other clubs downgrading their status, Huddersfield Town began to bifurcate their elite and community provision by implementing plans to provide a full spectrum of football provision for junior age groups through the community and charitable arm (Huddersfield Town Association Football Club, 2022).

In 2016, Brentford FC withdrew from the EPPP system altogether. Again, citing strong competition for recruiting the best young players with other clubs in London, the board stated:

> the development of young players must make sense from a business perspective ... in a football environment where the biggest Premier League clubs seek to sign the best young players before they can graduate through an Academy system, the challenge of developing value through that system is extremely difficult.
>
> (Brentford Football Club, 2022)

Similar to Huddersfield Town, Brentford implemented a new player recruitment and development pathway centred on an elite squad of around 18 players aged 17–21 to 'stand Brentford apart as a stand-out option for the most talented young players.' However, taking a different approach to junior provision, Brentford sought to strengthen ties with the club's Community Sports Trust through Football Development Centres in order to identify talent from the local community and ensure the best young players remain a part of a system that had a pathway of progression to the development squad and the first team.

The relatively recent successes and gains of the England male youth and senior teams in international tournaments point towards positive implementation outcomes (Webb et al., 2020). However, there has been a lack of independent evaluation or empirical research on how the EPPP has been implemented and enacted by the various stakeholders working in the system and less still on those models that have been implemented and enacted as alternatives to the EPPP. Nor have there been any efforts to independently evaluate recent policy and strategy implementation on player development in the youth female game.

Conclusion

It is likely that professional sport clubs will remain on the periphery of UK government sport policy goals given their operational modus operandi in the commercial/private sector, whilst continuing to contribute to the implementation of wider social policy goals through charitable foundations. To date, much research on policy implementation and enactment has utilised concepts and theoretical frameworks developed to analyse public and third sector policies formulated by government. The positionality of professional sport clubs does raise the question as to whether such concepts and frameworks are suitable for adoption in analysing implementation and enactment within professional sports clubs themselves. That said, recent work on enactment of policy in professional sports clubs highlighted in this chapter has begun to demonstrate that policy implementation is mediated by the co-operation of a range of policy actors that draw upon their discretion, skills and abilities which inevitably shapes the resulting outputs and outcomes. The organisational capacity of professional sports clubs to implement their own policies also seems important, which hitherto is a neglected area of focus on professional sports clubs. Moreover, whilst the work of FiTC departments of professional football clubs has received much attention, particularly the evaluation of programme work which contributes to the implementation of wider government social policy goals, there is a paucity of evidence of the work undertaken by policy actors and how this shapes the programme outcomes. Here, much more rigorous independent evaluative research is required if we are to more adequately appraise the actual outcomes of such programmes, which should also take account of prevailing policy contexts, mechanisms of implementation and enactment by policy actors in contributing to government goals.

PRACTITIONER REFLECTION AND INSIGHTS

Tranmere Rovers in the Community implementation of programmes

Steve Williams, Community Development Officer, Tranmere Rovers in the Community and Louise Edwards, Community Officer, Tranmere Rovers in the Community

The community section gained charitable trust status in 2007, which meant we became self-financing from the club. Charitable trust status helps with bidding for community projects from external funders. The vice chairman and managing director of the football club sit on the board of trustees for the charity, so there is a good connection between the community and professional operations, where we can draw on their expertise, and players, to make appearances at programmes and help promote them. The charity operates across four different but overlapping core themes: (i) inclusion, (ii) education, (iii) health and (iv) sports participation (mainly in schools). We have a diverse range of funding sources for our programmes. As with other community trusts, we are linked with the EFL Trust, who point funders towards us for national programmes such as FFIT fans and Premier League Kicks, as they access and distribute core funding from Sport England and the NHS. We also develop our own projects and funding streams, which often happen through local networks, so we are able to tap into the needs of the local community. For example, we have recently linked up with the nearby Deen Centre in Birkenhead, which is an Islamic organisation and a place of worship open to all people and a centre for the whole community to use for communal activities. We noticed the females at the centre were accessing the community gym at the club, so we invited them in for football sessions which we now have funding for. Just by simply offering football sessions during daytime periods when the facility was free and convenient for the group, we have been able to demonstrate improved physical health outcomes.

We ran a programme called Active Rovers funded by the NHS which targeted men over 40 who were overweight. We used football as a hook to engage them with physical activity by playing football. Through this we were able to refer men to relevant NHS services to help support them to lose weight. In addition, there were also positive social outcomes too, as many of the participants engaged because of the opportunity to develop friendships. There were then spin-offs such as walking football and football for mental health programmes. Because of the track record of successful delivery, when national programmes such as FIT Fans are introduced, we are approached to apply for funding. FIT Fans runs for 12 weeks for a cohort of 30 men and 30 women who must have a certain level of BMI and be over the age of 35. The key is to make the activities very social in order to get the educational elements of healthy eating and the physical activities such as walks, walking football and Soccercise. After 12 weeks we sustained the outcomes by bringing back previous participants to speak with the new cohorts. Working with partners has also helped sustain the health outcomes, as we are able to signpost the participants to other programmes in the locality. In addition, we were noticing that outcomes other than health were being achieved, but not being captured or measured as part of FIT Fans which was purely focused on weight and physical health gains. Many of our participants are from low socio-economic backgrounds and many are isolated and live on their own. Participants have expressed to us how the social engagement that comes with being part of the programme has also impacted positively their mental health. We, along with other community trusts, have fed this back to the EFL Trust and expect future delivery of the programme to try to develop and capture mental health outcomes alongside the physical. Not only this, but we include people on the programme that we don't have funding for. A lot of people under the age of 35 are also overweight and they need the programme as much as those in the target range, so we don't turn them away.

It used to be a case of 'get the funding first and worry about the monitoring and evaluation at the end,' but these days it is very stringent. Different funders ask for different evidence. For example, Premier League Kicks wanted a video of evidence from the participants and how the programme has allowed them to meet the outcomes. Evidencing the outcomes has been difficult over the years for us. When one programme is completed, we are concentrating on delivering other programmes simultaneously, which means attention to capture the evidence is less of a priority than meeting the actual outcome. The evaluation reports go to the funders which sometimes come back in asking for further evidence and case studies.

What works particularly well for us as an organisation is the small number of staff we have delivering these programmes. There are ten in the team who work across different programmes. We have to be flexible and diverse, working across more than one programme at once. The approach is to offer programmes to coaches employed at the charity to see who is interested, and then support them to undertake any associated training and education to deliver things like educational workshops or mental health support for participants. Most of the time participants tell us delivery is successful because of the relaxed atmosphere and continuity of seeing the same staff. As funding comes up, we embed it in the programmes we are already delivering and offset it against people's jobs, rather than staff wages being dependent on the delivery of one programme. That is how we have been able to sustain a stable staffing base which participants get to know and helps successful implementation of the programmes we deliver. This continuity of staffing on programmes means we are able to get to know the participants well and develop trust. As such, we are able to match participants with programmes that are suitable to their needs. There are some challenges, for example, one of us oversees the Premier League Kicks programme largely alone whilst working on other programmes, whereas other bigger clubs may have more staff devoted to it.

The programmes are KPI led, but what works well is working in conjunction with the funders to develop the right KPIs and compromise between the targets the funder wants and the capacity we have to deliver. At times, however, the funding bids are written by people who are not on the ground, because they are more aware of the political and government agendas and which keywords are needed on the funding applications. This sometimes leads to the development of KPIs that are too difficult to achieve. So, communication between us on the ground and others at management level in the club is needed.

Tranmere Rovers and the Implementation of Youth Development

Paul Morrison, Head of Football/Futsal Operations and Safeguarding, Tranmere Rovers in the Community

When the EPPP was introduced, the club felt it was necessary to comply with it in order to continue what was a well-respected youth development programme. The youth department would produce players on a fairly regular basis who were then sold on to make a profit for the club, often for millions of pounds. The EPPP was top-down in practice, but clubs were able to adopt their own practices within the overall framework and structures required. Prior to the EPPP, it was common for coaching staff to undertake multiple roles. This was largely by chance and fortune when some coaches had other expertise so they could double up in their roles, for example, as an education link or physiotherapist. The EPPP formalised roles alongside minimum certification, so staff were employed to perform discrete roles. This more structured approach was needed in areas such as safeguarding and welfare and the medical roles. Removing these responsibilities from the coaches was better, allowing them to concentrate on coaching and signposting any welfare or medical issues to the relevant roles.

The EPPP is a great help to safeguarding as it specifies what should be in place. The EFL support is good too. For example, the EPL and EFL provide guidelines to clubs to develop comprehensive provision through sample policy templates and PowerPoints. It is not often we have to enact these, but when a safeguarding issue arises, we have these policies to refer to. We have monthly area meetings with other safeguarding officers in the North West group, led by a representative from the EFL. This maintains good relationships with local clubs as we can share best practice and feedback up the chain to the EFL of any problematic areas we may collectively be experiencing. The expectations are relevant to each club, no matter what level. It also funds 17 hours for a safeguarding officer. The main downside is it expects the same safeguarding standards from a Premier Club to a League 2 club, but a Premier League club compared to us will be able to allocate more staff to it. In my own opinion, there should be one person at least full-time for safeguarding, whatever the league status of the Club. For example, I was head of safeguarding whilst also head of youth development phase and a practising coach that made up my full-time hours, but I never felt I dedicated the 17 hours to safeguarding.

Meeting the requirements of the EPPP was not straightforward. The demands placed on the club meant the restructuring of resources to comply with Category 3 classification. The club had to move from one coach per team to employ two coaches. This also meant there were existing staff who did not have that level of qualification, which they needed to successfully complete to ensure the academy was compliant with the EPPP regulations. This was difficult, as the academy traditionally operated on recruiting coaching staff through word of mouth. We had to negotiate with local partners to hire facilities to ensure the standard and capacity of facilities met the requirements of the EPPP, as the academy did not have the capacity to operate from one site. Once we had demonstrated this, the academy was licensed to operate at Category 3. This meant the club could draw down £360,000 worth of funding annually to operate. However, the size of the staff base was quite small in comparison to other bigger clubs' academies, and full-time academy staff still performed more than one role.

The academy had to provide a philosophy and curriculum on coaching and developing players. This was the responsibility of the academy manager and heads of age groups, positions we did not have until the EPPP stipulated so. How we did this was up to us. But the EPPP provided lines of accountability from academy manager down to the age group coaches who were managed by a phase lead (foundation U9s–U12s, youth development U13s–U16s and professional development U16s–U18s) which prior to the EPPP were only loosely in place. So, implementation of the EPPP provided the youth section with a clearer structure and more defined roles than hitherto. Whilst this caused some friction, as coaches, for example, were now more accountable to heads of their phases, once the positions were embedded, it became easier to operate the academy functions. This occurred alongside the stipulation that all coaches must be, or be training towards, at least UEFA B level, and latterly the FA Youth Awards. One of the key differences these developments made to coaching practice was the need to keep the session moving and all players actively involved. For example, prior to the EPPP, a lot of coaching practice at the club was characterised by stopping the session in a structured and progressive way, so that demonstrations could be shown to players and an explanation provided leading to an objective for the session. There became a fear of stopping the session, and putting kids in lines, and coaches talking too much. This was in part influenced by the performance management tool introduced with the EPPP, where the player performance clock demanded players complete X amount of hours training or playing time. We needed to provide evidence for each player which would be audited to ensure we were implementing the required practices to comply with EPPP regulations. As part of this, coaches were also required to evaluate player development targets against the objectives for each micro cycle (weekly sessions) and the meso cycle (6–12-week player reviews) and the macro cycle (season objectives). We struggled at first, as coaches had never been required to do much administration work, and some were very resistant and did not see the value in it. To complete the required paperwork for audit, full-time staff were often taken out of coaching for three months to compile and present all of the necessary paperwork. My own view is that coaching under EPPP tends to be viewed by coaches as 'what we have to do to satisfy what auditors want.' There was less emphasis than before on what we think players need, when earlier more bias was on developing individuals. There is too much emphasis on paperwork to evidence implementation. Individual targets are set out, but this is more of a tick-box exercise than a thoughtful process to satisfying EPPP requirements ahead of player developmental needs. It's also easy to tick a target as achieved when deeper insight might question this.

Due to the constraints of facility provision to provide the requisite number of contact hours, it was common for age groups to regularly replace their football training with gym-based sessions, which meant at times, some groups were actually getting less football practice than prior to the EPPP being implemented. This was also to account for the paperwork to satisfy the auditors that the club complied with the player clock. So, we fulfilled the requirements of Category 3 status in terms of hours, but not by necessarily offering the required footballing provision. Whether this impacted player development is hard to establish.

Despite being in the EPPP system, the number of players progressing into first-team football dwindled. Due to the regulations, players were being recruited to higher-level clubs' academies for a very small compensation fee (£3,000 per year for 9–11-year-olds, £12,500 per year for 12–16-year-olds). Combined with this, larger clubs in the North West were not only recruiting to and operating age group squads but also shadow squads and development centres which they financed separately to the EPPP. This competition made the recruitment and retention of players increasingly difficult year on year. At the same time, the club suffered successive relegations from League 1 into non-league football. This meant the central funding for the EPPP Category 3 licence continued for one full season, half the following season and was removed altogether in the third season out of league football. The club attempted to continue to fund the academy along the lines of Category 3 licence regulations, albeit with a reduction in staff numbers. However, this became unaffordable, and the pattern of player recruitment described above became even more acute. Therefore, a decision was made at board level to restructure the academy to offer provision at the 16-year plus age group, disband all the junior age groups and direct funds towards first-team provision. The youth development model implemented was to recruit players being released from the bigger clubs' academies based on similar premises to Huddersfield and Brentford. Alongside this, a college was set up to provide post-16 education alongside playing opportunities in Association of Colleges football competitions and to provide links with high-level semi-professional non-league clubs to provide football experience. So far, it has been difficult to 'graduate' players to the first-team squad in this model, although two players have been provided with first-team contracts.

References

Anagnostopoulos, C., Byers, T., & Shilbury, D. (2014). Corporate social responsibility in professional team sport organisations: Towards a theory of decision-making. *European Sport Management Quarterly, 14*(3), 259–281. https://doi.org/10.1080/16184742.2014.897736

Anagnostopoulos, C., & Shilbury, D. (2013). Implementing corporate social responsibility in English football: Towards multi-theoretical integration. *Sport, Business, and Management: An International Journal, 3*(4), 268–284. https://doi.org/10.1108/SBM-05-2013-0009

Ball, S. J. (2003). The teacher's soul and the terrors of performativity. *Journal of Education Policy*, *18*(2), 215–228. https://doi.org/10.1080/0268093022000043065

Brentford Football Club. (2022). Club statement: Brentford academy restructuring. Retrieved June 17, 2022, from https://www.brentfordfc.com/news/2016/may/club-statement-brentford-academy-restructuring/

Cobourn, S., & Frawley, S. (2017). CSR in professional sport: An examination of community models. *Managing Sport and Leisure*, *22*(2), 113–126. https://doi.org/10.1080/23750472.2017.1402694

Curran, K., Drust, B., Murphy, R., Pringle, A., & Richardson, D. (2016). The challenge and impact of engaging hard-to-reach populations in regular physical activity and health behaviours: An examination of an English premier league 'football in the community' men's health programme. *Public Health*, *135*, 14–22. https://doi.org/10.1016/j.puhe.2016.02.008

Department for Culture, Media and Sport/Strategy Unit. (2002). *Game plan: A strategy for delivering government's sport and physical activity objectives*. DCMS/Strategy Unit.

Department for Culture Media and Sport. (2015). *Sporting future: A new strategy for an active nation*. DCMS.

François, A., Bayle, E., & Gond, J. P. (2019). A multilevel analysis of implicit and explicit CSR in French and UK professional sport. *European Sport Management Quarterly*, *19*(1), 15–37. https://doi.org/10.1080/16184742.2018.1518468

Gamble, R., Hill, D. M., & Parker, A. (2013). Revs and psychos: Role, impact and interaction of sport chaplains and sport psychologists within English premiership soccer. *Journal of Applied Sport Psychology*, *25*(2), 249–264. https://doi.org/10.1080/10413200.2012.718313

Gammelsæter, H. (2010). Institutional pluralism and governance in "commercialized" sport clubs. *European Sport Management Quarterly*, *10*(5), 569–594. https://doi.org/10.1080/16184742.2010.524241

Green, C. (2009). *Every boy's dream: England's football future on the line*. A&C Black.

Grix, J., & Carmichael, F. (2012). Why do governments invest in elite sport? A polemic. *International Journal of Sport Policy and Politics*, *4*(1), 73–90. https://doi.org/10.1080/19406940.2011.627358

Haycock, D., Jones, J., & Smith, A. (2020). Developing young people's mental health awareness through education and sport: Insights from the tackling the blues programme. *European Physical Education Review*, *26*(3), 664–681. https://doi.org/10.1177/1356336X20942

Hindley, D., & Williamson, D. (2013). Measuring and evaluating community sports projects. In J. L. Paramio Salcines, K. Babiak, & G. Walters (Eds.), *Routledge handbook of sport and corporate social responsibility* (1st ed., pp. 317–327). Routledge.

Houlihan, B., & Lindsey, I. (2012). *Sport policy in Britain*. Routledge.

Huddersfield Town Association Football Club. (2022). Restructuring of academy at Huddersfield Town. Retrieved June 17, 2022, from https://www.htafc.com/news/2017/september/restructuring-of-academy-at-huddersfield-town2/

Hunt, K., Wyke, S., Bunn, C., Donnachie, C., Reid, N., & Gray, C. M. (2020). Scale-up and scale-out of a gender-sensitized weight management and healthy living program delivered to overweight men via professional sports clubs: The wider implementation of Football Fans in Training (FFIT). *International Journal of Environmental Research and Public Health*, *17*(2), 584–616. https://doi.org/10.3390/ijerph17020584

Mellor, G. (2008). 'The Janus-faced sport': English football, community and the legacy of the 'third way'. *Soccer and Society*, *9*(3), 313–324. https://doi.org/10.1080/14660970802008942

Mills, A., Butt, J., Maynard, I., & Harwood, C. (2012). Identifying factors perceived to influence the development of elite youth football academy players. *Journal of Sports Sciences*, *30*(15), 1593–1604. https://doi.org/10.1080/02640414.2012.710753

Morgan, S. (2013). The premier league: A commitment to social responsibility. In J. L. Paramio Salcines, K. Babiak, & G. Walters (Eds.), *Routledge handbook of sport and corporate social responsibility* (1st ed., pp. 251–262). Routledge.

Mountjoy, M., Rhind, D. J., Tiivas, A., & Leglise, M. (2015). Safeguarding the child athlete in sport: A review, a framework and recommendations for the IOC youth athlete development model. *British Journal of Sports Medicine*, *49*(13), 883–886. http://doi.org/10.1136/bjsports-2015-094619

Nesti, M., & Sulley, C. (2014). *Youth development in football: Lessons from the world's best academies*. Routledge.

O'Gorman, J., Partington, M., Potrac, P., & Nelson, L. (2021). Translation, intensification and fabrication: Professional football academy coaches' enactment of the elite player performance plan. *Sport, Education and Society*, *26*(3), 309–325. https://doi.org/10.1080/13573322.2020.1726313

Oliver, M., & Parker, A. (2019). Safeguarding, chaplaincy and English professional football. *Religions*, *10*(10), 543–557. https://doi.org/10.3390/rel10100543

Parnell, D., Cope, E., Bailey, R., & Widdop, P. (2017). Sport policy and English primary physical education: The role of professional football clubs in outsourcing. *Sport in Society*, *20*(2), 292–302. https://doi.org/10.1080/17430437.2016.1173911

Parnell, D., Stratton, G., Drust, B., & Richardson, D. (2013). Football in the community schemes: Exploring the effectiveness of an intervention in promoting healthful behaviour change. *Soccer and Society*, *14*(1), 35–51. https://doi.org/10.1080/14660970.2012.692678

Pringle, A. (2009). The growing role of football as a vehicle for interventions in mental health care. *Journal of Psychiatric and Mental Health Nursing*, *16*(6), 553–557. https://doi.org/10.1111/j.1365-2850.2009.01417.x

Pringle, A., Zwolinsky, S., McKenna, J., Daly-Smith, A., Robertson, S., & White, A. (2013). Effect of a national programme of men's health delivered in English premier league football clubs. *Public Health*, *127*(1), 18–26. https://doi.org/10.1016/j.puhe.2012.10.012

Pringle, A., Zwolinsky, S., Smith, A., Robertson, S., McKenna, J., & White, A. (2011). The preadoption demographic and health profiles of men participating in a programme of men's health delivered in English premier league football clubs. *Public Health*, *125*(7), 411–416. https://doi.org/10.1016/j.puhe.2011.04.013

Richardson, K., & Fletcher, T. (2020). Community sport development events, social capital and social mobility: A case study of premier league kicks and young black and minoritized ethnic males in England. *Soccer and Society*, *21*(1), 79–95. https://doi.org/10.1080/14660970.2018.1506334

Roe, C., & Parker, A. (2016). Sport, chaplaincy and holistic support: The Elite Player Performance Plan (EPPP) in English professional football. *Practical Theology*, *9*(3), 169–182. http://doi.org/10.1080/1756073X.2016.1221638

Rutherford, Z., Gough, B., Seymour-Smith, S., Matthews, C. R., Wilcox, J., Parnell, D., & Pringle, A. (2014). "Motivate": The effect of a football in the community delivered weight loss programme on over 35-year old men and women's cardiovascular risk factors. *Soccer and Society*, *15*(6), 951–969. https://doi.org/10.1080/14660970.2014.920628

Sanders, A., Keech, M., Burdsey, D., Maras, P., & Moon, A. (2021). CEO perspectives on the first twenty-five years of football in the community: Challenges, developments and opportunities. *Managing Sport and Leisure*, *26*(1–2), 7–21. https://doi.org/10.1080/23750472.2020.1771198

Tears, C., Chesterton, P., & Wijnbergen, M. (2018). The elite player performance plan: The impact of a new national youth development strategy on injury characteristics in a premier league football academy. *Journal of Sports Sciences*, *36*(19), 2181–2188. https://doi.org/10.1080/02640414.2018.1443746

The Football Association. (1997). *Charter for quality*. The Football Association.

The Football Association. (2001). *Football development strategy 2001–2006*. The Football Association.

The Football Association. (2011). *The football association national game strategy* (pp. 2011–2015). The Football Association.

The Football Association. (2014). *The FA chairman's England commission report*. The Football Association.

The Premier League. (2011). *Elite player performance plan*. The Premier League.

Van Hoecke, J., Schoukens, H., & De Knop, P. (2013). Quality and performance management of national sport organizations: Measuring and steering the performance of the distribution network. In P. Sotriadou & V. De Bosscher (Eds.), *Managing high performance sport* (pp. 119–146). Routledge.

Webb, T., Dicks, M., Brown, D. J., & O'Gorman, J. (2020). An exploration of young professional football players' perceptions of the talent development process in England. *Sport Management Review*, *23*(3), 536–547. https://doi.org/10.1016/j.smr.2019.04.007

Wilson, R., & Anagnostopoulos, C. (2017). Guest editorial: Performance strategies for meeting multiple objectives: The case of professional sport teams. *Sport, Business and Management*, *7*(2), 114–120. https://doi.org/10.1108/SBM-03-2017-0017

Zeimers, G., Anagnostopoulos, C., Zintz, T., & Willem, A. (2018). Corporate social responsibility (CSR) in football: Exploring modes of CSR implementation. In S. Chadwick, D. Parnell, P. Widdop, & C. Anagnostopolous (Eds.), *Routledge handbook of football business and management* (pp. 114–130). Routledge.

Chapter 12

Conclusions

Learning Lessons from Implementing Sport Policy

John Hayton, Iain Lindsey and Marc Keech

At the end of the introductory chapter, we contended that:

> In bringing together academic and professional practitioner contributions … we hope the book will provide readers with a rare opportunity to consider an integrated dialogue between different viewpoints that can often be unnecessarily and detrimentally separated. Furthermore, in seeking to draw together themes identified and discussed across the book in a concluding chapter, our intention is to help readers identify central issues in implementing sport policy in the UK, consider the extent of their potential generalisability to other countries and suggest potential developments for future policy, practice and research.

Edited volumes, such as this, often invite comments regarding the differential nature in quality, consistency and continuity of the contributions. But, at their best, and particularly when based around a particular theme or a different line of enquiry, edited collections can provide a stimulus to the analysis of the field. Whilst in no way anticipating and/or over claiming any contribution that this book may make, we set out with the intention of providing readers with a collective synthesis and response to the question(s) of what has worked and what hasn't worked in sport policy with reference specifically to organisations in the UK (and predominantly in England). In one sense, the pragmatism of 'what works' or 'what hasn't worked' echoes the ideology of the 'New' Labour government of 1997–2010, and also represents the potential to oversimplify the complexity of issues the chapters have raised. Nevertheless, each of the chapters provides examples of how policy has been implemented by organisations who themselves must continually respond to the conditions and context in which they operate.

So as to provide an overarching conceptual framework for the book, we set out to critically examine the following three points that were earlier identified in Chapter 1, namely:

- changes and continuities in the positioning of different organisations in national sport policies and respective implementation approaches over time;

DOI: 10.4324/9781003162728-12

- the consequences of national sport policies and implementation approaches for different organisations engaged with sport; and
- how recognised sport policy outcomes reflect approaches towards implementation through different organisations.

Hence the aim was to not only provide authors with a coherent structure and purpose to their contribution, but it was also to add value to the debates regarding the implementation of sport policy. These debates are certainly enhanced across the book by the highly expert practitioners who have offered insightful reflections that complement the academic analyses of sport policy implementation. These contributions are much appreciated, given the highly pressed time that practitioners have available and, in some cases, limits in the information that some felt that they could publicly share. Nevertheless, these practitioners have certainly added to the richness of understanding of the work and challenges in implementing sport policy. With these points in mind, we now return to the three points identified above to draw conclusions and provide a more coherent and detailed synthesis of the contributions.

Positioning of Organisations in Sport Policy Implementation

From our broad overview of sport policy over time in the introduction to this book, specific aspects of sport policies have been given further recognition in subsequent chapters. Particular changes and granularities in national policies have been further identified as important across different implementing organisations. One issue that comes through as a result is that implications for implementing organisations do not necessarily depend on traditional distinctions between scales or levels of policy change (e.g., Hall, 1993, cited in Houlihan & Lindsey, 2013). Shifts in policy goals, which may normally be considered as the most significant change, certainly do have significant implications for implementing organisations as, for example, has been the case since *Sporting Future* (HM Government, 2015) gave more explicit orientation towards wider social policy goals for sport and Sport England's (2021) subsequent *Uniting the Movement* gave strengthened priority towards physical activity as well as sport. Nevertheless, chapters also indicate how more specific policy initiatives, and an ongoing sense of policy overload or initiativitis, which may be theorised as representing lower levels of policy change (Hall, 1993), do also bring significant implications including ongoing, destabilising uncertainty for implementing organisations.

Differing levels of policy uncertainty and initiativitis are recognised in different areas of sport policy. In part due to the construction of the book, the collection of chapters gives less attention to elite sport policy than community and youth sport policy. This balance of interrogation may also implicitly reflect the differing levels of continuity across these policy areas. Chapman and Reed's contributions make clear how UK Sport has been able to plot a steadier course for elite sport due to

210 John Hayton et al.

continued policy stability for this area over time. In community sport (and physical activity) policy, there may alternatively be something of a magnifier effect whereby shifts in governmental focus become reflected in changes in Sport England's operations with ongoing consequences for various implementing organisations across the sector. Somewhat differently again, Ives's chapter emphasises how a significant change of government and their school sport policies can reorientate or undermine a whole set of organisations.

It is not sport policies alone that have significant consequences for some of the types of organisations covered in the book. A broad indicator of this point is the extent to which chapters by Dowling and Harris, Kamperman and Rankin-Wright, Keech and Wilkinson, and O'Gorman recognise that wider government approaches to performance measurement continue to be recognised as being influential across various implementing organisations in sport, despite policy rhetoric in *Sporting Future,* and from the Conservative government more widely, shifting away from such an implementation technique. More specifically, public sector organisations involved with sport are especially affected by developments in wider policy areas. Partington, Morby and Robson particularly show how the wider austerity imposed on local authorities since 2010 has significantly affected their role in and contribution to sport and physical activity implementation. Similarly, Ives's chapter considers how intersecting shifts and initiativitis in education policy together with dramatic changes in PE and school sport policy have constrained the capacity of schools to effectively deliver outcomes for young people.

A finding that unites many of the chapters is how the extent of focus and priority towards different organisations and types of organisations changes with policy over time. Policy has directed different resources to different NGBs over time, but Dowling and Harris also note how recent policy shifts associated with *Sporting Future* and *Uniting the Movement* have seen NGBs generally being deprioritised and receiving collectively less funding for their role in community sport. On the other hand, greater integration of sport and physical activity policy has brought increased engagement of and with public health organisations, even though Brown and Beacom recognise they rarely have a role in direct provision. Ives presents a further example of different types of organisations coming to the fore and diminishing in implementation importance respectively as policy changes. The dismantling of School Sport Partnerships from 2010 and the subsequent policy decision to fund the PE and Sport Premium have meant that there has been limited impetus to develop provision in secondary schools whilst specialist staff with particular expertise have been removed from key positions in the implementation chain. Instead, the direction of the PE and Sport Premium to primary schools has resulted in generalists, and primarily head teachers, having a more important role and has also consequentially led to massive expansion in private coaching companies providing services and delivering in schools. Similar prioritisation can also be identified within subsets of particular types of organisations, as Adams and Edson have recognised in the extent to which policy has focused on formalised and regulated 'heavy' voluntary sports clubs and pushed more informal and spontaneous 'light' clubs towards becoming more like the former type.

An overarching assessment may also be reached that policy developments over time have led to increases in the scale and diversity of organisations that are involved in sport policy implementation. Besides Brown and Beacom's explicit consideration of public health agencies, chapters by Mori and O'Gorman, respectively, recognise expansion in third-sector organisations, including those in the 'sport-for-development movement' and in the role of community organisations associated with professional sports clubs. Policy impetus towards the intentional use of sport to contribute to wider social outcomes has certainly been a key factor in the expansion of such organisations. Moreover, policymakers have recognised the limited local community connections and, ultimately, constrained potential to increase grassroots activity that some more established sporting organisations, including NGBs, may have. Perhaps voluntary sports clubs have also suffered something of a diminution of their policy status due to their focus on members and traditional sporting offers, whilst other types of organisations from the non-profit sector (such as charitable arms associated with professional sport clubs and foundations) have proven well placed and receptive to delivering to such wider physical activity and social goals.

These factors relate to the remarkable admission in Sport England's (2016) *Towards an Active Nation* strategy that 'we have only a few proven delivery models and providers we can confidently back, so we need to expand the supply chain on which we rely' (p.11). The distribution of resources by Sport England has consequently encouraged new and different organisations to become more involved in implementation of sport policy. Their core 'funded partners' increased from 107 in 2015–2016 to 134 in 2020–2021, and it was partly a factor of necessity during the Covid pandemic and lockdowns that led to a massive, almost six-fold rise in the total number of organisations to receive Sport England funding in 2020–2021 (National Audit Office, 2022). While such an expansion in organisations funded to enhance 'grassroots participation in sport and physical activity' was regarded positively by the National Audit Office (2022), a counterpoint is the potential for increasing the long-standing problem of fragmentation across the sport and recreation sector.

Nationally directed approaches to overcoming the challenges that fragmentation poses for implementation do show signs of adaptation over time. Mori points to the increase in third-sector 'broker' organisations, some of which are Sport England-funded, taking a role in providing a link between national funding and local delivery. The promotion of partnerships that was such a strong feature of sport policy under Labour has continued more recently, at least in policy discourse and rhetoric. Different degrees of change are evident in practice though. Ives laments the discontinuation of Labour's School Sport Partnerships that connected networks of secondary and primary schools. On the other hand, Active Partnerships may no longer formally represent partnerships between NGBs and local organisations but, as Keech and Wilkinson's chapter indicates, their role in brokering local co-ordination

212 John Hayton et al.

has perhaps become even more central to sport policy implementation. A continuing question, and one considered further in the remainder of the chapter, is whether policy levers available within sport are sufficient to enable approaches to co-ordination to be effective and ultimately deliver desired and desirable outcomes.

Consequences of Sport Policies for Organisations

Because of widening emphasis upon sport to contribute to health and social outcomes and concomitant expansion and diversity of implementing organisations, those bodies (e.g., UK Sport, Sport England and NGBs, local authorities, Active Partnerships, and public health agencies) translating and enforcing top-down (e.g., government and Sport Council) imperatives and overhanging policy targets have become heavily reliant on a ranging tapestry of organisations external to themselves. Many organisations have therefore become responsible for targets and measures upon which factors external to their own performance come to bear, thus reinforcing organisational interdependence. Sport England, for example, have held an increasingly contractual relationship with many and wide-ranging organisations that they fund in return for specific outcomes; Active Partnerships operate in a not too dissimilar fashion to enable local partners to grow sport and physical activity; whilst local authorities have shifted from direct providers to enablers and co-ordinators across a wider range of stakeholders, with NGBs reliant on Active Partnership networks, schools and VSCs to deliver their strategies and achieve targets. It has already been noted that the health agenda has transcended wider public policy, yet public health agencies possess limited capacity to directly implement objectives and so the DCMS and Sport England have become re-aligned to help drive, *inter alia*, national physical and social well-being outcomes, pulling a myriad range of stakeholders into this policy space, and creating, as Brown and Beacom describe, hyper-complexity for policy and practice.

Relatedly, NGBs and other organisations have found themselves situated within a policy environment wherein they are challenged to balance, as Dowling and Harris put it: 'the internal negotiation and external navigation of multiple, often competing and contradictory policy objectives which are often enforced upon them as a result of their funding/resource-dependencies.' In the case of local authorities, Morby, Partington and Robson articulated that the rhetoric of localism espoused by central government and a concomitant sense of autonomy is often mediated by performance management requirements that extend centralised control over local councils and which can serve to deviate from bottom-up, 'what works' implementation which Katy Bowden, for one, ascribes success to. Dowling and Harris further explicated that key decisions made by NGBs at the national level struggle to resonate with local-level delivery agencies often because they fail to reflect local circumstances – and this can create tension between NGBs and agencies such as VSCs who will operate to shield their services and their members' needs. Differences in values and beliefs across the community sport system have revealed diffuse priorities amongst providers that speak to the complicated nature of top-down policy implementation. A prime example is where health-related objectives come to clash with competitive sport objectives in and through the apparatus of organisations which are charged with their implementation. As a case in point, Chapter 5 demonstrated the disconnect between the aims of a local authority to increase general participation levels and the divergent priorities and approaches of the NGBs that were also commissioned to provide accessible sport and physical activity opportunities.

The book has illustrated that, in many cases, 'street-level' implementation of policy is overly distant from its policy definers and translators. NGBs, for example, have commonly been pulled closer to the influence of UK Sport and Sport England due to a dependency on performance-based funding. Lacking the capacity to deliver their policies at the local level, NGBs look to Active Partnerships, local clubs and schools to develop their sports and accomplish their targets. Whilst heavily reliant upon such organisations in the pursuit of their own goals and agendas, and representing principal agents of sport policy, organisations such as NGBs and Active Partnerships have no direct authority over local-level deliverers who may have a diverse set of priorities. As we have seen, in the absence of such control, organisations 'on the ground,' such as VSCs, employ discretion in how and to what extent they choose to implement policy, thereby obscuring or limiting the ability of governing body actors to explain 'what works.' It is clear, therefore, that the policy aims and processes of higher tier authorities do not always reflect the context, beliefs and values of VSCs. NGBs would appear to inadvertently produce tension with VSCs, particularly as they are considered to have insufficiently consulted and negotiated with clubs on intended policy outcomes and how these should be achieved and implemented.

In a challenging financial climate, the manifold third-sector organisations that contribute to the domains of sport and health have increasingly sought to diversify their funding streams, often prioritising sources such as central government departments, clinical commissioning groups, public health agencies, trusts, foundations and corporates. Kevin McPherson suggests that, whilst this has moved many third-sector organisations closer to central policy, it may alter their priorities and lead to mission drift in organisations originally set-up with a remit for sport, as they reorientate towards health and social objectives. Across public health, as it is across the broad funding landscape for sport and physical activity, core funding budget constraints have led to competition for externally funded projects amongst an array of third-sector organisations and projects, which, as Brown and Beacom state, are more often than not time-limited, thus bounding implementation by limiting continuity and operational scope. Indeed, the resource-dependence and financial scarcity that characterise the challenging climate that stakeholders in sport and physical activity find themselves in can mean that organisational self-preservation is prioritised more than anything else, presenting an atomised complexion of a community sport policy system that is comprised of many individual units rather than truly representing a collective or communal system, and this breeds inter-organisational competition.

Responding to an ever-shifting political and economic landscape, organisations have had to adapt to policy and funding changes over time, and one key and ongoing transformation has been to pursue a 'modernisation' agenda. Whilst this impetus to become more 'professional' may bring about some positive developments in organisations (for example, Swim England's creation of a Research and Insight Team to inform strategy, professional sport academies adopting more structured safeguarding practices, and many third-sector organisations developing the wherewithal to seek revenue diversification), the book has revealed that such policy agendas can also prove problematic. For example, pressures placed on VSCs to modernise their structures and further professionalise their services and personnel creates tension between these organisations and the NGB they are affiliated to. Such expectations may not necessarily align with the priorities of clubs and the needs of their members, and they also tend to increase volunteer workload, which can in turn pull volunteers away from direct service delivery. Whilst VSCs take their place as policy 'agents,' Chapter 10 illustrated the capacity of these organisations to resist – collectively – policy imperatives transmitted downward from higher-tier organisations, employ discretion where they deem necessary to prioritise the interests of their members and act on their own terms and under their own initiative when reorganising their operating structures.

The modernisation of NGBs has had implications on their internal culture, as well as their ability to direct policy implementation via their affiliate organisations, and the relationships that they have with them. Dowling and Harris speak of NGB empire building which typically feeds 'top heavy' business models that have increased numbers of managerial staff and are orientated towards profit making. Such a 'business model' has ironically weakened NGB influence over organisations such as VSCs – in part, because they deploy less professional delivery support staff 'on the ground' – whilst they remain, to differing extents, somewhat reliant upon VSCs to achieve key policy targets that they have been charged with by organisations such as the Sport England. To compound this issue, the book highlights that NGBs, particularly those of large size, may lack soft skills and need to develop communication, brokering, negotiation, and conflict resolution skills to operate effectively in the multi-faceted community sport environment wherein much sport engagement rests upon the work of, for example, VSCs.

Furthermore, organisations such as NGBs, and in some cases third-sector organisations, have experienced an influx of staff from non-sporting professional backgrounds, and whilst adding skills and benefits to operational areas such as branding, marketing and commercial enterprise, this corporate shift can engender alienation and division amongst established sports staff. Not only can this lurch to a more corporate business orientation sit uneasily with professional 'sports people' – who may question whether user needs are appropriately understood and provided for – Ian Freeman also commented that it can lead people to act out of self-interest, and to the detriment of collaboration. Consequently, such a culture can lead to a drain of committed, passionate, professional sports personnel from the sector. What is more, organisations such as Swim England can experience a

Conclusions 215

frequent turnover of staff, and this can undermine the consistency and continuity of practices and principles underpinning long-term policy implementation and the oversight that it receives.

Third-sector organisations have increasingly recruited or trained staff to undertake bidding and revenue-generating activities, often taking staff away from face-to-face sport delivery. As most funding arrangements are outcome linked, staff constructing the bids build-in targets and indicators against which the organisation's performance can be measured. However, as the officers for Tranmere in the Community highlight in Chapter 11, such indicators and targets are often too unrealistic to fully achieve in practice, and at the same time do not encompass wider outcomes observed by facilitators, suggesting a disconnect between back office and 'front of house' organisational units. Such a lack of communication not only fails to consider the realistic capacity of such programmes, but it perpetuates overreaching and potentially threatens the organisation's credibility and good standing for receiving further funding in future.

Indeed, many chapters reported that the implementation of policy could be hindered by limitations of knowledge, expertise and leadership amongst personnel involved at this stage of the policy process. In the context of high-performance sport, Kamperman and Rankin-Wright emphasise the need for greater inclusive leadership at the higher rungs of the talent pathway in order to strengthen the implementation of equality and diversity imperatives, whilst also positioning the role of national equity organisations as crucial vehicles by which to provide the necessary upskilling of the sporting workforce in the key aspects of inclusion, cultural competency and unconscious bias. Separately, and in respect of primary schools, Ives notes the difficulties that generalist primary school teachers have in developing PE and school sport due to a well-documented lack of confidence, training and experience in this area of the curriculum. On the other hand, where PE and school sport provision is outsourced, it is done so to coaches and external companies of limited qualifications and knowledge of the pedagogical principles underpinning PE which distinguish its purpose and practice from that of traditional sport-centred activity.

Issues of knowledge, expertise, and leadership become further apparent in the context of organisational efforts to achieve wider public health and social objectives that transcend sport for sports sake. As we have seen, the coupling of sport and health agendas has ebbed and flowed since the publication of *Game Plan* in 2002. Yet, as Brown and Beacom explicate, physical activity – as a key dimension of preventative public health – once an area of policy spillover has now undergone wholesale adoption into the sport policy agenda, whereby physical and mental health outcomes may now be seen to supersede traditional sporting outcomes. Maxine Rhodes, as the leader of an Active Partnership, highlighted in Chapter 6 the importance of different skill sets that staff now require to work across different sectors and across political, professional and community boundaries. Active Partnerships and other organisations can offer opportunities to upskill staff in these ways of working. Yet, amongst grassroots voluntary sports clubs as a different yet central provider of sport in England, many may not have the capacity or inclination

216 John Hayton et al.

to readily produce physical activity-related outcomes, prioritising instead core services and the needs of an often-homogeneous member base. When it comes to the domain of elite sport however, many of the implementation approaches (e.g., target setting, organisational communication and internal and external relations, and skills) discussed here have been enacted more substantially or effectively in seeking elite sport success.

Recognisable Sport Policy Outcomes as a Consequence of Implementation

As sport policy has evolved since the 1980s, implementation processes have taken greater account of the intended results, or as defined in the UK government's (2015) *Sporting Future* strategy, headline outcomes. Policies do not succeed or fail on their own; their progress is dependent upon the process of implementation. Equally, authors across the book have found it challenging to reflect on the outcomes as opposed to the processes of implementation. But it is in the area of *recognisable policy outcomes as a consequence of implementation* that sport needs to think more carefully about the schism between its own limitations and what it claims to achieve. The discussion of implementation in sport policy has often been illustrated by the gap between expectations arising from policy formulation and the results from implementation. This discussion is perhaps not as considered as it might be. What was previously identified as a policy implementation 'gap' has been supplemented in recent years by complex systems thinking, informed by considerations of unpredictability, nonlinearity and adaptability. Contrastingly, the lessons that have been learnt through multiple iterations of sport policy development in the UK have facilitated understanding of not only how and why policies and programmes have been implemented in the way they have been but what has been learnt from them. Sport claims it *has* learnt how implementation can often be a 'major stumbling block in the policy process' (Lester and Goggin, 1998, p. 1) and has subsequently operationalised relevant changes. Nevertheless, authors in this book have commonly faced challenges in identifying (existing) evidence of outcomes and impact that can be explicitly linked to policies and their implementation. Systematic measurement of outcomes, however, (such as those expressed in *Sporting Future* (HM Government, 2015), rather than more simplified quantitative outputs, is now an expected consequence of policy implementation.

The effectiveness of policy implementation and specific interventions in sport often relies upon either anecdotal evidence or more quantitative measures of success. At the elite level, as Chapman outlines, the UK has enjoyed a remarkable run of success, and the achievement of policy objectives as measured through medals and performance on the global stage. But, increasingly, the recognition of that success has been tempered by the potential of elite environments to deliver negative, unintended but damaging consequences to those who are involved. Thus the 'no compromise' approach to elite sport funding has itself been compromised when implemented successfully, resulting in unhealthy behaviours and cultures within the organisational settings and systems. Thus, the systemic drivers of elite sport success – specifically, highly focused policies, accountability and the rewarding of success itself with further funding – may well have changed the elite sport system but potentially to the detriment of the health and well-being of a large number of individual athletes, coaches and support staff.

The success of policies aimed at participation is much more difficult to evaluate, given the moving targets, shifting expectations and complexity of the organisational landscape. Short-termism has mitigated the long-term impact of policy development and formulation. Slightly contrary to successes in elite sport, there have been some indications of failure in increasing participation, as exemplified most prominently in the chapter on NGBs. DeLeon and DeLeon (2002) noted that delivery agents may be more reliable elements of an implementation system if they are involved in policymaking processes from the start. But the centralised decision-making processes and tighter controls, especially financially, which have underpinned policies aimed at increasing participation in local communities, have not led to sustained increases in participation. As alluded to in the section above on the consequences of sport policies for organisations involved in the implementation process – and as Brown and Beacom, Keech and Wilkinson, and Adams have all illustrated through their respective contributions – the weight, amount and complexity of external processes and variables are both beyond the control of sports organisations and often are barriers to the determinants of the relative success of policy implementation. Like the organisations that design them, programmes are automatically under threat when reliant upon single sources of funding and thus limit the potential of what they can achieve. Indeed, as both policy design and programme implementation has often not lasted long enough for sustainable benefits to occur systematically, the continued redesign and/or rebranding of organisations, such as the Active Partnerships or the re-emergence of Local Delivery Pilots almost 20 years after the initiation of Sport Action Zones, exemplify what might be seen as a cyclical process of re-implementation.

When examining larger, more expensive projects, the National Audit Office (2013) identified several factors which led to underachievement in policy delivery due to over-optimism. Of these, issues of complexity and the underestimation of the challenges of implementation, the misunderstanding of stakeholders in terms of the challenges which organisations have been set and taken on, and issues of behaviour and incentives, relating to short-termism and the culture of organisations seeking to demonstrate accountability, have all hindered implementation and delivery of sport policy outcomes. Thus, policies formed at a national level have encountered challenges of inconsistent local implementation, especially where divergent forms of governance at the local level have related to organisations with some degree of political autonomy, who are able to shape implementation in relation to their local context (Braithwaite et al., 2018). Furthermore, as Adams, Kamperman and Rankin-Wright, and almost all of the practitioner responses have illustrated, those involved in strategic policy formulation cannot succeed without an effective idea of what does actually happen at the point when policy and beneficiary or end user

218 John Hayton et al.

meet. As the introduction to the book identified, this is the basis for a bottom-up approach to policy implementation and illustrates the relative influence of discretionary power in determining the efficacy of policy.

As Sport England's approach to co-designing its 2021 strategy, *Uniting the Movement*, illustrated, a greater emphasis on community-led approaches recognises the stubborn inequalities which have underpinned the overall fall in the proportion of people participating weekly in sport since the early 1990s (Weed, 2016). Participation in sport requires comprehensive multifactorial solutions in which there needs to be recognition of the interaction between individuals, activity settings and influences on behaviour, not least of which is the enjoyment which individual participants gain from their participation. But, as many of the chapters have made clear, different organisations (sometimes of the same type and sometimes implicitly) have their own desired outcomes, which have differing alignments (or not) with national policy objectives. So, the consideration in the overall/national picture is often seen in relation to the outcomes determined/desired by national policymakers. But that is not necessarily the sole relation between policy (implementation) and outcomes if consideration is given to the extent to which organisations may be achieving their own desired outcomes and how that is affected by policy and implementation. Moreover, a centralised approach to sport policy has engendered the construction of systems in which the 'professionalisation' of voluntary sports organisations and their members is a key indicator of capacity, rather than the relationships and partnerships across policy sectors, which are necessary to address required social policy outcomes associated with increased participation.

There is an implicit sense by some practitioners (more so in third-sector organisations) that specific outcomes are reached despite not necessarily being officially recorded or accounted for – in some cases, this is because of a lack of time to do so, yet in others, and somewhat paradoxically, there is an admission that there is a lack of know-how within such organisations about how to provide enough or the 'right' evidence to demonstrate outcomes. The presence of such knowledge limitations in relation to processes such as monitoring and evaluation in organisations responsible for direct sport delivery highlights an important gap for governing and steering bodies such as NGBs, local authorities and Active Partnerships to address – without developing this capacity, it will remain difficult to understand 'what works' due to a disjunct between what is delivered and what is measured, and especially in respect of wider social objectives that transcend sport activity.

Theoretical Insights into Sport Policy Implementation

In seeking to make wider sense of the trends in sport policy implementation from across the book, it is imperative to link back to the theories of policy implementation that were introduced in Chapter 1, which spanned top-down, bottom-up and principal-agent approaches to analysing policy implementation as well as related conceptualisations of policy enactment. It is also necessary to recognise that sport policy is contextually embedded in a wider UK system of governance that is, and

Conclusions 219

has historically been, highly centralised (Houlihan & White, 2002). Similarly, a top-down approach has characterised sport policy implementation across time and across many of the areas covered in this book. It would be a surprise to find otherwise given the extent to which impetus and funding for sport policy is now driven by national government.

That is not to say that a top-down approach to sport policy implementation is uniformly applied or without deviation or change. Those at the 'top,' whether that be in government or in the national sport agencies covered in Chapter 2, cannot demand the 'perfect compliance' from implementing agencies in sport that early top-down theories indicated as a key criterion of effective policy implementation. Governmental involvement in sport has increased at a time when there have been broader changes in the different mechanisms used to steer implementation from the top and, in the preceding sections, we have highlighted the examples of conditionalities applied to funding, setting and monitoring of targets, and the instigation of different organisational structures that differ in specificity and in depth across the different sport policy areas that the book encompasses. Reference has also been made to Sport England's *Uniting the Movement* strategy that, at least, seeks to soften central steering of local policy and practice and, at best, may enable or promote greater control at local level. PE and school sport is another area in which, since the advent of Conservative-led governments in 2010, there has been significant lessening of key central steering mechanisms. While not necessarily problematic in itself, there is perhaps a salutary lesson whereby possible scope for more bottom-up development of PE and school sport has been squeezed as a priority for schools when other aspects of their provision remain subject to centralised imperatives to pursue national political priorities for education.

Different theoretical lenses can help make further sense of the implications of approaches to implementation of national sport policies. For Matland (1995), as outlined in Chapter 1, implications for and in implementation are shaped by the extent to which there is ambiguity (or, conversely, clarity) in overarching policies and how much policies may generate conflict (or, conversely, agreement) amongst stakeholders involved with implementation. Relatively unambiguous policies may make for top-down implementation, but outcomes and effectiveness may then be determined by the sufficiency of available resources, where there is low conflict or, when conflict is higher, by the extent of power that those driving policy from the top can bring to bear over implementing agencies (Matland, 1995). We can recognise the former in the case of elite sport, whereby the combination of highly focused policy together with the provision of substantial resources has resulted in effective implementation towards the goals of winning Olympic and Paralympic medals. However, in focusing on the goals that policymakers set, as top-down theorising in general does, it is important not to lose sight of alternative effects of implementation, as has been manifest in undesirable implications for athlete well-being as the drive towards elite success has continued unabated.

As the previous sections indicate, top-down approaches to improving participation in community sport have been unlike those for elite sport in that they evidently have not had the same level of success in relation to national policy goals. Assessing reasons for what may be termed as 'policy failure' draws us back to Chapter 1 where we cited conditions presented by Sabatier and Mazmanian (1979) and Cairney (2019) that may be required for effective top-down policy implementation. Crucial amongst these in the case of community sport are those regarding the effective structuring of the implementation process and the need for minimal dependency relations across policy levels and organisations. It is questionable as to whether grassroots sport policy can be implemented in ways to meet these conditions. Again, the book and its contributions collectively demonstrate the profound complexity across the sets of organisations involved in the implementation of community sport (and physical activity) policy. At best, between national and local levels, there are cascading 'principal-agent' relationships with Sport England having developed contractual relationships with NGBs and other organisations such as Active Partnerships, who in turn may be considered as 'principals' seeking to implement through other organisations such as voluntary sector clubs. While not necessarily in explicit conflict, as Matland (1995) would term it, chapters have indicated various forms of indirect or inherent resistance on behalf of these and other implementing organisations. There remains, for some third-sector sport organisations, a historical culture and continuing ethos of autonomy that is inevitably in tension with policies that are governmentally and public-sector driven. The recent expansion of organisations explicitly positioned to deliver the wider social outcomes desired by policymakers (as encompassed in Chapters 6, 8 and 11) may offer a more 'compliant' (Cairney, 2019; Sabatier & Mazmanian, 1979) set of implementing agents, but have also added to the complexity of the overall implementation structure.

Emerging strongly from the book, and as indicated by the many questions that remain as to 'what works' in driving successful policy outcomes, particularly in non-elite sport, is the sense that the experiences and perspectives of practitioners directly involved in the implementation of sport policy are not widely accounted for in academic research, and so this can only take our analysis and interpretation so far. As Lucy Moore argues when reflecting on sport policymaking and implementation in relation to sport governing bodies, limited attention has been 'paid to the biographies and daily working practices of the individuals who constitute these key stakeholder organisations in relation to policy formation and execution' (2021, p. 180), and such neglect limits deeper understanding of the effectiveness of policy design and delivery.

Policy enactment therefore presents an especially useful theoretical tool to understand what goes on amongst organisations implementing sport policy and to unpack variation amongst implementing agencies' responses to national policies both across diverse types of organisations and within particular types of organisations. In our introduction to the book, we engaged with the work of Ball and colleagues, who have stressed that evaluating the success of policy implementation is very difficult, and it can be hard, if not impossible, to discern which implementation processes may lead to intended, unintended or less than desirable outcomes.

As Ball et al. (2012) state, 'policy making and policy makers tend to assume "best possible" environments for implementation' (pp.148–149) and seldom 'take account of the complexity of institutional policy enactment environments' (p.9) in which such texts and associated discourses are rendered into contextualised practices. Throughout the book, we have gained a sense of how policy enactment is constrained or enabled in organisations by specific and overlapping contextual factors, which often stand to detract from the conditions that Sabatier and Mazmanian (1979) and Cairney (2019) highlight as conducive to top-down implementation success (such as access to the necessary resources and the effects of wider socio-economic conditions acting upon an implementing agency).

The constraining nature of organisational context upon policy enactment is well illustrated across the book. For example, the professional and occupational cultures contextual dimension is instantiated by the increasing business orientation of NGBs, which has been shown to elicit tension between professional sport staff and senior leaders, as well as a disconnect with non-sporting corporate staff – ultimately fomenting a divisive effect on policy implementation. Elsewhere, the responses to external policies by VSCs are very much mediated according to the situated contextual dimension, as their principal focus is on the needs and expectations of their members. What is more, when it comes to implementing equality policy in sport in the UK, Kamperman and Rankin-Wright highlight the need for action to remove barriers to participation at the grassroots level and urge more incisive outreach to under-represented communities. This in particular implicates the situated and material contexts of VSCs in that they may be characterised by a homogeneous membership whose own needs may be their primary focus, and they may lack the staff resource to undertake outreach recruitment. Relatedly, Kamperman and Rankin-Wright highlighted how funding-linked high-performance outcomes set by UK Sport have suppressed the work of NGBs towards equality targets, demonstrating the effects of the interplay of external (e.g., 'no compromise' approach) and material (funding and staffing) contextual dimensions on organisational commitment to enacting equality, diversity and inclusion policy.

References to 'performance' and 'performance cultures' are not surprising given Ball and colleagues' (2012, p.139) explication of the general regime of the state that is 'decisively focused on performance', and which is intimately bound to processes of evaluation and surveillance that together constitute 'a form of power which is automatic and generalised.' Such forms of power are operationalised via policy technologies which steer the enactment of policy by delivery agencies in line with national imperatives by exerting sets of pressures downwards through the delivery chain. The increasing embeddedness of policy technologies have, therefore, coincided with devolving governance systems. Performativity is one such policy technology that is both explicitly and implicitly apparent across the chapters of this book, to which we will now evince some examples of its insidiousness in the enactment of sport policy. When sport investment relies upon targets creating performance cultures centred on their measurement of progress against them, Ball (2003) suggests that tactical approaches that engender short-term gains are sought, even though the distribution of such efforts will have social consequences. In the local authorities chapter, Katy Bowden provides further illustration of this point by highlighting that due to pressures to achieve targets, NGBs focused their efforts to increase sports participation in typically more affluent areas where engagement was more easily mobilised, thus boosting performance in relation to external targets. As a further example, in Chapter 9, Ives and Watkinson speak to the initiativitis experienced in the school system through which a series of policies reproduce the technology of performativity and thus perpetuate 'the relentless pursuit of the unattainable' as their enactment will be mediated by material and contextual factors (Barker, 2010, p.100, cited in Ball et al., 2012).

Throughout the book, various chapter authors refer to the intensification of policy actors' roles, for example, the increasing administrative load experienced by professional football academy coaches and the growing time commitments required of volunteers in grassroots sport clubs (as evidenced by academic and practitioner contributions in Chapters 10 and 11). Such examples speak to an increased volume of what Ball refers to as 'second order' activities – as opposed to 'first order' activities that entail the direct delivery of sport 'on the ground' – that 'are the work of performance monitoring and management' (Ball, 2003, p. 221). O'Gorman explained that in an environment characterised by increasing accountability, work auditing and perceived managerial surveillance, professional coaches resorted to strategic fabrications in the documenting and enacting of their duties to present a conforming and policy-compliant impression of themselves and their conduct, accounts which may not necessarily have reflected 'the day-to-day working practices and environment.'

As Ball states, 'performativity produces opacity rather than transparency' in terms of policy implementation as information produced as to 'what works?' becomes obfuscated and distorted via widespread acts of fabrication that are occasioned within systems of recording and reporting of and on practice (2003, p. 215). In any case, the excessive demands of second-order activities can detract from the energy and focus that the practitioner has available to implement progressive pedagogical or organisational inputs (Ball, 2003; O'Gorman et al., 2021). In combination with the insecure employment conditions that many sports workers face, the consequences of performativity can have an estranging effect on their professional identity and a detrimental impact on their social and psychological well-being (Ball, 2003; Braun & Maguire, 2020; Kessler, 2021; O'Gorman et al., 2021).

Prominent questions arise when considering the implications of performativity on policy implementation. One such question being, how can we truly know what means and methods of implementation might work and for what reasons if we are to assume that reporting practices are so laden with fabrications? Another, relatedly, is how can policy auditors gain an accurate reflection of how policy is implemented and what this looks like in practice? Sabatier and Mazmanian's (1979) five conditions for effective implementation encounter several problems when considering the policy technology of performativity: the implementation process may be offset by the accounting processes built in to record it; policy actors' commitment to the goals become frayed due to an intensified workload that detracts from direct delivery, and accountability mechanisms have not been appropriately informed by and negotiated with key workforce representatives.

We have highlighted the compliance–discretion balance intimated by Cairney (2019) as necessary to successful policy implementation, yet returning once more to the context of VSCs, Daniel Edson has stressed that clubs place their members' needs and user services at the heart of their decision-making, inferring a leadership agency which tempers their engagement with the performative dimensions encouraged within their environment. According to Edson, the ability of VSCs to exercise such discretion has, in part, been aided by an increased reliance of the NGB on the clubs to deliver their objectives because of its changing governance and workforce structures, thus altering the power gradient between the two and buttressing the position of the VSC in this relationship.

To encapsulate a rounded picture of our theoretical application of a policy enactment framework, we turn once more to the context of equality and inclusion. Kamperman and Rankin-Wright contend that audit and outcome-based approaches to equality seldom evidence genuine change because they tend not to focus the necessary attention on the structures, cultures and processes that continue to marginalise those who experience inequalities and discrimination in sport. Under critique, Kamperman and Rankin-Wright state that organisational efforts to establish inclusive policies often amount to 'vague and poorly developed rationales' that largely reflect rhetorical and performative commitments to social justice – a scenario aided by overarching equality frameworks that may merely require the development of an equality policy and action plan, but not evidence of their efficacy. Kamperman and Rankin-Wright refer to such depthless organisational responses as a form of 'lip service.' Ball (1997, 2000, 2003) explained that such textual accounts (e.g., the development of equality policy and an action plan by a sports organisation, absent evidence of actual change to the organisation) serve an accountability function whilst also presenting a version of the organisation that appears responsive to their 'consumers.' It could be suggested that such strategies of impression management are geared towards reputation enhancement and income maximisation to strengthen an institution's market position (Ball, 1997, 2000). Yet, as Ball (2000) acknowledged, the demands for performativity close down the possibilities for social justice and equity. Instead, Kamperman and Rankin-Wright contend that equality policy must go beyond an outcome-based compliance approach towards a process-orientated approach characterised by firm institutional commitment and real action that is facilitated by strategic and structural change. To the effects outlined here, the technology of performativity would appear to conspire against both Sabatier and Mazmanian (1979) and Cairney's (2019) proposed conditions for effective policy implementation on account of often ambiguous and poorly communicated policy, a lack of political commitment of institutional leaders and wherein one policy objective may be undermined by conflicting priorities.

Pertinently, Ball et al. (2012) – in reference to the study of education – state that the analysis of policy implementation is often de-politicised, and the same could be argued in the domain of sport policy. Sports work and the enactment of policy are bound up with emotion, and sports workers will have differing professional philosophies and dispositions towards their work, will be at different stages of their career/role to the next person and will have had different experiences of policy – all of these factors inform a policy actor's personal discursive archive which stands to shape their response and feelings to a contemporary policy and how that policy may influence their practice (Ball et al., 2012). The expert practitioner contributions throughout this book, as well as academic chapters, convey a sense of the variety of individual roles through which policy is enacted in sport and how the nature and positioning of one's role may colour and shape that individual's responses to policy. To illustrate this diversity of sport workers' roles, we can include paid staff in sport organisations, volunteers in community sport clubs, those professionals whose wider roles in education and health overlap with sport and physical activity, or vice versa, and those employees of 'broker' organisations who sit and serve as a conduit between many of the types of organisations focused on in this book. A policy enactment framework not only enables us to uncover the material and social contexts in which policy agencies render policy into practice, but it also encourages us to examine the individual subjectivities of the policy actor (and all policy actors, not just senior leaders within organisations) that come to bear on policy delivery – facets of the policy process which have, until recently, been left underexplored in the domain of sport policy.

This then leads us to the potential limitations of our theoretical analysis in sport policy. The book amplifies the importance of both zooming in (as per Moore, 2021) as well as zooming out (i.e., looking at the sector as a whole, or at least multiple implementing organisations, as the book has attempted to do so). But it is likely that this needs a theoretical toolbox, rather than just individual theories. We as editors (and many of the contributors) have been able to link types of policy to what has happened in implementation. But, at present, our analysis is more limited in linking what happens in implementation to resultant outcomes. The pace of change in sport policy dynamics, and the common condition of short-term funding, has resulted in constant changes in organisational context. Consequently, organisations have finite capacity to implement policies that aim to change the behaviour of intended participants or beneficiaries and, ultimately, achieve outcomes of social action or change.

Implementation involves action to enact a policy, but the intended outcomes illustrate the impact of action on the policy 'problem.' Due to the constantly changing nature of policy imperatives, the disconnect and obscurity between processes of implementation practices in sport and the expected outcomes of those practices affects our ability as analysts to unpack and examine those organisational actions that lead directly to intended policy outcomes. In turn, this affects our ability to demonstrate outcomes that match expectations of policymakers. The action from policy statements is, in the case of elite sport, aimed at a narrow arena of success within systems and through performance measured by medals. The success of policies aimed at participation is much more difficult to evaluate, given the moving targets, shifting expectations and complexity of the organisational landscape. But in environments aimed at broader and more primary social policy objectives, action has most frequently exhibited itself as programmes, procedures, regulations or practices. Sport policy, as a field of study, has been getting better at theoretical/

Conclusions   225

methodological approaches to evaluation. Perhaps this demonstrates the need to work back from them to implementation issues and, ultimately, policy? But largely, we're stuck with theories that emphasise one stage of the policy process or another.

Conclusion

Understanding policy implementation processes in sport is important because of the extent of funding from the public purse. At its core, we have sought in this book to develop greater understanding of what Sager and Gofen (2022, p. 1) term the 'implementation arrangements' in sport, namely the combinations of 'institutional setting and organisational design' that define the 'context within which policy seeks to achieve its goals.' In doing so, the book has offered some key insights which show how implementation of sport policies reflects a process involving change over time, which is characterised by the actions of multiple organisations and their actors and is influenced by varying contexts throughout.

There is some positivity across the book about the potential of recent sport policy developments, namely Sport England's *Uniting the Movement* strategy and some early responses to problems resulting from top-down elite sport policies. These developments may offer opportunities for more responsive implementation processes. Yet the National Audit Office (2022) report, *Grassroots Participation in Sport and Physical Activity*, shows that policy change without changes in system structures and cultures is the recipe for constant failure. Policy implementation needs to reflect sport and physical activity as being strongly connected to many, wide-ranging, issues. In particular, the challenge for organisations working at a national level is how they can effectively enable or implement local delivery. Often, policy actors such as some of those reflected in this book have not recognised that their lived experience rarely relates to the communities they are seeking to serve and support. Consequently, their impact has often been limited. Whilst national leadership can facilitate change through policy and strategy, improvements in sport policy implementation can only occur at the point of delivery and, thus, the importance of our analysis must be effectively conveyed to those beyond the realms of academia.

References

Ball, S. J. (1997). Good school/bad school: Good school/bad school: Paradox and fabrication. *British Journal of Sociology of Education, 18*(3), 317–336. http://doi.org/10.1080/0142569970180301

Ball, S. J. (2000). Performativities and fabrications in the education economy: Towards the performative society. *Australian Educational Researcher, 17*(3), 1–24. http://doi.org/10.1007/BF03219719

Ball, S. J. (2003). The teacher's soul and the terrors of performativity. *Journal of Education Policy, 18*(2), 215–228. http://doi.org/10.1080/0268093022000043065

Ball, S. J., Maguire, M., & Braun, A. (2012). *How schools do policy: Policy enactments in secondary schools*. Routledge.

Barker, B. (2010). *The pendulum swings: Transforming school reform.* Trentham Books.

Braithwaite, J., Churruca, K., Long, J. C., Ellis, L. A., & Herkes, J. (2018). When complexity science meets implementation science: A theoretical and empirical analysis of systems change. *BMC Medicine, 16*(63). http://doi.org/10.1186/s12916-018-1057-z

Braun, A., & Maguire, M. (2020). Doing without believing – Enacting policy in the English primary school. *Critical Studies in Education, 61*(4), 433–447. http://doi.org/10.1080/17508487.2018.1500384

Cairney, P. (2019). *Understanding public policy* (2nd ed.). Macmillan.

DeLeon, P., & DeLeon, L. (2002). What ever happened to policy implementation? An alternative approach. *Journal of Public Administration Research and Theory, 12*(4), 467–492. http://doi.org/10.1093/oxfordjournals.jpart.a003544

Hall, P. A. (1993). Policy paradigms, social learning, and the state: The case of economic policymaking in Britain. *Comparative Politics, 25*(3), 275. https://doi.org/10.2307/422246

HM Government (2015). *Sporting Future: A new strategy for an active nation.* Cabinet Office.

Houlihan, B., & White, A. (2002). *The politics of sports development: Development of sport or development through sport.* Routledge.

Houlihan, B., & Lindsey, I. (2013). *Sport policy in Britain.* Routledge.

Kessler, M. A. (2021). Performative enactments of teacher evaluation: Two preservice teachers and the edTPA. *Policy Futures in Education, 19*(1), 44–62. https://doi.org/10.1177/1478210320940132

Lester, J. P., & Goggin, M. L. (1998). Back to the future: The rediscovery of implementation studies. *Policy Currents, 8*(3), 1–9.

Matland, R. E. (1995). Synthesizing the implementation literature: The ambiguity-conflict model. *Journal of Public Administration Research and Theory, 5*(2), 145–174. https://doi.org/10.1093/oxfordjournals.jpart.a037242

Moore, L. (2021). Inside out: Understanding professional practice and policy making in UK high-performance sport: A process sociological approach. *International Journal of Sport Policy and Politics, 13*(1), 179–185. http://doi.org/10.1080/19406940.2020.1844274

National Audit Office. (2013). *Over-optimism in government projects.* National Audit Office.

National Audit Office. (2022). *Grassroots participation in sport and physical activity.* National Audit Office.

O'Gorman, J., Partington, M., Potrac, P., & Nelson, L. (2021). Translation, intensification and fabrication: Professional football academy coaches' enactment of the elite player performance plan. *Sport, Education and Society, 26*(3), 309–325. http://doi.org/10.1080/13573322.2020.1726313

Sabatier, P., & Mazmanian, D. (1979). The conditions of effective implementation: A guide to accomplishing policy objectives. *Policy Analysis, 5*(4), 481–504.

Sager, F., & Gofen, A. (2022). The polity of implementation: Organizational and institutional arrangements in policy implementation. *Governance, 35*(2), 347–364. https://doi.org/10.1111/gove.12677

Sport England. (2016). *Towards an active nation.* Sport England.

Sport England. (2021). *Uniting the movement.* Sport England.

Weed, M. (2016). Should we privilege sport for health? The comparative effectiveness of UK government investment in sport as a public health intervention. *International Journal of Sport Policy and Politics, 8*(4), 559–576. https://doi.org/10.1080/19406940.2016.1235600

Index

accountability: national sport policymaking 63; PE and School Sport (PESS) 160; sport council 22; voluntary sports clubs (VSCs) 180–181

Achieving Racial Equality: A Standard for Sport 117–118

Action Sport programmes 79

Active Leeds 86

Active Partnerships 57, 59–61, 66–67, 69, 70, 85, 104, 211–212; Active Sports Guide 60; County Durham Sport (CDS) 71–73; performance measures 61; staff 215–216

Active People Survey 3–4, 27, 88

Activity Alliance 125–129

Advisory Sports Council 20–21

Advocacy Coalition 94–95; Framework 94–95; Monitoring and evaluation 61; Multiple streams 95; Performance Management and Improvement 68; standardisation 118–119; VSC 178–179

Ahmed, S. 68; 'The language of diversity' 121

asset-based community development (ABCD) 139–141, 143

asymmetric governance 68, 180, 181

Ball, S. J. 12–14, 196, 222, 223

'Big Society' initiative 4, 176

Black Lives Matter (BLM) 119–120

Blair government: modernisation 2–3; *see also* New Labour government

bottom-up approach to policy implementation 9, 43–44, 53, 153, 218

Brighton Declaration on Women and Sport 117

budget: local authorities (LAs) 82–83; *see also* funding

Cairney, P. 8, 220, 223

Carter report 62–63, 81–82

charities 116, 138, 142; Tranmere Rovers in the Community 199–204

Choosing Activity: A Physical Activity Action Plan 99–101

Clinical Commissioning Groups (CCGs) 95, 103

coaching: Elite Player Performance Plan (EPPP) 196, 204

Coalition government 4; 'Big Society' initiative 4; *Creating a Sporting Habit for Life* 26; local authorities under 82–83; physical activity agenda 101–103

Code for Sport Governance 22

Commission for Race Equality (CRE) 117

community sport 5, 41, 42, 69, 134, 138–139, 145–146, 199; deficit reduction approach 141–142; delivery models 139–142; Football Fans in Training (FFIT) 194; Football in the Community (FiTC) 192–194; funding 49; local reach 48–49; resources 44–45; role of NGBs as policy implementers 43–45, 48–50; street-level bureaucracy (SLBy) 177–181; *see also* third-sector organisations (TSOs); voluntary sports clubs (VSCs)

Community Sport Networks (CSNs) 63, 81

Compulsory Competitive Tendering (CCT) 10, 59, 79

Conservative government/s: austerity 4; 'Big Society' initiative 176; Health of the Nation (HotN) 98; 'Levelling Up' 85;

228 Index

local authorities (LAs) 78–80, 83–85; neo-liberalism 137–138; Thatcher 135–136
corporate social responsibility (CSR) 192–193
Council of Europe (CoE), European Sport for All Charter 135
County Sport Partnerships (CSPs) 44, 57, 59, 61–65; appraisal 66; core services 64; funding 62; *see also* Active Partnerships
Covid-19 97; equality policy impacts 120; impact on local authorities (LAs) 83–85; physical activity impacts 104
Creating a Sporting Habit for Life 102
Crouch, T. 65–66
Cunningham Report 28

Department for Digital, Culture, Media and Sport (DCMS) 31, 41, 42, 95, 136; Carter report 81–82; *Creating a Sporting Habit for Life* 27, 82; 'Sport in our Communities' report 85–86; *Sporting Future: A New Strategy for an Active Nation* 40, 70
Department for Levelling Up, Housing and Communities 85
Department of Health 97
Department of National Heritage (DNH), *Sport: Raising the Game* 21
disabled people 125–129; equality policy 118; physical activity 126–128
diversity 121, 124; Team GB 122; *see also* equality policy

education policy 152–154; *see also* school/s
Elite Player Performance Plan (EPPP) 195–198, 201–204
elite sport 6, 39, 42, 190; funding 40, 216–217; *see also* professional sports clubs
enabling authorities 80
English Sport Council *see* Sport England
equality policy 223; *Achieving Racial Equality: A Standard for Sport* 117–118; Covid-19 impacts 120; disabled people 118, 125–129; high performance versus inclusion 121–122; implementation challenges 121–124; inclusion 124; language 124; legislation 117; New Labour 118; organisations 117; outcomes over processes 122–123; racial 117–118; rhetoric versus real action 124; Sporting

Equals 120; standardisation 118–119; women's rights 117; *see also* race and racial equality
Equality Standard, The: A Framework for Sport 118–119
evidence-based policy 3, 101, 200–201

facility management 81, 142; Leeds City Council 86–87
football clubs 107–110, 199; chaplains 197; Elite Player Performance Plan (EPPP) 195–198; social policy implementation 192–194; youth development policy implementation 195–198
Football Fans in Training (FFIT) 194, 200
Football in the Community (FiTC) 192–194
funding 2, 22; community sport 49; CSPs 62; diversified models 138; elite sport 40, 216–217; local authorities (LAs) 79, 83; national governing bodies (NGBs) 24–25, 33–34; National Lottery 21, 58; needs-based 141; 'no compromise' approach 41; PE and School Sport (PESS) 158–160; performance measures 3–4; private 5; public health 96; school sport 152; third-sector organisations (TSOs) 144; UK Sport Council 24

Game Plan 3, 26, 41, 62, 98–99, 136–137, 155, 180, 191
Gove, M. 158
governance 7, 14, 178; asymmetric 68, 180, 181; voluntary sports clubs (VSCs) 179–180
Great Britain Sports Council: Sport for All campaign 136; *Sport in the Community: The Next Ten Years* 21, 79
Green, M. 20–22
Grix, J. 64, 68, 70, 181

health: inequality 97; preventative 96; social determinants 96, 97; *see also* public health
Health and Social Care Act 102–103
Health of the Nation (HotN) 98
high-performance sport 21, 23, 25, 27, 42, 215
Houlihan, B. 22, 39, 64, 76, 80, 94, 143, 173, 180

implementation: bottom-up approach 9, 43–44, 53, 153; capacity building 11–12;

Elite Player Performance Plan (EPPP) 196–198; equality policy 121–124; failure, reasons for 11; future challenges 85–86; 'gap' 6; local authorities (LAs) 76; 'no compromise' approach 6; outcomes 216–218; partnership approach 6, 153, 156–157; PE and Sport Premium 160–161; physical activity agenda 94; principal-agent theory 10; research 11; role of NGBs 42–45, 48–50; Sport England 26–27; stages 10–11; street-level 213; theoretical insights 218–225; through professional sports clubs 192–194; top-down approach 7–8, 43, 53, 80–81, 212–213; underachievement 217–218; VSCs and 181–182

inclusion 116, 124, 223; disabled people 126–129; versus high performance 121–122; *see also* inequality

inequality 73, 87, 96, 116, 138, 223; gender 117, 123; health 97; 'Levelling Up' 85; racial 117–118; *see also* equality policy

International Olympic Committee (IOC) 24

key performance indicators 196, 201
Kick It Out campaign 117

Labour government/s: modernisation 4, 22; partnerships 3; *Playing to Win: A New Era for Sport* 26, 27; 'sport for sport's sake' 26; *A Sporting Future for All* 3; voluntary sports clubs (VSCs) 176

leisure trusts 81, 84

'Levelling Up' 85

Local Area Agreements (LAAs) 101

local authorities (LAs) 63, 135, 210, 212; budget cuts 82–83; Carter report 81–82; Community Sport Networks (CSNs) 81; under Conservative government 78–80, 83–85; contracts 81; Covid-19 impacts 83–85; funding 79; future challenges 85–86; grant aid 83; Leeds City Council 86–89; under the New Labour government 80–82; oversight 85; policy implementation 85–86; public health 102–103; relationship with central government 76–77; Sport Development Officers (SDOs) 79, 80; unitary authorities 77–78; Wolfenden report 77

Local Delivery Pilots (LDPs) 84, 99

Local Exercise Action Pilots (LEAPs) 101

local government 77; under Coalition government 82–83; electoral process 78; local authorities (LAs) 77; modernisation 80; parish councils 78; public health 102–103; services 78; two-tier 78; unitary authorities 77–78

Local Government Act 77, 100–101

Local Strategic Partnerships (LSPs) 100–101

Localism Act 82, 142

Major, J. 2, 154

Marmot Review 97

mega events 89

modernisation 2, 4, 22, 176, 179, 214; local government 80; sport 3

Monitoring and Evaluation framework 61

Multiple Streams Framework (MSF) 95

mutual aid 173, 178, 180–181

national governing bodies (NGBs) 6, 22, 23, 29, 37, 50, 82, 210, 212; during the 1980s 39–40; during the 1990s 40; commitments 41; community sport 42–45, 48–50; contractual arrangements 10, 26, 81, 212; diversity targets 123; 'earned autonomy' 40–41; evolving role from 1960 to 2021 38–42; funding 24–25, 33–34; internal structure 38; medal-winning potential 24–25; modernisation 214; Olympic sport 40; priorities and roles 42–44, 48; skills shortage 49; transparency 50–51; and VSCs 172; Whole Sport Plan approach 26; Wolfenden report 39; *see also* voluntary sports clubs (VSCs)

National Health Service, Strategic Health Authorities (SHA) 99

National Lottery 21, 40, 58, 79–80; *see also* funding

neo-liberalism 137–138, 179

New Labour government: equality policy 118; *Game Plan* 3, 26, 98–99, 136–137, 155, 180; local authorities (LAs) 80–82; Policy Action Teams (PATs) 136; public health policy 98–101; social inclusion 137; Third Way 136–137

New Public Management (NPM) 2, 4–5, 10, 39–40, 179–180

NICE guidelines for physical activity 103

'No Compromise' approach 6, 25, 30, 34, 41

230 Index

Olympic Games 6, 122
outsourcing 81; PE and school sport 161–162
oversight, local authorities (LAs) 85; *see also* governance

participation 7, 32, 42, 65, 217–218; increasing 26; targets 69
partnership/s 3, 5, 69–70, 72–73, 137, 153, 163, 180; Active Partnerships 66–67; approach 10, 60, 153–154, 156–157; County Sport Partnerships 44, 61–65; Local Strategic Partnerships 100–101; multi-agency 137; under New Labour government 80; origins 58–59; School Sport Partnerships 5, 155; Sport England 26–28; UK Sport Council 25; *see also* Active Partnerships; County Sport Partnerships (CSPs)
PAT 10 report 62
PE, School Sport and Club Links (PESSCL) 152, 156
PE and School Sport (PESS) 152–154, 163; accountability 160; decision to cut funding 158; future of 162; historical and political context 154–155; outsourcing 161–162; reinstatement of funding 158–160; *see also* school/s
PE and Sport Premium 159, 210
PE and Sport Strategy for Young People (PESSYP) 152, 155, 158, 164
performance: culture 14, 221–222; versus inclusion 121–122; management tools 80; measures 3–4, 196, 210
performativity 13, 222–223
Phillpots, L. 68, 181
physical activity 5, 7, 65, 72, 94, 100, 107, 200; challenges 105–106; under Coalition government 101–103; Covid-19 impacts 104; demographics 88–89; disabled people 126–128; economic impact 87; 'five-a-week' 98; *Let's Get Moving* 102; Local Delivery Pilots (LDPs) 84; New Labour agenda 98–101; NICE guidelines 103; in school 152; third-sector engagement 104; whole-systems change 84; *see also* public health
Playing to Win: A New Era for Sport 26, 82
policy documents: *Achieving Racial Equality: A Standard for Sport* 117–118; *Creating a Sporting Habit for Life*

27, 82; equality 118; *Game Plan* 41; *Playing to Win: A New Era for Sport* 26, 82; *Sport in the Community: The Next Ten Years* 21, 79; *Sport: Raising the Game* 2, 98, 154; *Sporting Future: A New Strategy for an Active Nation* 4, 27, 32–33, 42, 65, 83–84, 119, 138; *A Sporting Future for All* 3, 80, 118; *The Talent Plan for England* 29; *Towards an Active Nation* 27, 211
political opportunity structure 172, 173, 181; configuration of power 175; formal institutional structure 174; informal procedures and prevailing strategies 174–175; for VSCs in England 175–177
Positive Futures 142
preventative health care 96
Primary Care Trusts (PCTs) 99
Primary Health Care model 96
principal-agent theory 10, 21, 172, 177, 220
private sector funding 5
professional sports clubs 190–191, 199; Elite Player Performance Plan (EPPP) 195–198; Football in the Community (FiTC) 192–194; social policy implementation 192–194; and UK government 191–192; *see also* football clubs
proportionate universalism 138
public health 94; Clinical Commissioning Groups (CCGs) 103; under Coalition government 101–103; under Conservative government 98; domains 97; funding 96; interventions 96, 100; under New Labour government 98–101; organisations 97; physical activity agenda 95; preventative 100; Public Service Agreements (PSAs) 100, 101; workforce 100
Public Service Agreements (PSAs) 100, 101
Purnell, J. 41, 64

race and racial equality 117–118; Black Lives Matter (BLM) 119–120
Race Representation Index (RRI) 120
Regional Sport Boards (RSBs) 63

Sabatier, P. 6–8, 10–11, 220
School Games network 158–159, 164
School Sport Partnerships (SSPs) 5, 155–157, 164–165

school/s 152; competitive sport 102, 158–159; curriculum reform 153–154; PE and Sport Premium 159–161, 165; Public Service Agreements (PSA) targets 101; Sportsmark/Sportsmark Gold 155
social determinants of health 96, 97
social inclusion 98; New Labour government 137
Socio-Ecological Model (SEM) 96
Specialist Sports Colleges (SSCs) 155–157
Sport and Recreation Alliance 120
sport council/s: accountability 22; Advisory Sports Council 20–21; governance 22; Great Britain Sports Council 21; Sport England 21–22; UK Sport 21–22
Sport Development Officers (SDOs) 79, 80
Sport England 20–22, 30, 32–33, 39; Active Partnerships 57, 59–61; Active People Survey 27; Active Sports 80–81; *Everyday Sport* campaign 100; *Framework for Sport in England* 57; funding 2; monitoring 26–27; Monitoring and Evaluation Framework 61; *National Framework for Sport in England* 41, 61–62; partnerships 26–28, 211; policy implementation 26–27, 30–31; priorities and roles 25–28; *The Talent Plan for England* 29; *Towards an Active Nation* 65, 68, 211; *Uniting the Movement* 27–28, 32–34, 70, 71, 73, 84, 88–89, 120, 128, 138, 218; voluntary sports clubs (VSCs) 172
Sport in the Community: The Next Ten Years 21, 58, 79
Sport: Raising the Game 2, 21, 26, 58, 79, 98, 154
Sporting Equals 117, 120
Sporting Future: A New Strategy for an Active Nation 4, 26, 42, 65, 70, 83–84, 119, 126–127, 138, 173, 191, 216
Sporting Future for All, A 3, 80, 118
'Sporting Giants' 29
Sports Development Council (SDC) 135
staff/ing 214; Active Partnerships 215–216; County Durham Sport (CDS) 71; Swim England 52–54; third-sector organisations (TSOs) 215; Tranmere Rovers in the Community 201; voluntary sports clubs (VSCs) 185–186
standards: *Equality Standard, The: A Framework for Sport* 118–119; Sportsmark/Sportsmark Gold 155

Strategic Health Authorities (SHA) 99
street-level bureaucracy (SLBy) 95, 172, 177–182, 186
sugar tax 160
Swim England 51; Athlete Development Support Pathway (ADSP) 53; Covid-19 impacts 84–85; funding 54; Long-Term Athlete Development (LTAD) 53; outcomes 52; Research and Insight Team 52–54; staff 52–54

Tackle It campaign 117
talent programmes 28–29; Elite Player Performance Plan (EPPP) 195–198, 201–204; equality, diversity, and inclusion (EDI) 125; football 195–198
Thatcher, M. 135
Third Way 136–137
third-sector organisations (TSOs) 104, 139, 142, 147–148, 211–213; asset-based community development (ABCD) 139–141, 143; funding 144; staffing 215; voluntary sports clubs (VSCs) *see* voluntary sports clubs (VSCs)
top-down approach to policy implementation 7–8, 43, 53, 80–81, 153, 158, 212–213
Towards an Excellent Service (TAES) 68
Tranmere Rovers in the Community 199; Active Rovers 200; funding sources 199–200; implementation of youth development 201–204; staff 201
transparency, national governing bodies (NGBs) 50–51
trusts: charitable 199; leisure 81, 84; Primary Care 99; *see also* charities

UK Sport Council 20–22; focus on event hosting 25; funding 2; government funding 24; grant aid 24–25; implementation of government policy 30; mission creep 25; national governing bodies (NGBs) 23–24; 'no compromise' approach 23; Olympic and Paralympic sports 24; partnerships 25; *The power of our differences* 120; priorities and roles 22–25; remit 32–33; talent programmes 29; World Class Programme (WCP) 23–24
United Kingdom; National Lottery *see* National Lottery

Uniting the Movement 5, 27–28, 70, 84, 88–89, 128

voluntary sports clubs (VSCs) 171, 211, 221, 223; accountability 180–181; collective action 183–184; configuration of power 175; formal institutional structure 174; governance 179–180; heavy 178–179; informal procedures and prevailing strategies 174–175; light 178–179; and NGBs 172; policy implementation 181–182; political institutionalism 172–173; political opportunity structure 173–177; professional staff 185–186; rugby 185, 186; street-level bureaucracy 177–181, 186

Wanless, D., *Securing Good Health for the Whole Population* 99
welfarism: community sport 134–135; needs-based funding 141
White, A. 39, 80
Whole Sport Plans 26, 27, 41, 82, 87–88; Swim England 52
whole-systems change 84, 89
Wolfenden report 20, 39, 77, 135
women, equality in sport policy 117, 123
workforce, community sport 144; *see also* staff/ing
World Health Organisation (WHO) 96

Youth Sport Trust (YST) 40, 153–154, 156, 164